Stavros Panayiotou

God, Subjectivity and the Self

A Comparative Study between Levinas and
Kierkegaard

Stavros Panayiotou

God, Subjectivity and the Self

A Comparative Study between Levinas and
Kierkegaard

Bibliografische Information der Deutschen Nationalbibliothek
Die Deutsche Nationalbibliothek verzeichnet diese Publikation in der Deutschen Nationalbibliografie; detaillierte bibliografische Daten sind im Internet über http://dnb.d-nb.de abrufbar.

Bibliographic information published by the Deutsche Nationalbibliothek
Die Deutsche Nationalbibliothek lists this publication in the Deutsche Nationalbibliografie; detailed bibliographic data are available in the Internet at http://dnb.d-nb.de.

Cover picture: Photo 263586526 © agl tbnn | Dreamstime.com

This monograph is mainly based on the author's PhD dissertation which is successfully submitted and approved by Sofia University "St. Kliment Ohridski".

ISBN: 978-3-95538-042-7

WiSa

Hannover-Stuttgart 2024

To my mother — whose non-reciprocal love has been the
ethical anchor of my life

ACKNOWLEDGMENTS

First, I owe a kind appreciation to my wife Polina Orphanou, who patiently encouraged me to publish this book. I would also like to express my deepest gratitude to the individuals whose support and guidance have been instrumental in the completion of this book. First and foremost, I extend my heartfelt appreciation to Prof. Aneta Karageorgieva and Prof. Nikolai Mihailov, for their invaluable insights and scholarly guidance throughout the research process. I am also deeply grateful to Prof. Richard Cohen and Prof. Sophie-Grace Chappell, whose comments and feedback have been crucial in shaping the ideas presented in this book, especially on the works of Emmanuel Levinas. I am also indebted to Prof. Ioannis Trisokkas, Prof. Ioannis Christodoulou, and Dr. Sebastian Stein, who patiently read the whole draft enriching the book with their endorsed comments. Sincere thanks also go to my editors Dr. Louise Rebecca Chapman and Dr. Matthew Gill, who are always prompted to edit and improve the content of my research topics. Furthermore, I would like to express my gratitude to my colleagues and fellow researchers, Dr. Piotr Pietrzak and Dr. Venera Russo, who have shared their perspectives and engaged in insightful conversations during conferences and workshops, enriching the depth of this comparative study. To my friends and family, whose unwavering support and understanding have been a constant source of inspiration, I extend my deepest thanks. It would be unfair to overlook the hospitality and patience of the libraries' staff, who provided me with access to all philosophical databases and rare collections related to Levinas' and

Kierkegaard's texts enthusiastically. My thanks are due to all the librarians and archivists, who assisted me with all sorts of queries; the library of Sofia University; the Gennadios Library and the library of National and Kapodistrian University, the French library in Athens; the library of Cyprus University, the Center of Philosophical Studies in Cardiff University, the public library and the online library of the Open University of London, the Danish center of Kierkegaardian Studies in Copenhagen and the center of Levinasian Studies in Kaunas. I would also like to thank Dr. Alina Jugel, the *Ibidem-Verlag* representative, who provided her invaluable assistance during the publication process. Last but not least, I extend my gratitude to the readers, whose curiosity and interest in philosophical exploration make the pursuit of such inquiries all the more meaningful. This book stands as a testament to the collaborative spirit of intellectual inquiry, and I am grateful to all who have played a part, no matter how small, in bringing these ideas to fruition. To sum up, I would like to add that solid, robust and sound arguments that surfaced from this book is definitely result of a hard work and collaboration between me, my mentors and discussion with other scholars. However, I personally accept all responsibility for any misconceptions and errors.

Stavros S. Panayiotou

This book is mainly based on the author's PhD dissertation approved by the Faculty of Philosophy, Sofia University, "St. Kliment Ohridski"

LIST OF CONTENTS

ABSTRACT

On the one hand, due to Hegelian totality and the Heideggerian manifestation of being *qua* being, subjectivity cemented itself within an epistemological framework that seems quite sufficient to proclaim itself absolute and divine. In addition, Descartes's *cogito* has been considered as the culmination of the cognitive dominance over metaphysics, aesthetics, and ethics. On the other hand, the post-Hegelian critique of the thinking subject influenced several continental thinkers across Europe to present a new postmodern interpretation based on ethical metaphysics and intersubjectivity as well as faith and religion. The former ideal of ethics was first introduced by Emmanuel Levinas, and the latter line of thought was explored by Søren Kierkegaard, the founder of existential philosophy. Levinas defends the thesis that it is the "Other" who gives a meaning to the self and not the opposite. Overcoming the notion of self-reflection of the thinking subject and fundamental ontology, he proposes a different interpretation of the notion of subjectivity by claiming that what really matters is the moral responsibility for the "Other" and that the primordial relation between me and the "Other" starts from the "Other" and not from the self. For Levinas, God commands me through the face of the "Other", but it is my responsibility to understand and answer. In this comparative study of Levinas and Kierkegaard, I argue that, on the one hand, Levinas believes that God exists outside of the cosmos, I can seek only His trace through the other person, and hence I cannot be in a direct relation with God as I am a finite human being and God is transcendence (infinity). That is why God disappears from human relations after sending the "Other" to me and subjugating me as a hostage. God leaves all human affairs in our hands. In them God is a presence to the point of an absence. I am therefore a subject because of God's commandment and subjection that awaken my thinking and consciousness. My personality as a self-consciousness is secondary and constitutes my "I" in comparison with my moral subjection as "me", which is primary. On the other hand, for Kierkegaard, I am responsible directly to God and my responsibility is a matter of my faith; the religious life does not coincide with ethics and is sometimes absurd if it is measured by ethical norms.

INTRODUCTION

i. Aims and Objectives of Study

This study is an original work[1] that aims at shedding some additional light on the postmodern philosophical tradition as regards the philosophical insights of two prominent thinkers: Emmanuel Levinas (1906–1995) and Søren Kierkegaard (1813–1855).[2] Although other authors have thoroughly sketched Levinas's[3] and Kierkegaard's philosophical accounts,[4] especially Merold Westphal in his work *Levinas and*

---

[1] In the main body of this study there are some parts containing phrases or extracts from published texts of mine or of other scholars. However, all references and quotations from other thinkers or published works are carefully acknowledged and cited. There are also several excerpts from Levinas's and Kierkegaard's works which yet again are fully cited and carefully highlighted with quotation marks. For instance, Levinas's work *God, Death and Time* (2000) is specifically used and thoroughly analyzed in this study (citing several extracts from it) since from my point of view it is one of Levinas's most important works, evaluating the most significant implications concerning the notion of God and how death and time are integrated with ethical norms. It is worth mentioning from the beginning that in footnotes, at the bottom of each page, references concerning monographs, books, articles, volumes, chapters of various editions, translations into English, etc., contain only brief information, i.e. the first letter of the author's name, surname, title, date and page(s). For a complete list of works cited, see the bibliography (after the conclusion). References in the main body of the study are marked in parentheses, i.e. (surname date: pp.). Books are cited in *italics*, and articles (in journals and volumes) in quotation marks.

[2] I do not intend to examine all materials and fields of study regarding Levinas and Kierkegaard. I rather focus only on three aspects: God, subjectivity, and selfhood, as well as whether these three subjects are linked to time and death. Levinas seeks answers through ethics as first philosophy, and Kierkegaard develops his arguments in terms of faith and (neo-)Christian religion. Authors' full names are mentioned only once. After the first mention, I just use the surname in the main body and the first letter of names in the footnotes.

[3] I prefer to use singular genitive case with 's instead of s', i.e. Levinas's thought, Descartes's *cogito*, and plural genitive case with s', i.e. researchers' work. However, I do not change the type of citation of other authors' style in footnotes and the bibliography.

[4] Apart from the above monographs concerning comparisons of Kierkegaard and Levinas, productive and valuable studies have also been written by C. Welz,

Kierkegaard in Dialogue (2008) as well as in the study *Kierkegaard and Levinas: Ethics, Politics and Religion*, edited by Aaron Simmons and David Wood (2008), this study is focused especially on the broad field of metaphysics and social phenomenology on the one hand and on philosophy of religion and ethics on the other. What I present in this study mainly raises questions without necessarily seeking genius dogmatic answers, but mostly in order to bring to surface a new dialectic that sometimes is adopted by both thinkers and sometimes provides an objection to and/or a discrepancy between Levinas's and Kierkegaard's philosophical thought. Specific research questions seek to explore arguments on how Levinas and Kierkegaard think about God, persons, and subjectivity. It is common knowledge that the two major modern philosophical traditions, the analytic and continental schools, interpret (if it is possible to do so) God, His relation to persons (if there is such relation), and subjectivity from extremely different angles. For instance, the analytical point of

---

"The presence of the transcendent — transcending the present. Kierkegaard and Levinas on subjectivity and the ambiguity of God's transcendence" (2007, 149-176); idem. "Present within or without Appearances? Kierkegaard's Phenomenology of the Invisible: Between Hegel and Levinas" (1997, 470-513); C. Welz and K. Verstrynge (eds.), *Despite oneself: Subjectivity and its secret in Kierkegaard and Levinas* (2008); P. Sheil, *Kierkegaard and Levinas: The subjunctive mood* (2010); P. Kemp, "Another Language for the Other: From Kierkegaard to Levinas" (1997, 5-28); B. T. Prosser, "Conscientious Subjectivity in Kierkegaard and Levinas" (2002, 397-422); D. Murphy, "Levinas and Kierkegaard on Divine Transcendence and Ethical Life: Response to Donald L. Turner and Ford Turrell's 'The Non-Existent God'" (2007, 383-385); A. Hurst, "Kierkegaard, Levinas and the Question of Escaping Metaphysics" (2000, 168-187); A. Wells, "On Ethics and Christianity: Kierkegaard and Levinas" (2012, 71-80); Brothers, R., "Ethics of Ethics, Law of Laws: Kierkegaard, Levinas and the Aporia of Substantive Identity" (1999, 54-68); R. C. Reed, "The Binding of Abraham: Levinas's Moment in Kierkegaard's Fear and Trembling" (2017, 81-98); M. Westphal, "Levinas, Kierkegaard and the Theological Task" (1992, 241-261); S. Moyn, "Transcendence, Morality, and History: Emmanuel Levinas and the Discovery of Soren Kierkegaard in France" (2004, 22-54).

view explores arguments related mostly to the Enlightenment tradition and from the English-speaking world using an epistemological-psychological framework (through the fields of experimental philosophy, neuroscience, philosophy of mind, case studies, and other-worldly scenarios). In contrast, the continental line of thought deals with philosophical accounts from other traditions (most of the original sources are non-Anglophone) such as those of French, German, Austrian, Italian, Russian, and Danish thinkers (in the fields of phenomenology, ontology, ethics, aesthetics, psychoanalysis, existential dialectics, and metaphysics).

The aim of this study is mainly to explore philosophical arguments that are found in Levinas's and Kierkegaard's writings in order to provide a clear picture of persons, their essence and existence, their relations (and the extent thereof) to God, and subjectivity as regards time and death. After considering the most significant primary sources and secondary literature on this topic, the main aim is to deduce Levinas's and Kierkegaard's views related to God, subjectivity, and the self. I intend, in parallel, to find out and answer as sufficiently as possible, through Levinas's and Kierkegaard's arguments, questions such as: What is it to be a person? Can we define God beyond ontotheology? Is ethics first philosophy? Are faith and ethics inseparable? Are there several notions of time? Can we surpass death? Why are, for Levinas, responsibility and "Other"-ness necessary and sufficient conditions of subjectivity? Does responsibility precede freedom and if yes, how? How and why does ethics precede (fundamental) ontology?

Though Levinas was Jewish and Kierkegaard Protestant Christian, Levinas was influenced by Kierkegaard's existentialism[5] and his tendency to develop his philosophical perspectives within a religious framework. Especially the 'early Levinas'[6] spent his first academic years studying and discussing philosophical issues revealed by his famous predecessors Edmund Husserl (1859–1938) and Martin Heidegger (1889–1976), who were the first continental philosophers — after Aristotle and Plato — who revived the forgotten, disregarded and eliminated science of ontology, and, as Maria Dimitrova points out, 'we have to clear it up from the patina of time in order for it to flare up again'.[7] On the other hand, the 'later

---

[5] It is quite clear through the works of early Levinas that he had thoroughly read and interpreted Kierkegaard's ideas, especially on subjectivity and the relation between humans. See, for instance, B. T. Prosser, "Conscientious Subjectivity in Kierkegaard and Levinas" (2002, 397-422); S. Moyn, "Transcendence, Morality, and History: Emmanuel Levinas and the Discovery of Soren Kierkegaard in France" (2004, 22-54); B. A. Walter, *Communication and Response-ability: Levinas and Kierkegaard in Conversation*, ch. 1: "Levinas, Kierkegaard and the Ethical Demand" (2014, 1-34); M. Westphal, "The Many Faces of Levinas as a Reader of Kierkegaard" (2008b, 1141-1162); J. McLachlan, "Beyond the Self, Beyond Ontology: Levinas' Reading of Shestov's Reading of Kierkegaard" (2010, 179-196).

[6] This definition varies, as several scholars specializing in Levinas assert that he started his philosophy insisting on Judaic religious thought; however, during his philosophical academic scholarship — and after the Holocaust where his family was executed in concentration camps in the so-called Great German Reich — he definitely changed his philosophical method from existentialism to ethics. It is not meant here that ethics covers only the social and political discussion developed within an ordinary sense, but mainly, what it is to be ethics, according to Levinas, is the field "wherein paradox of the infinite appears progressively in relation to the finite". See E. Levinas, *God, Death and Time* (2000, 202). For Levinas's view on phenomenology in his early philosophical stage see W. Heng, "Levinas' Phenomenology of Sensibility and Time in His Early Period" (2008, 105-121).

[7] For a brief generic discussion on Levinas's views regarding analytic and continental philosophy and his relation to Husserl and Heidegger and their most important implications, see M. Dimitrova & P. Pietrzak, "Interview with Maria Dimitrova on Emmanuel Levinas's Philosophy" (2018, 184). For early Levinas's work and its critique of Heidegger's fundamental ontology, see J. Taminiaux, "The early Levinas's reply to Heidegger's fundamental ontology" (1997, 29-49);

Levinas'[8] makes a change of orientation of immense importance by dedicating the rest of his life to developing a prominent philosophical work on social phenomenology and ethics as the holiness of the holy.[9] This is a crucial point which could be compared to Kierkegaard's faith and philosophy of religion through the broad field of existentialism. It is worth mentioning that what really matters for Levinas is to make clear that ethics as 'First Philosophy' needs to escape from modernity and its disastrous results at the time of his work.[10] Levinas, apart from ethical metaphysics and phenomenology, as developed by Husserl and Heidegger, was also quite interested in politics and justice (Peperzak 2007, 197-214). Levinas often claimed that human beings are obliged to escape from sameness by giving priority to "Other"-ness and closeness, as ethics is a matter of the holiness of the indirect,

---

B. Bergo, "What Is Levinas Doing? Phenomenology and the Rhetoric of an Ethical Un-Conscious" (2005, 122-144).

[8] 'Later Levinas' is a definition given by thinkers who specialize in Levinas's ethics referring particularly to the reversal of Levinas's thought after *Otherwise than Being or Beyond Essence*, where Levinas totally escaped from Heidegger's 'ontological shadow' as well as from the phenomenological process of Husserlian *Pure Ego*, completely defending ethics as 'First Philosophy'. For 'later Levinas', see A. Peperzak (ed.), *Ethics as First Philosophy: The Significance of Emmanuel Levinas for Philosophy* (1995); A. Yampolskaya, "Prophetic Subjectivity in Later Levinas: Sobering up from One's Own Identity", (2019, 1-12).

[9] J. Derrida himself provides a significant phrase — that apparently Levinas said to Derrida during their philosophical conversations in France — during his speech at Levinas's funeral: "I am always struck by a remark record by Levinas: You know one often speaks of Ethics to describe what I do, but what really interests me in the end is not Ethics — not Ethics alone — but the holy; holiness of the holy, and that makes Levinas such as a fascinating and enlightening figure not just for Philosophy but for anybody; theologians too, anyone interested in the great questions for human living" (Derrida 1999, 4).

[10] H. Marcuse in his book *One-Dimensional Man* (2006) clearly describes the dramatic dismantling of ethics during modernity where individuals' freedom, their critical and negative thinking, have been absorbed by the mass production and the technological rationality of liberal capitalism.

non-reciprocal, and asymmetrical holy.[11] Yet, according to Kierkegaard, what matters is the covenant between mankind and God but not through the 'strict secularism' of the established Church and the Westernized high clergy. Transcendence, according to Kierkegaard, is above and beyond secularism and fundamentalist criteria (Quinn 1998, 349-375; Malantschuk 1971, Hannay 1982).

ii. Outlined Structure of the Book

This study is separated into three parts. Part One pays particular attention to metaphysics and social phenomenology, covering a brief introductory section of the history of philosophy: How have we arrived at ethics and social phenomenology through ancient and modern philosophy? Is epistemology a necessary and sufficient condition for ethics and Christian ethics? Part One also discusses the insufficient analytical tradition of 'Criterialism' as well as the Orthodox patristic tradition as a problematic condition of the self. This chapter is quite important in order to show how Levinas's and Kierkegaard's arguments concerning the notion of the self and subjectivity in continental philosophy emerged. This part takes into consideration subjectivity and ethical subjectivity in Levinas and Kierkegaard, keeping a distance from Husserl's and Heidegger's ontology and developing in detail Levinas's response to fundamental ontology.

---

[11] The above terminology is thoroughly discussed in a separate chapter below. For a generic discussion of holiness, see Caruana, J., "'Not Ethics, Not Ethics Alone, but the Holy': Levinas on Ethics and Holiness" (2006, 561-583); R. I. Sugarman, "Through the Lens of Levinas: Preliminary Reflections on Holiness (Leviticus 19)" (2013, 129-143); P. Theisohn, "Reading the Beyond. Lévinas — Literature, Holiness, and Politics" (2008, 61-80).

Part Two deals with infinity, transcendence, and ethics as first philosophy. It explores the argument as to whether we can speak of God beyond ontotheology, unpacking Levinas's responsibility and Kierkegaard's alternative of faith. It deals with the peculiarity of ontological transcendence as immanence. Both Levinas and Kierkegaard raise objections to immanence and knowledge. However, they present their arguments by developing different philosophical methods. Levinas defends the "witnessing of the Saying" (Levinas 1969, 48, 260; idem. 1991, 5-7, 37, 45-48, 153-162) and the non-reciprocal asymmetrical relation between human beings and God (Levinas 1969, 225; idem. 1991, 84, 158) while Kierkegaard claims that transcendence is identified and tautological with faith through a reciprocal and direct interconnection between man and God such as the direct Abraham-God relationship (Goodman 1996, 24-27; Ferreira 1998, 207-234; Mackinnon 1993, 107-125). Part Three covers the discussion on subjectivity and death and their relations with time. Levinas raises an objection to *conatus essendi*,[12] claiming that the good precedes being and presence through the progressive route of diachrony, departing from his phenomenological predecessors (Levinas 1991, 57, 163; Coe 2018, 116, 159, 219). On the contrary, for Kierkegaard, time and death have a religious eschatological teleology with which human beings can achieve a direct relation to God through their faith, love,

---

12   Levinas rejects the notion of conatus essendi as a rotten theory, which infringes on the importance of the "Other", giving priority to sameness and ontology. He claims that "the individuation or super-individuation of the ego consists in being in itself, in its skin, without sharing the conatus essendi of all beings which are beings in themselves [...] The subject resting on itself is confounded by wordless accusation [...] Already the position of the subject is a deposition, not a conatus essendi". See E. Levinas, Otherwise than Being (1991, 118, 127). See also E. Wyschogrod, "Ethics as First Philosophy: Levinas reads Spinoza" (1999, 202-204).

and forgiveness (Watts 2014, loc. 2094-2190). The analysis of the bulk of this research is summarized in a Conclusion based on the implementations and results of the arguments of this project exploring Levinas's and Kierkegaard's aspects regarding God, subjectivity, and the self.

iii. Brief Introduction to Levinas's Life and Philosophical Works

> "I cannot, nor would I even try to,
> measure in a few words the oeuvre of Emmanuel Levinas.
> It is so large that one can no longer glimpse its edges."
> (Derrida, 1999, 4).

Levinas was born in 1906 in Kovno, Lithuania, and he died in Paris on Christmas Day, 1995. It would not be hyperbole to allege that he does not fit into any philosophical tradition. Instead, he seems to develop a vehement critique of Western philosophy. He was an academic philosopher making his first steps in the tradition of phenomenology, but he was also deeply imbued with the intellectual spirit of Judaism and expertise in Talmudic studies and the Torah. He influenced not only postmodern and post-structural French philosophers but liberation theologians as well. The "Other", which is the other person,[13] is the dominating theme in his philosophical writings. This is the reason that he begins with the "stranger, the meek and the humblest", who confronts me and calls me to respond and calls me therefore to radical responsibility.

---

[13]   The "*Other*" with capital "O" expresses (a) the allegoric infinite Other, something that it is extremely different and exterior to the *egotic* self-enclosed Being (b) as well as the idea of God as the Absolute Other. The *other* in lower case ("o") refers to human beings.

This is what he called ethics[14] and, indeed, for Levinas, philosophy begins with ethics. He talks about ethics as first philosophy. Ethics, according to Levinas, does not merely have the meaning of being good or gentle to others or offering charity to social institutions. Ethics, as Levinas says, is an optics, "the spiritual optics" (Levinas 1969, 78). As Levinas points out in his work *Difficult Freedom*, "Ethics is an optic, such that everything I know of God and everything I can hear of His word and reasonably say to Him must find an ethical expression" (Levinas 1990, 17). What matters for Levinas is the ethical relation: humanity as grasped in interpersonal relations, which are imbued with traces of infinity and which promise access to transcendence.[15]

---

[14]   Levinas separates ethics from ontology (the study of beings *qua* beings) by using the term 'good' as a necessary and sufficient condition of ethics, something that is precluded by ontology. Levinas underlines that "to be good is a deficit, a wasting away and a foolishness in being; to be good is excellence and elevation beyond being; the very possibility of the beyond" (Levinas 1998b, 69). M. Eskin correctly infers that Levinasian ethics can be divided into three principal senses: "ethics as a philosophical discipline going back to Socrates; as Levinas's own philosophical discourse; [and] as a human being's fundamental relation to and concern for the other human being, which is the subject of Levinas's philosophical discourse" (Eskin 2000, 30).

[15]   Transcendence in Levinas has a major twofold manner: (a) To show that transcendence is used as a noun, which means God, and that God has nothing to do with (and is irreducible to) immanence, and (b) the usage of the term as verb: to *transcend* "the essence or the move of knowable being which carries on its being in presence; […] it transcends immanence" (Hand [ed.] 1989, 180). Regarding the argument of Levinas's trace see M. Dimitrova, *In Levinas' Trace*, (2011). A. Peperzak also provides a very satisfying definition of transcendence by saying that transcendence (if we consider it the definition of God or not), is for sure beyond and otherwise than being and it has nothing to do with cognition, experience, or knowledge. It refers to another dimension exterior to any human's mental capacities, beyond the frame of subjectivity and cognition, consciousness, intentionality, and inner properties. Transcendence thus can be defined only through an ethical concept (Peperzak 1997, 162-170). Transcendence therefore is the departure from the immanence of the known (Bruns 2004, 35).

Levinas lived among various cultural traditions: Jewish, Russian, German, and French. His family belonged to an Eastern European tradition of Judaism, but, unfortunately, they were executed during Nazism. However, his wife Raisa and his daughter Simone were spared thanks to Maurice Blanchot, who assisted them in finding refuge in a monastery in the south of France. Levinas had his first philosophical interest in the works of Fyodor Dostoevsky (1821-1881),[16] who provided him with his first motivation to study ethics and philosophy. The quote that changed his academic career by making him take an interest in philosophy came from Dostoevsky's work *The Brothers Karamazov*:[17] "We are all guilty of everything and everyone, and I, more so than all the others" (Levinas 1998b, 72; Jodalen and Vetlesen [eds.] 1997, 48). In 1923, Levinas moved to Strasbourg, where he met Henri Bergson (1859-1941), from whom he received a significant philosophical influence. In 1928, he began his philosophical studies in Freiburg with Edmund Husserl, the 'father of modern phenomenology', and, most importantly, he came under the tutelage of Husserl's successor Martin Heidegger. Levinas always considered Heidegger's *Being and Time* one of the most important philosophical works in the Western world.

Levinas placed his philosophical work in a three-dimensional model derived from the Bible, characterizing it as one in which the Jewish moment mainly shaped his academic

---

[16] For Dostoevsky's religious/philosophical aspects, see J. Frank, *Dostoevsky: The Mantle of the Prophet, 1871-1881* (2002) and M. Holquist, *Dostoevsky and the Novel* (1977).

[17] See F. Dostoevsky, *The Brothers Karamazov* (1970) and W. J. Leatherbarrow, *Fyodor Dostoevsky: "The Brothers Karamazov"* (1992).

future as an ethics philosopher: (a) 'The Lord thy God is One', (b) 'Love your neighbor as yourself', and (c) 'Sacrifice a lamb in the morning and another at dusk' (Levinas 1990, 19).[18]

Humans, according to Levinas, are not merely beings. In a lecture on Judaism, Levinas claims that "the Jewish man discovers man before discovering landscapes and towns. He is at home in a society before being so in a house. He understands the world on the basis of the Other rather than the whole of being functioning in relation to the earth" (ibid., 22). Understanding the world on the basis of the Other is the basic idea that underlies his most famous book, *Totality and Infinity*.

Levinas in general wonders how the Other could enter my world without simply being reduced to that world or without infringing on my world. That is, in short, how does one avoid the other being reduced to the self due to some dependent 'victim-status'? Indeed, this is the question that I am going to address in the first part of the book. If we want to venture a general remark on this issue, we may assume what Levinas is trying to say with the above question or, rather, the way he seeks to address it. However, the two most important books written by Levinas, *Totality and Infinity* and *Otherwise Beyond Being or Beyond Essence*, are not easily read and are not meant to be. They both manifest a tendency to go back and

---

[18] Among the scholars who studied Levinasian thought in the 20th century, this phrase is quite peculiar. This opinion given by another rabbi is not so familiar in the Judaic theological tradition. However, for Levinas, it is of immense importance and he gives approval to this third commandment using it in several ways throughout his academic career. From my point of view, Levinas uses it to link the practice of ritual with that of justice. The second commandment, he says, "indicates the way which the first is true and the third indicates the practical conditions of the second" (Levinas 1990, 19) through the daily act of fidelity to the law, which is an extremely necessary and sufficient condition for monotheistic Jewish religion. Thus, through this cyclical dialectic, the commandments of God are met, and justice is done.

repeat the same point from slightly different angles. Derrida said that there is a "return and repetition always of the same wave against the same shore in which however as each return recapitulates itself it also infinitely renews, and it reaches itself." (Derrida 1978, 398, n. 7). What Levinas proposes is not a Socratic dialogue in which you are gently brought to understand in a logical manner a particular idea by answering a list of questions. It is more like what is implied in the title *Totality and Infinity*: that is, we need to transit from totality into infinity, overcoming being *qua* being and immanence.

Levinas also endeavors to rebuild a robust argument against *logos* (logic) and *nous* (mind), exploring the fact that whatever is universal and fundamental must only be related to ontology and not to transcendence. Western tradition, for Levinas, is fully based on knowledge, apprehension, experience, and immanence.[19] He is thus against the conventions of Western thought. Shaping and formatting the above analytical mode of being in the Western philosophical tradition, the "Other", unfortunately for Levinas, has been forgotten, totalized into a system which is dominated and controlled by the "Same". This conviction comes from a deeply felt antagonism to Heidegger's work *Being and Time*. However, it is worth noting that there is no intention to infer that Levinas became rapidly disillusioned with Heidegger's or Husserl's collusions with Nietzscheanism.[20] On the contrary, Levinas in his first

---

[19]   In order to clarify that Levinas separates his ethics from the Western philosophical tradition, I cite below an excerpt from R. Bernasconi's article "'Only the Persecuted': Language of the Oppressor, Language of the Oppressed", (1985, 85), who underlines that "Levinas's achievement is that he has developed a philosophy that arises from the non-philosophical experience of being persecuted".

[20]   Concerning the relation between Levinas and Nietzsche on God, subjectivity, and death, see J. Stauffer and B. G. Bergo (eds.), *Nietzsche and Levinas: "After the*

philosophical stages showed his absolute admiration for both Heidegger and Husserl, as he shared especially with Heidegger a common focus on human subjectivity. However, there are several differences between Heidegger's and Levinas's thoughts on subjectivity.

Heidegger has been considered the first philosopher after Plato who raised the question of "Being" in contemporary philosophy. In parallel, Heidegger was the first continental thinker who criticized that the search for meaning belonged absolutely to mathematics, psychology, and positive science. Heidegger, like Levinas, made a profound turning point in continental philosophy by alleging that the search for meaning should focus on man. At this point, Levinas distances his theory from Heidegger's allegation that "Being" alone as "*Dasein*" can justify the search for meaning. On the contrary, for Levinas, the face-to-face in a direct relationship is what matters. Having this in mind, Levinas sets up an alternative approach which makes personal-ethical responsibility to others the starting point (Barber 2008, 642-643) against Heidegger's being and Rene Descartes's famous phrase "[ego] cogito, ergo sum" – "I think, therefore I am" (Descartes 1644, 28). As regards *cogito*, several thinkers misunderstand its relation to Levinas's thought. Ethically speaking, in my opinion, there is a huge ethical gap between *cogito* and Levinas's "face".

> "Levinas' ethical subject is defined by an anarchic responsibility prior to rational deliberation; the good has chosen me before I have chosen it. [...] Bensussan describes this 'having to respond' as 'immemorial: it goes way back and precedes all questions I can ever ask myself concerning the reasons why

---

Death of a Certain God" (2009, 116-133, 214-231); J. L. Kosky, "After the Death of God: Emmanuel Levinas and the Ethical Possibility of God" (1996, 235, 237).

I have responded or not.' The logic of this argument is found in Descartes' *cogito ergo sum*: in doubting thinking, I am thinking; one cannot negate thinking. Similarly, one cannot negate responsibility, for trying to do so is itself a response, not only to the other but before and for the other" (Smith 2016, 97).

In my opinion, Levinas would argue against this combination of propositions. Although Felicity Smith correctly noted that the "ethical subject defines by anarchic responsibility prior to rational deliberation" (Smith 2016, 97), she misused the function of this proposition in terms of immanence. Descartes's ethics (as well as Hegel's totality) explores ontological criteria in order to speak about selfhood.[21] *Cogito* is not a doubting of thinking, but an ontological method to infer that knowledge precedes ethics and consciousness precedes responsibility. Smith, on the one hand, correctly gives priority to the immemorial which "precedes all questions". On the other hand, however, "the logic of this argument" (referring to Gerard Bensussan) has nothing to do with Descartes's *cogito*, since the latter is developed through a rational process: by thinking, even doubting thinking, an ontological aporia remains. Therefore, it would be mistaken to compare Descartes's *cogito*, which stands on inner criteria, with Levinas's

---

[21]   For instance, G. L. Bruns provides a valuable statement in order to clarify Levinas's position against the *cogito*: "In the Levinasian encounter with the other, I can no longer comport myself as a cogito, a self-contained rational subject, a Hegelian consciousness conceived as a *pour soi*, that is, a power of representation or intentionality in pursuit of its own sovereignty. I now exist in the accusative, no longer an *I* but a *me* someone now at the disposal of — answerable to and for — another. I am my responsibility *prior* to any freedom of choice" (Bruns 2004, 34). Therefore, it is clear that *cogito* is completely outside Levinas's ethical phenomenology and it cannot be compared to the face. Encountering the other as an equal interlocutor in terms of freedom we automatically lose the radical generosity toward the stranger that Levinas proposes as a necessary and sufficient condition of selfhood. The other, for Levinas, can be an interlocutor but not an equal to me, since, in this way, heteronomy gives to autonomy something that it is not ethical. Concerning the other as an interlocutor, see E. Levinas, *Basic Philosophical Writings* (1996, 5-9).

responsibility, which is based on ethical intuition.[22] We cannot therefore interpret Levinas's ethical responsibility through the lens of a Westernized moral sense. Dimitrova correctly underlines that "morality should not be a form of legislation, encompassing the unwritten rules of one community or another, but, instead, must be understood *au sense extra-moral*" (Dimitrova 2011, 16).[23]

Levinas posits an ethical I: "I am called therefore I am", or "You *are* therefore I am" (Marcus 2007, 515). The I exists not in the nominative, but in the accusative case as "me"; as

---

[22] T. G. Casey makes a useful distinction between Levinas's and Descartes's views on the idea of the infinite and responsibility: "Levinas is ultimately dissatisfied with Descartes's own presentation of the idea of the infinite [as well as how responsibility is attached to the idea of selfhood] because it remains within the realm of knowledge and of ontology. It cedes too much to knowledge, and the latter becomes overweening. Since Descartes's priority is the search for knowledge, he neglects the potentially revolutionary features of the idea. Levinas instead wants a humility that does not belong to knowledge but to ethics" (Casey 2003, 390).

[23] Descartes interprets morality as inseparable from ontology, as a criterion, which is based on legal, social, psychological, and cognitive criteria. On the other hand, Levinas attaches the word *extra-* onto morality, i.e. *extra-moral sense*. By attaching the word *extra-*, Levinas gives an infinite character to morality expressing ethics, as first philosophy. M. Dimitrova cogently explains the ethical function of *extra*-moral repercussions in Levinasian thought and how the term *extra-* changes the philosophical meaning: "morality (as obedience to rules) and extra-morality (as caring for the Other) [...] Transcendence (of the outer world) and extra-transcendence (of the Other); passiveness (in sensitivity) and extra-passiveness (in the closeness of the Other); desire (directed at the objects of the world) and metaphysical extra-desire (towards the Other and infinity, revealed by the encounter with him); sociality (as belonging to the whole of society) and extra-sociality (as responsibility for others); justice (according to legislation) and extra-justice (according to moral saintlessness); rationality (as providing the foundation of 'I can') and extra-rationality (as questioning myself and seeking a better justice)" (Dimitrova 2011, 17-18). In parallel, Kierkegaard also provides an irrational sense of morality, but through his Christian ethics, by saying that love cannot be sensual and rational: "By the sensual, Christianity means the carnal, the selfish [...] and it is just because of this that Christianity harbors a suspicion about earthly love and friendship" (Kierkegaard 1949, 44). For true subjective love, there are two necessary and sufficient presuppositions, as Kierkegaard claims: "In order to be able to recommend love [as a subjective truth], inward self-abnegation and outward sacrificing disinterestedness are both required" (Kierkegaard 1995, 301).

Adrian Peperzak correctly points out, "the self in the accusative [*se, soi-même*] is the core of human significance" (Peperzak 1997, 104). In the same manner, Levinas argues that phenomenology is moving beyond the vision of essences, tracing thoughts and intentions, not merely back to the whole horizon, as Husserl pointed out. Consciousness thus for Levinas, as is thoroughly analyzed in the bulk of this research, is a necessary but not sufficient condition to justify subjectivity. The most important thing is to find a path to speak philosophically above and beyond knowledge, experience, and 'onto-theo-logy'. This is therefore the main task of this book: to ascertain Levinas's and Kierkegaard's insights as to whether it might be possible to escape from immanence, presence, consciousness, and 'onto-theo-logy'.

iv. A Brief Introduction to Kierkegaard's Life and Philosophy

"At a certain point, I thought I had to distance myself from what was called 'philosophy of existence' [...] But it is Kierkegaard to whom I have been most faithful and who interests me; most: absolute existence, the meaning he gives to subjectivity, the resistance of existence to the concept or the system — this is something I attach great importance to and feel very deeply, something I am always ready to stand up for." (Derrida 2001, 40)
"Kierkegaard's philosophy has marked contemporary thought so deeply that the reservations and even the rejections it may elicit are yet forms of that influence" (Levinas 1996, 71)

Kierkegaard was a Danish philosopher, theologian, and social critic who lived in the 19th century.[24] He is considered the 'father of existentialism'. He was born in Copenhagen in 1813 and during his childhood adopted religious principles

---

[24] Concerning Kierkegaard's life, see G. Joakim, *Kierkegaard: A Biography* (2005).

similar to those of his father. He composed twenty-two books, which are divided into aesthetics, ethics, and religion. He died at age forty-two of spinal disease.

In his most famous works *Either/Or* and *Fear and Trembling*, Kierkegaard intended to awaken us to our inner deceptions and psychological sentiments. He vehemently criticized our normal life, which standardizes a one-dimensional way of life, as Herbert Marcuse claimed a century later. The Danish bourgeoisie and the members of the established Danish church were two of his most hated groups whose vehemently criticized throughout his life. He also rejected a simple, relaxing way of life, trying to show the Danish people that they had lost the real meaning of life. As he contends:

> "When I became older, when I opened my eyes and saw reality I started to laugh and haven't stopped since. I saw the meaning of life was getting a livelihood, its goal acquiring a titular office, that love's rich desire was getting hold of a well-to-do girl, that the blessedness of friendship was to help one another in financial embarrassment, that wisdom was what the majority assumed it to be, that enthusiasm was to make a speech, that courage was to risk losing ten dollars, that cordiality consisted in saying 'You're welcome' after a dinner, that fear of God was to go to communion once a year. That's what I saw, and I laughed." (Kierkegaard 2004, 29).

At the same time, Kierkegaard was especially caustic about the 19th-century understanding of love (Evans 2004). Everywhere he looked during his youth, Kierkegaard saw intolerable incompatibility and impossible choices. This led him to one remarkable existential dilemma in *Either/Or* regarding marriage: "Marry and you will regret it. Do not marry you will also regret it. Marry or do not marry you will regret it either way" (Kierkegaard 2004, 31).[25]

---

[25]   This "either/or" statement is for Kierkegaard the essence of all philosophy.

Kierkegaard influenced several existentialist thinkers of 20th century such as Jean-Paul Sartre, Albert Camus, and Heidegger. Especially his work *The Concept of Anxiety*, published in 1844, in which he paid particular attention to the word 'angst', has been read and discussed with considerable interest.[26] As Kierkegaard also wrote, "life can only be understood backwards, but must be lived forwards" (Dalton 2001, 3). Our constant angst means that "happiness is more or less written into the script of life" (Watts 2014, loc. 361-1052).

For him, Christianity is not merely a cosmic ideological religion.[27] Kierkegaard was not interested in justifying the Christian church by rational criteria or an idolatrous concept as Catholics and the Orthodox do; instead, he presented a dramatic 'leap of faith' (McDonald 2017, ch. 5). We need to get rid of reason and rationality in order to approach true faith: "to believe is indeed to lose the understanding in order to gain God" (Hong and Hong [eds.] 1980, 38).

---

[26] The most comprehensive secondary source concerning Kierkegaard's notion of anxiety (angst) from my point of view is A. Gron's *The Concept of Anxiety* (2008).

[27] Religion, philosophically speaking, can be divided into several categories depending on which field we refer to: Religion as (a) culture (related to cultural and social norms), (b) as ideology (fundamentalism through political and social ideology such as the Crusades, jihad and ISIS), (c) as object of research (as an academic discipline among scholars), (d) as a set of propositions (to prove/disprove religious theories epistemologically as the Greeks did: i.e. theists/atheists), (e) as theology (as a relationship with the sacred, the holy and the scriptures), and (f) as morality (whether religion is reduced to a kind of morality, see Kant's conception of religion). (Pirhayati and Rezaei 2019, 72). This study aims at thoroughly examining religion regarding the two latter points: (e) Kierkegaard's theology (through faith) and (f) Levinasian ethics concerning subjectivity, God, and selfhood in relation to time and death as well as whether we can speak for all of these philosophical accounts beyond "being". Levinas underlines that we need to be careful of using the term religion since it must not be confused with theology, mystery, and sacredness. Levinas contends that the term religion must declare "the relation with human beings, irreducible to comprehension", distancing itself "from the exercise of power", by "rejoining the Infinity in human faces" (Levinas 1996a, 8).

Kierkegaard invokes the example of God's command to Abraham and its 'monstrous paradox'. We must believe, according to Kierkegaard, "even though faith violates human rationality, nature and morality" (West 1996, 142). "It is the absurdity of religion which proves its unique value, its irreducibility" (ibid., 125). According to Kierkegaard, it is folly to try to prove God's existence (Moore 2002, 74-76). It is also worth noting that Kierkegaard, though he insists on Christian faith and religious principles, is vehemently against what he calls, 'Objective Christianity', which falsely provides biased historical evidence by establishing the Church's dogma. Faith, he asserts, is a necessary and sufficient condition of subjectivity, emphasizing his existential exploration and providing examples from the Old Testament such as that of Job and Abraham to support his arguments for the 'leap of faith'. As Vasiliki Tsakiri states, "Abraham's exercise of freedom converges with the leap of faith, which for Kierkegaard happens always within the realm of the finite but opens up human singularity towards the infinity" (Tsakiri 2009, 60).

Concerning singularity and/or the 'Single One', we need to be quite careful not to misidentify Kierkegaard's singularity with Levinas's singularity.[28] The latter contends that

---

[28]   Singularity is of immense importance for Levinas in order to raise his objection to ontological process which developed through universality and particularity. Levinas states that "the oneself is a singularity, prior to the distinction between the particular and the universal. It is, if one likes, a relationship, but one where there is no disjunction between the terms held in relationship, a relationship that is not reducible to an intentional openness upon oneself, does not purely and simply repeat consciousness in which being is gathered up, Singularity is based on the irreducibility of the infinite outside totality" (Levinas 1991, 108). Levinas argues that we need to transit from the absolute to the singular other, where the other resides not only as being-in-the-world but mainly is beyond the cosmos without infringing on her individuality. In no way is the other absorbed by the "Same" (Ferro 2012, 26-51). Both Levinas and Kierkegaard

the singularity of a moral subject depends on asymmetrical, indirect, and non-reciprocal attributes while the former defends—through faith, repetition (Kierkegaard 1983, 46), secrecy, silence, and absurdity—the direct, immediate, and reciprocal relation to God. The leap of faith, therefore, moved by the principle of the absurd, converts finitude into infinity and a return to the finite yet again. This is because God allows it to be done; "since for God everything is possible, everything becomes also possible in the finite world by virtue of the absurd" (Tsakiri 2009, 60).

Kierkegaard provides a quite different perspective concerning the notion of faith and its relation to reason. He claims that reason has nothing to do with faith, and faith has nothing to do with rational reason. He not only puts a huge gap between them, but also he creates a separate existential framework in which faith surpasses human understanding. In this way "he renews the theological tradition of fideism for

---

developed a vehement critique of Hegel's universality. They believe that Hegel's totality wrongly manifests ethics with history and knowledge. Hegel's totality which includes all aspects of the universe is not accepted by Levinas and Kierkegaard since the *Geist* consists of immanence and speculation. Awareness of the self as Hegel construed it is integrated into a supra-individual entity in-itself whose normative canons rule method, action with a universal process. Levinas raises an objection to Hegel's speculative philosophy by saying that the concept of totalization as power and dominance of the self and as a decision of free will must be excluded. Levinas and Kierkegaard agree on this fact, but the former provides an ethical argument and the latter a religious one. Both thinkers strongly reject the absorption of the "Other" in the "Same" as in Hegel and Heidegger. According to Levinas, "there exists a tyranny of the universal and of the impersonal, an order that is inhuman though distinct from the brutish. Against it, man affirms himself as an irreducible singularity, exterior to the totality into which he enters, and aspiring to the religious order where the recognition of the individual concerns him in his singularity, an order of joy which is neither cessation nor antithesis of pain, nor flight before it" (Levinas 1969, 242). For a full discussion of singularity, especially concerning Levinas's ethical singularity, see L. Guenther, "'Nameless Singularity': Levinas on Individuation and Ethical Singularity" (2009, 177-187); S. Hanlon, *Levinas Singularity and the Restless Subject* (2009, 84-128).

which religious faith is diminished rather than strengthened by its reduction to merely human reason" (Hollander [ed.] 1960, 7). Kierkegaard develops a more radical version of fideism, highlighting that "religious faith not only does not require the support of reason but is essentially at odds with it" (Kierkegaard 1989, 43).

Kierkegaard rejects both objective knowledge and contemplative theory as they make no useful contribution to understanding human life. Thus, religion and faith cannot be reduced to theory. Religious moral systems cannot be justified with philosophy and rationalism; religion is a matter of faith, not a mental demonstration of the inner representation of ethical images. The truths of religion, according to Kierkegaard, belong to "the sphere of subjective existence" (West 1996, 119). Existence can be only understood subjectively, from within. Also, Kierkegaard gives priority to ambivalence, dread, and anxiety, which play a crucial role in achieving freedom (ibid., 121-124). Human beings are, according to Kierkegaard, "a mixture of the animal and the divine; a synthesis of the infinite and the finite, of the temporal and the eternal, of freedom and necessity" (ibid., 122). For him, "personhood is a synthesis of possibility and necessity. Its manner is therefore like breathing (respiration), which is expiration and aspiration" (Kierkegaard 1989, 70).

Kierkegaard compares freedom with contemporary mass society where people despair obeying rules and living in the "mediocre and the average" (West 1996, 122). By raising the issue of despair, Kierkegaard leads human beings to rethink their destiny to return to religious faith (as a Protestant). "Only a self which comes to a self-conscious decision to accept God overcomes despair [...] only religion answers to the fully self-conscious individuality of authentic existence" (ibid., 124).[29] Summing up Kierkegaard's existential subjectivity of religious faith, we may assert that, through his inward renewal of faith, Kierkegaard also sheds additional light on the subjective existential truth of the human condition.

Moreover, paradox, in Kierkegaard, is of immense importance to both subjectivity and religion. To fully understand Kierkegaard's paradox, firstly, we must reconsider humans' condition of possessing a rational mind. My existence, according to Kierkegaard, is a happening which paradoxically emerges as an elusive phenomenon beyond objectivity. Objective uncertainty is something that surfaces between me and the subjectivity of myself:[30]

"When subjectivity, inwardness, is truth, then truth, objectively defined, is a paradox; and that truth is objectively a paradox shows precisely that subjectivity is truth [...] The paradox is the objective uncertainty that is the

---

[29] The notion of despair is of immense importance in Kierkegaard's philosophy. Several secondary sources pay particular attention to this matter. See, for instance, M. Theunissen, *Kierkegaard's concept of despair* (2005), especially the first two parts (ibid., 1-104). M. T. Mjaaland states that "Despair [...] presuppose[s] a certain consciousness of being a self and thus consciously relating to oneself. The basic structure of conscious despair is double or twofold: in despair not willing to be oneself, and in despair willing to be oneself. This double origin of the sickness unto death makes it necessary to analyze it dialectically" (Mjaaland 2011, 82).

[30] Kierkegaard underlines that pure Christian faith can be revealed not in theory but only in practice, 'imitating' Christ's deeds, as God-man Christ suffered during his human life. As M. Dooley correctly mentions, "Kierkegaard's antipathy to organized Christianity, or Christendom, sterns from his belief that the genuine ethical message the Christ-figure brought through his deeds and actions has been occluded by the powers that be as a means of self-preservation and self-deification. To practice Christianity, however, requires that one affirm what is out of power, what the law looks at with suspicion, and what offends and repulses our most sacred beliefs and mores. In other words, to have faith in the God-Man requires standing with him in lowliness and suffering for the truth as he did". See M. Dooley, *Politics of Exodus* (2001, 142).

expression for the passion of inwardness that is truth [...] The eternal, essential truth, that is the truth that is related essentially of the existing person by pertaining essentially what it means to exist [...] is a paradox." (Hong and Hong (eds.) 2000, 207-208).

v. Convergence and Variance of Levinas and Kierkegaard

If there is an opportunity to explore the debate of subjectivity and the "Self" on a solid basis, it can only be achieved through the existential philosophy and ethics which posit that personhood belongs to the metaphysics of existence and ethics rather than to the ontological essence of "Being". Before starting comparisons about the notion of the self and subjectivity in the works of Levinas and Kierkegaard, it would be appropriate to clarify the basis of the bulk of this study. It is prudent from the beginning to clearly declare that ethicists (Levinas) and existentialists (Kierkegaard) define human nature not by its predestined essence—ontologically—but mainly by man's actions—praxis (Dimitrova 2006, I.1, 15). Thus, this project mainly explores theses dealing with metaphysical, ethical, and existential perspectives rather than ontology and epistemology.[31] For Levinas, epistemology and ontology are like "twins" which must stay behind, giving priority to the face and to ethics as first philosophy: "the face takes philosophy outside the ambit of *ordo cognoscendi* leaving ontology and epistemology behind" (Jodalen and Vetlesen [eds.] 1997, 15). What matters is not the being *qua* "Being" but man as human. It is therefore urgent to ask

---

[31]   For instance, the Heideggerian methodology of being-in-the-world impacts the majority of the ontological standpoint of the self-rejecting subjectivity and activism giving priority to fundamental ontology of "Beings".

questions using the interrogative conjunction *why* rather than *how*, also preferring the term "ought to be" to "is". For Levinas, as Dimitrova points out, "Heidegger's wisdom is not an original or primordial truth. It deduces the personal from the ontological while the personal is ethical" (Dimitrova 2006, 16).

In this study, I argue that the (subjective) self merits an ethical and not an ontological task, comparing the ethical (to some extent) with the existential. Levinas, despite his great interest in Heideggerian ontology[32] during his time at the University of Strasbourg, later realizes that his phenomenology needs further elaboration in order to fabricate a more ethical phenomenology of exploring humans and not ontological beings *qua* beings. Hence, Levinas expresses his critique of Heidegger by claiming that the latter provides a quasi-phenomenological idea of the truth of beings *qua* disclosure (Tsakiri 2009, 65) and unconcealment. Concerning Heidegger's latter term as well as 'clearing' in *Being and Time*, Levinas contends that "the idea that a transcendence of the transcendent depends on its extreme humility enables us to glimpse a kind of truth which does not take the form of unconcealment. The humility of a persecuted truth is so profound that it will not even venture to present itself in the Heideggerian *clearing*" (ibid.). Levinas alterity seems to transcend beyond and above any Husserlian observative and epistemological preoccupations of bracketing the "I" (Hirst 2014, 187) and any

---

[32] G. L. Bruns gives a very cogent definition of Heideggerian ontology: "ontology means a concern with the unity of being or totality of all that is" (Bruns 2004, 31). Concerning Heidegger's notion of ethics and its relations to ontology, see J. Hodge, *Heidegger and Ethics* (1995). Regarding Levinas's critique of Heidegger's metaphysics and ontology, see A. T. Peperzak, "On Levinas's Criticism of Heidegger" (1997).

Heideggerian ontological implications. Levinas's insistence on alterity surfaced even before he raised ethics as first philosophy. Levinas, as Rudolf Bernet clearly points out, "had already exhibited in his first writings on time a particular attention to the question of alterity. In his question of the other (*aliud*) at the heart of the sameness of my experience of time, it is already the other person (*alter*) that Levinas is aiming at" (Bernet 2004, 86-87). Bernet, in the same vein, underlines a crucial fact on Levinas's subjectivity and time which contrasts with Husserlian epistemology and Heideggerian fundamental ontology: "he attempts to establish that the past itself, in its most originary sense, is not my past but the other's past. The famous analyses of the 'trace' and the 'immemorial' do nothing else than establish the idea of a past which has never been present" (ibid., 89).[33]

Levinas and Kierkegaard — though from extremely different philosophical backgrounds — both contend that personhood passes through total otherness. They both give priority to subjectivity rather than objectivity; the other has the character of subject rather than object. They also both link the ethical and the religious and "set them off as a region of self-transcending subjectivity thoroughly different from the violent objectivity" (Westphal 1992, 242). Levinas and Kierkegaard, in parallel, speak about the person underlining the signification of the other (human and divine), presenting their arguments by insisting on the relationship between (a) the "I" and the "Thou" and (b) the "I" and the divine other.

---

[33] Concerning Kierkegaard's view on time before death, see J. Davenport, *Narrative Identity and Autonomy*, 2012, especially ch. 5: "Selves in time before death: Kierkegaardian religious narrative unity" (ibid., 150-167); P. Stokes, *The Naked Self* (2015, 93-115).

However, I argue below in more detail that Levinas prefers the interconnection between the 'other and me' to the Buberian 'I-Thou' relation. In contrast, Kierkegaard (a Protestant) develops his existential theory concerning the concept of the self and subjectivity from a more spiritual Christian standpoint where a person has direct communication with God and with the other persons in 'secrecy' through individual prayer and without any interference from the community or the established church:[34] He thus advises his reader to "close your door and pray to God, then you have the highest a man can have love, your Saviour, then you have everything both in life and death, and disregard the differences, they neither add to nor subtract from" (Kierkegaard 1949, 58). Subjectivity, therefore, for Kierkegaard, does not depend on the immanence and knowledge which are both social characteristics that the established church promotes, but on actual transcendence.[35] For instance, Kierkegaard holds that "truth is subjectivity" (Kierkegaard 2009a, 159-212). This truth can be obtained by our actuality and not by absolute knowledge. What really matters for Kierkegaard is not what I know but what I ought to do (Kierkegaard 1951, 15). He claims that the I, as subject, needs to understand herself first before understanding others. This, we may say, is absolutely

---

[34]   H. L. Dreyfus, "Kierkegaard on the Self" (2008, 11-23); G. Pattison and S. Shakespeare (eds.), *Kierkegaard: The Self in Society*, (1998, 43-69).

[35]   This is the main reason that Kierkegaard, as J. Watkin states, "stresses the nonsocial aspect of a really Christianized human society" is that "he is worried that the Danish State Church has neglected Christian teaching about absolute renunciation of the life of immanence. If the Christian ethical-religious society is no different to a well-run pagan one, transcendence has been reduced to immanence: [That is] abstract humanity and numerical equality between man and man, the immanentalist principle of the greatest happiness [...] has replaced the individual's relationship to the transcendent God in eternity and reassured him in being a clever egoist" (Watkin 1990, 73).

opposed to Levinasian thought. Kierkegaard insists that the most crucial thing for someone to reflect her personhood is firstly to understand herself theologically: "to see what God really wishes me to do, the thing is to find a truth which is true for me [...] for which I can live and die" (Dreyfus 2008, 16). Kierkegaard, even if he rejects the analytic methodology of selfhood, that is, the prioritization of consciousness and empirical knowledge, starts from the inner self; he targets the self and then looks at the other. Levinas's ethics is exactly the opposite. It is the other who makes me think about myself. The subjective truth for Kierkegaard can be found in the strength of faith and not through the process of the immanent. As he puts it in his *Concluding Unscientific Postscript*, "the truth thus becomes an approximating whose beginning cannot be posited absolutely, just because there is no conclusion to have retroactive force; whereas any beginning [...] when *made*, does not occur on the strength of immanent thinking but is *made* on the strength of a decision, essentially on the strength of faith" (Kierkegaard 2009a, 159).

The above 'decision', we could argue, does not infringe on the face of the "Other", as ontology does, but returns to the "Same". Though Kierkegaard's argument seeks no selfishness of the ego (at least through his ethical and religious argument)[36], as the *cogito* does, it always seeks a direct man-God relationship. Always, for Kierkegaard, the 'I-Thou' relation has a divine prototype: the man-God relationship which

---

[36] We should not ignore that Kierkegaard's aesthetics gives priority to egotism and skepticism. However, as W. McDonald contends in his article *Soren Kierkegaard*, 2017, ch. 3, this model of aesthetics has been transformed by ethics since it was seen "to be emptily self-serving and escapist. [...] It fails to acknowledge one's social debt and communal existence".

is completed in faith. For Kierkegaard, faith in Christian ethics overcomes the church's dogma. As McDonald correctly puts it, faith for Kierkegaard "is not a matter of regurgitating church dogma. It is a matter of individual subjective passion, which cannot be mediated by the clergy or by human artefacts [...] but only on the basis of faith does an individual have a chance to become a true self" (McDonald 2017, ch. 5). This is one of the most crucial discrepancies between Kierkegaard and Levinas, where the latter would defend that becoming a true self does not depend on my enclosed individual faith but on my eternal responsibility for the other, something that indirectly is God's commandment, not mainly through the 'thou shalt love', as Kierkegaard suggests (Kierkegaard 1949, 37-74) but through the commandment 'thou shalt not kill'.[37]

---

[37] Levinas gives a concise definition of the phrase "thou shalt not kill" by underlining that "the Face is also the 'Thou Shalt not Kill'. A 'Thou-Shalt-not-Kill' that can also be explicated much further: it is the fact that I cannot let the other die alone, it is like a calling out to me" (Levinas 1998a, 104).

CHAPTER 1:
LEVINAS AND KIERKEGAARD ON GOD AND ONTO-THEOLOGY

1.1 Introduction

Levinas was one of the most prominent ethical thinkers of the 20th century whose works, especially *Totalité et Infini* (1961) and *Autrement qu'être ou au-delà de l'essence* (1974), raise the notion of the "Other" to the highest peak. Levinas has been called the philosopher of the "Other", defining ethics[38] as first philosophy. In his *Ethics as First Philosophy* (Kearney and Rainwater [eds.] 1996, 124-135), Levinas starts his analysis by sketching the problematic approach of the classical notion of knowledge and its severe pitfalls for humans and God. Levinas, in general, rejects the purely ontological relationship with the world that philosophy has traditionally prioritized with its exclusive concern for 'Being-as-totality'.[39] Levinas

---

[38] For Levinas, "Ethics is the field sketched out by the paradox of an Infinite in relation, without correlation, to the finite, beyond any [*doxic*] experience" (Levinas 2000, 200). We might paraphrase the term ethics by saying that ethics is synonym for a phenomenology of intersubjective responsibility far from a materialistic level of experience and autonomy. Several thinkers called Levinas's ethics metaethics or ethics of ethics. In my opinion, such views, regarding the definition and notion of Levinasian ethics, are not accepted.

[39] The theory of Being-as-totality is mainly explored by Hegel in his work *Phenomenology of Spirit* and Verene's work on recollection. See G. W. F. Hegel, *Phenomenology of Spirit* (1979) and D. P. Verene, *Hegel's Absolute* (2007); idem., *Hegel's Recollection* (1985). There is also another perspective concerning Hegel's being as totality in a more historical-Marxist framework in Kojeve's *Introduction to the Reading of Hegel: Lectures on the Phenomenology of Spirit* (1980). Concerning Levinas's insights on "Totality" and "I" see his work *Entre Nous* (1998a, 13-38). Regarding Kierkegaard's view on Hegel in general, see M. C. Taylor, *Journeys to Selfhood* (1980, 8, 105-121); J. Stewart, *Kierkegaard's relation to Hegel* (2003). For more details, see N. Thulstrup, *Kierkegaard's relation to Hegel* (1980, 279-381).

highlights that the self, "overcome by its awareness of the burden of its own being, is helpless in acquiring any relief from it" (Caruana 2007, 254).

This chapter deals with the broad field of ethics (Levinas, 1985; Skorupski 2010; Thomas 2004: Llewelyn 1995) and philosophy of religion (Yandell 1999; Kosky 2001, 131-196). It details Levinas's[40] and Kierkegaard's[41] arguments on whether we can approach God's essence and whether (and how) God can be revealed to us. Starting with the notion of Heideggerian ontotheology (Thompson 2005, 29-33)[42] and its relation to fundamental ontology[43] (Levinas 1998a, 1-11), I argue that we can "speak" of God beyond and outside ontotheology (Schrijvers 2006, 302-314; idem 2010, 221-233) by

---

[40]   The main comprehensive works by Levinas are *Totality and Infinity* (1969) and *Otherwise than Being or Beyond Essence* (2010).

[41]   A useful guide for a productive reading of Kierkegaard, especially on ethics, subjectivity, and the self, can be found in J. Caputo, *How to read Kierkegaard* (2007, ch, 3, 5, 9). The essential works of Kierkegaard are those about persons and their relation to other beings and God (2009, 2004, 1995). A well-structured essay concerning Levinas's and Kierkegaard's notions on divine transcendence can be found in M. Westphal, "Commanded Love and Divine Transcendence in Levinas and Kierkegaard" (2000, 200-223). A very useful guide concerning Kierkegaard's philosophical and religious aspects edited by E. F. Mooney, *Ethics, Love and Faith* (2008), gives particular attention to subjectivity, personal identity, and selfhood. See idem (2008, 11-23, 24-38, 2008b, 39-47). Concerning Kierkegaard's notion of self-love, see J. Lippitt, *The Problem of self-love* (2013) and J. Bukdahl, *Kierkegaard and the Common Man* (2001).

[42]   A quite valuable article concerning the transition from Heidegger's fundamental ontology to Levinas's deconstruction of the subject is D. Franck's "The Body of Difference" (2000, 3-29), where Franck opposes a "movement of transcendence internal to the Same" (ibid., 5).

[43]   It is worth noting from the beginning that Levinas intends neither to reject (fundamental) ontology based on the difference between beings and "Beings" nor to present ontology as a rotten philosophical discipline. Instead, he tries to ask whether it is fundamental (Dimitrova 2011, 19). As we shall infer in this study, he admits that first philosophy is not ontology but rather ethics which provides necessary and sufficient conditions to philosophize about God, subjectivity, and humans.

providing (intuitive)[44] arguments derived from the field of ethics and philosophy of religion instead of ontology (Critchley and Bernasconi 2004, 1-32). After discussing Levinas's and Kierkegaard's insights on God, I contend that these thinkers, even though they agree on several issues about God (Westphal 2008a, 45-72), interpret God's essence and His relation to human beings (if any) from different perspectives (Simmons and Wood [eds.] 2008, 99-121). Levinas points out that we cannot regard God or reflect God's substance/essence directly. It is impossible for us to reach or reflect God because He is infinite. Levinas believes in God's existence, but God, in Judaism (Putnam 2004a, 33-62; idem 1999, 93-134) is a transcendence unknowable for us.[45] We, as finite beings, cannot name, understand, or communicate directly with God. For Levinas, God is never experienced directly but only as a trace (or in the trace) whose "infinity is testified to in the infinity of responsibility to the hungry and the meek" (Kin

---

[44]   By saying intuition in philosophy, we mean "a nonsensible (non-thematized), nondiscursive faculty or method of knowing the truth about profound of difficult issues. Idealist (and ethicist) philosophers often appeal to intuition (and not to epistemology or metaphysics) and appeal to its great value (especially on religious, theological and ethical reflection). Intuitions (therefore) are starting points for philosophical reflection" (Martinich 2005, 192).

[45]   From Kierkegaard's philosophical perspective, there is a radical difference between Judaism and established Christianity since the former unites divinity and earthly life where the latter makes a division: "Judaism unites the divine and this life — [established] Christianity makes a division. The life of the true Christian will therefore be fashioned according to the paradigm which for the Jews is the paradigm of the ungodly man" (Watkin 1990, 70-71). For Kierkegaard, Judaism must be construed by true Christians as a biblical revelation which seeks absolute transcendence. However, Kierkegaard tries to promote a direct communication with God while Levinas insists on an asymmetrical relationship. For further details on Kierkegaard's view of Judaism and Levinas's reply to these challenges, see M. Fox-Muraton, "Election or the Individual? Levinas on Kierkegaard's Challenges to Judaism" (2012, 367-386).

2006, 99).[46] We can communicate with Him indirectly by the face of the "Other" (Waldenfels 2004, 63-81). The "Other" human is not a God but rather His only trace (Dimitrova 2011, 37-48).[47] It is impossible for humans (as finite persons) either to have direct communication with God or to reflect His essence.

> "The direct comprehension of God is impossible for a look directed upon him, not because our intelligence is limited, but because the relation with infinity respects the total Transcendence of the other without being bewitched by it, and because our possibility of welcoming him in man goes further than the comprehension that thematizes and encompasses its object [...] The comprehension of God taken as a participation in his sacred life, an allegedly direct comprehension, is impossible, because participation is a denial of the divine, and because nothing is more direct than the face to face, which is straightforwardness itself." (Levinas 1969, 78).

There is a clear statement in Levinas's work that clarifies that he is against the claim of any theology[48] to teach us what God

---

[46] In Kierkegaard, I am free to love the other before any call from her. This call comes not from the side of the other but is a duty of mine. Kierkegaard contends that it is my duty to love the neighbor, as does Levinas, even the "ugliest, the most wretched. "And what is the ugly? It is the neighbor whom one must love. One must love him; this is something that simple wise man knew nothing about; he did not know that the neighbor existed, and that one ought to love him" (Kierkegaard 1995, 301).

[47] At this point, I would really like to thank Maria Dimitrova who provided me with invaluable information concerning this issue.

[48] I am mainly referring to two specific types of theology: the mystical and rational theology with which Levinas (and I) strongly disagree contending that they both promote a form of idolatry. Below I provide an excerpt written by R. Urbano that it is of immense importance in order to clearly understand the above argument regarding several rotten implications of rational and mystical theology. "God is replaced with a sacred object. Moreover, he rejects rational theology because it thematizes God and reduces him to a mere concept. [...] God becomes a mere idea, and this leads to a kind of conceptual idolatry. [...] Rational and mystical theology weaken, if not destroy, God's transcendence and these two approaches presuppose that God can be accessed other than through one's ethical responsibility for the Other". See R. Urbano, "Approaching the divine: Levinas on God, Religion, Idolatry and Atheism" (2012, 51). A comprehensive study on Levinas's insights on ethics and theology in general can be found in M. Purcell's chapter "Ethics, Theology and the question of God" in

wants, creates, or expects. This is not Levinas's philosophical task. Contrarily, Levinas contends that metaphysics[49] must be seen as an ethical relation between humans (subject-subject relation) and not as violence (subject-object relation). According to Levinas, we are not in a position to say "truth" about transcendence, that is infinity, because we are finite beings, and transcendence does not dwell in immanence (Levinas 1998a, 179-180).[50] Man is responsible for discovering God's trace through the face of the "Other". Everything depends on man.[51] Transcendence does not depend on rational presuppositions or knowing, but, as Levinas points out, "transcendence is beyond being [...] not to be an absorption

---

Levinas and Theology (2006, 45-72). There is also a valuable note in Derrida's work *Religion* where he criticizes Heidegger's singularity between faith and belief, referencing also Levinas's view of "a faith in a holiness without sacredness" (Derrida 1998, 64). Concerning Derrida and Heidegger on phenomenology of religion, see P. Costello, "Towards a Phenomenology of Religion Across the Limits of Reason Alone" (2014, 106-126). Another paradigm that shows Levinas's objection to rational theology is evident in his text "God and Philosophy" (1989, 168), which underlines that "if the intellectual understanding of the biblical God, theology, does not reach to the level of philosophical thought, this is not because it thinks of God as a being without first explicating the being of this being, but because in thematizing God it brings God into the course of being [...] Rational theology, fundamentally ontological, strives to take account of transcendence in the domain of being by expressing it with adverbs of height applied to the verb being".

49 By metaphysics Levinas probably means transcendence and not the knowledge of beings *qua* beings as in analytic philosophy. In analytic philosophy several thinkers mistakenly equate metaphysics with epistemology, which is "the study of what can be known and how it is possible" (Martinich 2005, 191). Therefore, in analytic philosophy metaphysics as interconnected with epistemology means "the study of the most general features of reality" (ibid).

50 Levinas comprehensively explains his philosophical objection to ontology and immanence in his work *Of God Who Comes to Mind* (Levinas 1998b, 57-62).

51 This is a Talmudic principle which gives power to man as a master of God's indirect presence on earth. Levinas develops this thesis by contending that "the presence of God to the world, in the form of its soul, and in the light of this, the coherence of the whole system and the presence of the soul to each world, all depends on man" (Levinas 1994d, 159). Concerning Levinas's interest in Talmudic studies, see C. Chalier, "Levinas and the Talmud" (2004, 100-118.

in immanence [...] [it] is ethics which is not, in the last analysis, the *I think* (which it is at first) or the unity of transcendental apperception is, as a responsibility for another, a subjection to the other" (Hand [ed.] 1989, 178).

> "The life of the human individual sustains and gives life to the cosmos [...] *Being* is, through ethics and man. Thus, man is responsible for the universe. He makes and unmakes worlds, elevates and lowers them. God's reign depends on me. God has subordinated his efficacy—his association with the real and the very presence of the real—to my merit or demerit. And so, God reigns only by the intermediary of an ethical order, an order in which one being is answerable for another. The world is, not because it perseveres in being, not because being is its own *raison d'etre*, but because, through the human enterprise, it can be justified in its being. The human is the possibility of a being-for-the-other. That possibility is the justification of all existing (Levinas 1994d, 126).

For Levinas, "the Transcendent, infinitely other, solicits us and appeals to us", and in practice, ethically speaking, God's revelation can only be 'revealed' through the destitution in the face of the stranger, the widow and the orphan" (Levinas 1969, 78). In parallel, as Schrijvers correctly states, "I cannot identify myself with God, for, when confronted with the other, God seems to be absent" (Schrijvers 2011, 100).

Levinas himself does not impose his religion on us but invites us to think with him. The most important issue in Levinas's philosophy is not his faith but his ethics as first philosophy. The above statement will be discussed in a separate chapter analyzing the problem of personality. In the next subchapter, I give some brief examples on how Anglophone analytical thinkers understand philosophy (Sorell and Rogers 2003, 25-41) and how they explore the notion of the self-integrated into experience of knowledge (Chappell 2011, 1-27)[52] in sciences and naturalism (Christensen 2008, 205-312). I do not intend to expand on their philosophical accounts in depth since the aim of this study is mainly to analyze what Levinas and Kierkegaard say about persons, God, and subjectivity. It is ethics and philosophy of religion that is discussed in this study and not the discipline of ontology. As Dimitrova clearly states, "for Levinas, the notion of totality (understood ontologically by a traditional philosophy as the sum of all possible elements and their relationships identical with the Being or existence as a Whole) is derived *analytically* from thinking, which is viewed as the highest instance of synthesis of knowledge. Levinas opposes this philosophy with the idea of ethics prior to ontology" (Dimitrova 2011, viii).

1.2 God and Ontotheology

This sub-chapter deals with philosophical assumptions regarding whether we can provide valid arguments or a proper ethical intuition in order to answer (if possible) the question as to whether it is proper for us to hold that conscious human beings can be cognitively aware of God. Philosophical accounts concerning God integrated with man's thinking are a field that was initiated centuries before Christ. Socrates (470-399 BC) and especially Plato (427-423 BC)[53] together with

---

[52] Bibliographical citations of this study are extremely important to understand how analytic thought explores the notion of the self in contemporary philosophy (Chappell 2011, 26-27).

[53] For instance, Plato, in his work *Parmenides*, is against any ontological relations between God (τὸ Ἕν) and *logos*. He contends in Parmenides's dialogue that "[...] οὐδαμῶς ἄρα ἐστί τό Ἕν. Οὐ φαίνεται [...] τό Ἕν οὔτε ἐστίν [...] Οὐδ' ἄρα ὄνομα ἐστίν αὐτῷ, οὐδέ λόγος, οὐδέ τις ἐπιστήμη, οὐδέ αἴσθησις, οὐδέ δόξα. [...] Οὐδέ ὀνομάζεται, οὐδέ λέγεται, οὐδέ γιγνώσκεται" (Plato 1990 72, 142a). Tr. "The One

Aristotle (382-322 BC)[54] systematized the philosophy of religion during the fifth and fourth centuries BC. (Anton and Preus 1983, 1989, 1991, 1992). But it was Plotinus (204/5-270 AD)[55] who — having pre-Socratic influences — (Stamatellos 2007, 99-112; Grondin 2012, 3-6) initiated the "duality of the One" (τὸ Ἓν ἐν δυσὶ ὑποστάσεσι), which influenced several thinkers in the Middle Ages (ibid., 80-106) such as

---

cannot be shown. It is invisible, separated from the Being, which should be neither named, nor described not thought of nor known". For the hypothesis of the Idea and Good in Plato see J. Grondin, *Introduction to Metaphysics* (2012, 21-45).

[54] See Aristotle's *Metaphysics*, esp. book E', Z', Λ' and his consideration of being as being and "Being" as first philosophy (ibid. 46-55) and regarding ontotheology (ibid. 55-66). For Aristotelian ethics see Aristotle, *Nichomachean Ethics* (1998).

[55] Concerning Plotinus's *Metaphysics of the One*, see above J. Grondin, *Introduction to Metaphysics*, 68-73. Levinas refers to Plotinus's works several times. Levinas admired Plotinus's theological aspects, especially Plotinus's argument on "the One" (Τό Ἓν). The majority of Medieval and Byzantine philosophical and theological views were developed upon Plotinus's and Neo-Platonists' theology of the Ἓν. The most comprehensive monographies on Plotinus are written by H. J. Blumenthal, *Soul and Intellect: Studies on Plotinus and Later Neo-Platonism* (1993, 140-152), where he comments on the Ennead V, which analyzes the notion of the "One" and what it is to be intellectual. Also, see J. Bussanich, "Plotinus's Metaphysics of the One", 38-65 and K. Corrigan, "Essence and Existence in the Enneads", 105-129 (both texts) in L. P. Gerson (ed.), *The Cambridge Companion to Plotinus* (1996). Levinas argues that "Plotinus conceived the procession from the One as compromising neither the immutability nor the ab-solute separation of the One. It is in this situation, at first purely dialectical and quasi-verbal [...] that the exceptional signifyingness of a trace delineates in the world" (Levinas 1987a, 105-106). Presumably, Levinas derives several ideas from the fifth Ennead, where Plotinus explores his argument on the conception of the "One" and his attributes against intelligibility, humans, and absolute knowledge. For instance, Levinas might agree with Plotinus's position regarding the transcendence of the "One": §6. [The "One"] is beyond being. This is the requirement of negative theology (Gerson [ed.] 2018, 581). However, Levinas would disagree with Plotinus's generic remark that "the Intelligibles are not outside the Intellect" (ibid. 5.5 (32), 583). Levinas argues against this view since he believes that intelligibility is prior consciousness, will, and freedom. It is housed between me and the eternal *a priori* responsibility for the "Other". Levinas is familiar with Plotinus's texts, saying that "if you read the *Enneads*, the One doesn't even have consciousness of self, if it did have consciousness of self, it would already be multiple, as a loss of perfection. In knowledge, one is two, even when one is alone. Even when one assumes consciousness of self, there is already a split" (Levinas 1998a, 112).

Augustine[56] (354-430 AD) (ibid., 73-79), Maximus the Confessor[57] (580-662 AD), Aquinas (1225-1274 AD) (ibid., 95-98), and Anselm of Canterbury (1033-1109 AD) (ibid., 85-89), who brought into metaphysics questions about God and the philosophy of religion.[58] However, it was Heidegger who first initiated ontotheology into the philosophy of religion (ibid., 201-224), a term that is thoroughly explicated in this chapter.[59] Specifically, this chapter analyses whether we can speak of God beyond and above ontotheology. Before addressing arguments regarding Levinas's and Kierkegaard's insights on God and our subjectivity as a response to God's command, several terms must be defined.

By ontotheology[60], we mean the integration of thinking between beings *qua* beings and God. In simple words, ontotheology supports the radical replacement of religion,

---

[56] Regarding Augustine's philosophy of religion and theology, see his comprehensive works, *City of God* (1984) and *Confessions* (1987).

[57] The most reliable and comprehensive translation of Maximus the Confessor's texts is by P. Allen and B. Neil, *Maximus the Confessor and His Companions: Documents from Exile* (2002). See also T. T. Tollefsen, *The Christocentric Cosmology of St Maximus the Confessor* (2008, 64-137) and N. Loudovikos, *A Eucharistic Ontology: Maximus the Confessor's Eschatological Ontology of Being as Dialogical Reciprocity* (2010).

[58] Concerning philosophy of religion from ancient times to the twentieth century, see G. Oppy and N. N. Tsakakis (eds.), *The History of Western Philosophy of Religion* (2013).

[59] Immanuel Kant "invented" the term ontotheology, but it is Heidegger who systematized this term regarding the relation between theology and ontology. Kant remarks that the belief that one can actually "strive for a supposed contact with God" involves a "kind of madness" (Kant 1996, 169-70). In parallel, Heidegger points out that the "Onto-theological" constitution of metaphysics puts God in philosophy. And the question that must be answered is how the deity enters philosophy. In Kantian thought, there is a return to ontotheology "in which it determines the idea of God where God is posited as the totality of reality" (Levinas 2000, 154).

[60] One of the most "dangerous" pitfalls of ontotheology is the danger of "reducing God to another familiar object of our worldly experience which is a constant reality and threat in so much of theology and church life, often exploding into public life in the form of fundamentalism" (Min 2006, 114).

51

giving priority to consciousness and cognition as necessary and sufficient conditions to comprehend God. According to Kant, "ontotheology describes a kind of theology that aims to know something about the existence of God without recourse to scriptural or natural revelation through mere concepts of reason alone" (Halteman 1998). On the other hand, for Heidegger, "ontotheology is a critical term used to describe a putatively problematic approach to metaphysical theorizing that he claims is characteristic of Western philosophy in general" (Uttley 2016, 23, n. 16). Influenced by Western tradition, Heidegger "tries to turn existence into entities which can be understood and mastered through technological drive" (Minister and Murtha 2010, 1029). Ontotheology, according to Levinas, "consists in thinking of God as a being and in thinking being on the basis of this superior or supreme being" (Levinas 2000, 160)[61] and is a rotten theory since it "corrupts our thinking about God", and thus we need to "think God without Being" (Minister and Murtha 2010, 1029). From the exact time that God came into philosophy we can speak of ontotheology. In ontotheology, world and being are always "apprehended and comprehended by thinking" (Levinas 2000, 167). According to Heidegger, "the comprehension of being in its truth was immediately covered over by its function as the universal foundation of beings, by a supreme being, a founder, by God. The thinking of being, being in its truth, becomes knowledge (*logos*) or comprehension of

---

[61] Sometimes Levinas refers to God using Platonic terminology: The Good/God. Levinas claims that "the Good is, in spite of us" (Dimitrova 2011, 42). By this he means that even if God exists, he does not exist as the majority of people think, but it is impossible to think (as beings) how God evaluates human situations and issues.

God: theo-logy" (ibid., 123). However, when "being is immediately approached in the form of a foundation of beings, it
comes to be named God" (ibid.): and this is "onto-theology".[62] The more thinking and logic are developed, the more
we can speak of ontotheology. We can say that ontotheology
is in parallel to fundamental ontology.[63] The image of God
alone cannot be construed without the power of comprehension of beings. Thus. ontotheology needs the neo-technologi-
cal culmination of modernism in order to reveal itself. We can
infer that, for ontotheology, there is not God without beings
nor beings without God. God ($\Theta\varepsilon\acute{o}\varsigma$), the supreme infinite
"Being", is signified by "Beings", and beings are signified by
God. In the Western (Anglophone) philosophy of religion,
ontotheology is the middle term between God and beings
($\acute{o}\nu\tau\alpha$) *qua* beings. The Heideggerian being is an impersonal
power leading "to an account of history as impersonal

---

[62] Several thinkers assert that Levinas has no intention of totally infringing on
Heidegger's ontotheological insights, but of recasting them since he himself put
God in the conversation as well, although within an extremely different framework: through the face-to-face relation. For instance, A. Peperzak contends that
Levinas has no intention of infringing on or "destroying" Heidegger's thinking
on ontotheology, but he recasts and criticizes it as "a manifestation of the natural egoism which constitutes the elementary form of [immanent] life" (Peperzak
1997, 10).

[63] Choosing this mode of thinking, that is, by considering God as having the
power of knowledge and comprehension, we inevitably reduce God's essence
to that of beings. This is a huge mistake, as God, according to Levinas, is irreducible to human knowledge and "Physics". R. Scruton, supporting this thesis,
notes that God as well as subjects are not related to objects and physical laws.
It is only objects that are (which is why Levinas prefers the term "humans" to
"beings"): "Look for them [i.e. subjects] in the world of objects and you will not
find them. This is true of you and me; it is true too of God. *Physics* gives a complete explanation of the world of objects, for that is what 'physics' means. God
is not a hypothesis to be set beside the fundamental constants and the laws of
quantum dynamics. Look for him in the world of objects and you will not find
him" (Scruton 2012, 166). However, Levinas would proceed to clarify that God
cannot be understood directly either by the laws of quantum physics or by subjects.

destiny" (Kearney 2003, loc. 4733). The ethical stance of Levinas "is not an instrumental contract that the self of will to power […] makes" (ibid. loc. 4905) but an infinite command of goodness.

Meaning,[64] for ontotheology, necessarily has to be. Thinking is integrated with meaning. Thought and comprehension are inseparable from meaning. What is meaningful must be a necessary and sufficient condition for being. That is, being necessarily must confirm thought and knowledge. All these characteristics of fundamental ontology mean that we cannot speak of God outside the framework of ontotheology. However, ethics raises several objections to the arguments discussed above. For ethics, in general, God must be understood (if we ever can understand God) beyond ontotheology.[65] According to Levinas, "it is from a certain ethical

---

[64] Levinas gives proper attention to meaning in his work *Of God Who Comes to Mind* (1998b, 152-171).

[65] This is a very interesting point that needs further consideration. Even Levinas, who vehemently rejects ontotheology, which gives priority to rationality and teleology of reason (Courtney 2014, 248-291), "apologizes" to God and to himself because even outside ontotheology, he attempts to speak about the infinite (that is God) by expressing his thoughts and insights, even if he provides ethical implications (Levinas 1994, 30-50). For instance, in his work *Of God Who Comes to Mind*, he uses in the title the relative pronoun *who*. Thus, even if he wants to provide arguments against ontotheology he indirectly attributes human definitions to God since the relative pronoun *who* refers to humans: men and women. In the second chapter of that work he claims that "not to philosophize is still to philosophize" (Levinas 1998b, 55). Even if Levinas clearly rejects ontotheology by saying that the problem with ontotheology is that it is ultimately a kind of rational theology, that "in thematizing God [and attributing Him human conditions such as mind, voice, thinking, logic, etc.] Theology has brought Him into the course of being" (ibid.), he himself admits that he is obliged by speech to express his opinion that there is no opinion about God. However, he claims that by saying that there is no opinion about God we already express our opinion. This view is expressed by several thinkers who claim that ontotheology is inseparable from God-talk and God-discussion and that God who comes to mind comes necessarily to us in order to accept or raise questions about His essence and His relation to human beings. For instance, J. Robbins alleges that we cannot escape ontotheology even though we do not accept it. Ontotheology

54

relationship that one may start out on this search" (Levinas 2000, 125). Deriving from Plato's view that "Good"[66] (by which presumably here Levinas means the divine supreme God) is beyond being, Levinas builds up the structure of his "radical alterity" (Levinas 1991, 16; Robbins 2002, 142). As Levinas points out, there is an urgent need to distinguish philosophy from theology since "to philosophy belongs being and to Theology there is faith, revelation and God" (Robbins 2002, 147).[67]

It is worth noting that even though this chapter analyses and compares Levinas's and Kierkegaard's views regarding God and how beings are interrelated to God, we need to start with Heidegger in order to better understand the vital role of "Sameness" and "Otherness". Ontotheology gives priority to "Sameness", tying up logic with the relation between God and people. Thinking of God starts from beings and returns to beings themselves. In this way, the "Same" presses the "Other" to be absorbed and return to "Sameness" without revealing itself. Thus, the "Other" depends on the "Same" as

---

together with the issue of the death of God cannot be overcome since they are necessary and sufficient conditions for possible God-talk. By inventing and using the term God in any science, we automatically adopt ontotheology as a subsidiary factor for a God-talk. "For, the endeavor at overcoming remains trapped within ontotheology, and what is worse, it confuses this trap as the problem when in fact it is the very clue needed for thinking otherwise." (Robbins 2003, 3).

66 See Levinas's definition of "Good": "The Good invests freedom – it loves me before I love it. Love is love in this antecedence. The Good could not be the term of a need susceptible of being satisfied, it is not the term of an erotic need. a relationship with the seductive which resembles the Good to the point of being indistinguishable from it, but which is not its other. but its imitator. The Good as the infinite has no other. not because it would be the whole. but because it is Good and nothing escapes its goodness." (Levinas 1991, 187, n. 8).

67 Even though Levinas denies admitting that his work is theological, his work has several similarities to Karl Barth's "theology of language", especially when he tries to explain the notion of the "Saying" (Ward 1995, 147-170).

well as is addicted to and integrated into the latter. The "Other", according to ontotheology, is trapped by the "Same" and is unable to escape (Kearney 2003, loc. 4790). However, according to Levinas, "Otherness" is a separate version of oneself which is never adopted or absorbed by "Sameness". Only through my relation to the "Other" can I find God.

> "To be oneself is already to know the fault I have committed with regard to the Other. But the fact that I do not quiz myself on the Other's rights paradoxically indicates that the Other is not a new edition of myself; in its Otherness it is situated in a dimension of height, in the ideal, the Divine, and through my relation to the Other, I am in touch with God" (Levinas 1990, 17).

1.3 The Levinasian Priority of Ethics as First Philosophy over Ontotheology[68]

> "It is [for Levinas] a question of attaining, via the royal road of ethics, the supreme being, the truly being [...]. And this being is man, determined as face in his essence as man on the basis of his resemblance to God. Is this not what Heidegger has in mind when he speaks of the unity of metaphysics, humanism and onto-theology? [...] 'The Other resembles God.' Man's substantiality, which permits him to be face, is thus founded in his resemblance to God, who is therefore both the Face and absolute substantiality." (Derrida 1978, 142)

---

[68] Several thinkers who study Levinas agree with this statement; however, some of them, instead of ethics, use Levinas's phrase "Metaphysics precedes Ontology" (Levinas, 1969, 42) to explain the differences between Heideggerian ontology and Levinasian ethics. For instance, J. Grondin asserts that mistakenly "driven by its will to power and its egoism, ontology is transformed into first philosophy". He continues by saying that Levinas "in order to combat [without infringing on — as Levinas intention is not to infringe on or totally abandon Heidegger's ontology, but rather to put priorities on ontology and metaphysical ethics] its ontological imperialism proposes a terminological inversion: the primacy of the Same becomes that of the other, and ontology's primacy is transferred to ethics (here, Grondin analyses metaphysics as ethics and not as a science which investigates Being as Being neither as the fundamental [ontological] event] of our existence" (Grondin 2012, 244).

This subchapter offers some discussion and analysis of the Levinasian notion of God outside of ontotheology. Before discussing Levinas's arguments concerning God and His relation to human beings, it is urgent to discuss why Levinas considers ethics to be first philosophy[69] and how we can approach the relation between ethics, knowledge, and philosophy of religion.

Levinas, in his renowned article "Ethics as First Philosophy" (Kearney and Rainwater [eds.] 1996, 124-135), raises several objections to traditional classical knowledge, explaining that there are various disadvantages to the ontological basis that methodology stands for. The problem, as he points out, is that the classical notion of knowledge starts from immanence: "the ideal of rationality begins to appear as the immanence of the real to reason" (ibid.). The problem Levinas observes comes from a mistaken approach concerning the freedom of knowledge, which, according to classical tradition, is essentially the inspiration for the mind where (Hegelian) "wisdom of first philosophy is reduced to spirit as self-consciousness" (Aronoff 2010, 148, n. 295). "It is to be found in the concept of consciousness with the interpretation of *cogito* given by Descartes"[70] (Kearney and Rainwater [eds.]

---

[69]   That is to say, "Being only discovers itself by its being called [and not by its will] by the call [and not the will] of the other. Thus, before being comes responsibility, which implies a more originary origin than being itself" (Robbins 2002, 146).

[70]   It is important to briefly consider what the main difference in God in Levinas and Descartes is as both affirm the existence of God but within a different metaphysical framework. Even though Descartes admits that there is a God who is absolute and infinite, he "employs causal and ontological arguments to demonstrate that there is a God" (Bernasconi and Wood [eds.] 1998, 139). Levinas, who agrees on several positions with Descartes, especially that a subject has different thinking regarding his self and his finitude as well, "infinitude is the positive notion in terms of which the notion of man's finitude is understood"

1996, 125), described by Husserl as intentionality—"consciousness of something" (ibid.). Also, for Levinas, experience as human lived experience is interpreted wrongly in traditional lines of thought since they mistakenly express it as "collective and religious experience" (ibid.).

Levinas argues that Husserl's argumentation concerning intentionality and self-consciousness has a faulty basis.[71] According to Husserl, "knowledge is a 'filling out' that gratifies

---

(ibid., 142) underlines that one major difference with Descartes is that Levinas does not care to provide ratiocinative arguments on what it is to be God because we cannot say what God is. At this point I would like to express my sincere gratitude to my supervisor who patiently gave me specific directions on how I can reflect on Levinas's terminology about God, illeity, and transcendence as well as the way of differentiating Levinas's perspective on God from that of other thinkers, who, even though they admit the existence of God, they try to explain His existence with rational exegesis, something that for Levinas is absolute madness since we cannot compare with or think of infinity with our finite mind.

[71] Levinas agrees with the Husserlian dyadic relationship as a fundamental locus of concern and responsibility. Levinas also admits that he started his philosophical thinking on the "Other" from Husserl's idea that "the Other is the condition of correctness of my world and that each transcendence, including the transcendence of the outer world, exists for me and is comprehensible to me only by virtue of the transcendence of the Other". However, for Husserl, "both the Other and Transcendence are constituted in my immanence, whereas Levinas refuses to consider the Other as my *Alter Ego*" (Dimitrova 2011, 19-20). The "Other" calls me and teaches me how to transcend my potentials into infinity. Thus, I cannot escape responsibility and morality, which both precede my freedom and my decisions against my neighbor. In parallel, a second major problem with the Husserlian phenomenology of the "Other", Levinas claims, is that Husserl insists that the relation to the human other be understood as a relation of knowledge; the other can be understood as a relation of being: "our intuitive grasp of the other depicts him or her as a center of intentionality and hence as *alter ego*, as a sensuous-conscious subject" (Jodalen and Vetlesen [eds.] 1997, 5). Levinas discusses Husserl's view of the intentionality of consciousness (Levinas 1995, 37-52) and Husserl's method of intuition (ibid., 65-96), asserting that they provide an overall evaluation of phenomenology: noesis-noemata are revealed through the horizon of the intentionality of consciousness; that is, the latter is inseparable from the former. However, both terms, for Levinas, lack an ethical standpoint. Levinas argues that we need to make a step forward, from the intuition of essence to the philosophical intuition of existence: "Philosophical intuition must not be more directly characterized without mentioning the phenomenological reduction which introduces into the realm of phenomenology" (ibid., 135).

a longing for the being as object causing the world to be re-discovered as *noema*" (ibid., 127) where self-consciousness is a necessary and sufficient condition of knowledge. As Husserl points out, "all acts generally — even the acts of feeling and will — are 'objectifying' acts, original factors in the 'constituting' of objects, the necessary sources of different regions of being and of the ontologies that belong therewith" (Husserl 1931, section 117). For Levinas, "reduced consciousness rediscovers and masters its own acts of perception and science as objects affirming itself as self-consciousness and remains *a non-intentional* consciousness of itself" (Kearney and Rainwater [eds.] 1996, 127). Thus, Levinas suggests "a consciousness of consciousness, indirect, implicit and aimless without any initiative that might refer back to an ego" (ibid.).

Levinas also discusses another term, duration, by which he means "a consciousness that signifies not so much a knowledge of oneself as something that effaces presence or makes it discreet" (ibid.). This duration in phenomenological analysis remains "free from the sway of the will" (ibid.), and the most crucial thing is that it continues to be "absolutely outside all activity of the ego" (ibid.).

Levinas thus initiates, in contrast to Husserl, not ontological but transcendental phenomenology of the face where "the proximity of the other is the face's meaning" — there is a "face to face steadfast" (ibid., 130).[72] In contrast to the

---

72   I would agree with Grondin, who claims that "the Other is always a face, which can never be reduced to an idea I may have of it" (Grondin 2012, 244-245). This statement can be justified if we have a careful look at Levinas's phrase: "the way in which the other presents itself, exceeding the idea of the Other in me, we here name *face*" (Levinas 1969, 50). For Levinas, "the Other, *Autrui*, is not simply an *alter ego*, an *appresented* analogue of myself. He and I are not equals, citizens in an intelligible kingdom of ends...There is between us, an absolute difference. The Other is he to whom and in virtue of whom I am subject, with a

classical notion of knowledge, Levinas promotes and defends that [ethical] knowledge lies in the "Other" *prior* to any knowledge" (ibid.).

> "The Other (*l'Autre*) thus presents itself as human Other (*Autrui*); it shows a face and opens the dimension of height, that is to say, it infinitely overflows the bounds of knowledge. Positively, this means that the Other puts in question the freedom which attempts to invest it; the Other lays him- or herself bare to the total negation of murder but forbids it through the original language of his defenseless eyes." (Levinas 1996, 12)

To answer another crucial question concerning the relation between Christian ethics[73] and Levinas's ethics, for Levinas, the "Other" becomes my neighbor not in the same manner as the Christian dictum "Love your neighbor as yourself" but through a primordial concern about the "Other"; that is, "the Other becomes my neighbor precisely through the way the face summons me, calls for me, begs for me, and in so doing recalls my responsibility and calls me into question" (ibid., 131). For Levinas, responsibility exceeds the notion of "Being" as we know it in Heidegger's *Being and Time* and in Hegel's *Phenomenology of Spirit* or in other contemporary thinkers.[74] Being, according to Levinas, is not worth as much as

---

subjectivity that is heteronomy, not autonomy, and hetero-affection, not auto-affection. The Other is not the object of my concern and solicitude" (Bernasconi and Wood [eds.] 1998, 140).

[73] Even though there are hundreds of discrepancies between Christian ethics and Levinas's ethics, Christian thought derives several principles and aspects from Levinas's thought. See specifically a comprehensive article by A. T. Peperzak, "The Significance of Levinas's Work for Christian Work" in J. Bloechl (ed.), *The Face of the Other* (2000, 184-199). One of the most crucial discrepancies between Levinas and Kierkegaard is the term kenosis, that is, to abandon everything and everyone for the sake of the "Other". The latter term is being explored especially in Kierkegaard's Christology. See D.R. Law, *Kierkegaard's Kenotic Christology* (2013, 64-153).

[74] For instance, in Descartes, the self is the I of the *cogito* (cogito ergo sum), the center of consciousness leading to self-awareness and intentionality. In Spinoza and several analytic philosophers, being is enriched by additional emotions,

persons' relation to each other. Responsibility is beyond being and beyond being's immanence.

> "Responsibility goes beyond being. In sincerity, in frankness, in the veracity of this saying, in the uncoveredness of suffering, being is altered. But this saying remains, in its activity, a passivity, more passive than all passivity, for it is a sacrifice without reserve, without holding back, and in this non-voluntary — the sacrifice of a hostage designated who has not chosen himself to be hostage, but possibly elected by the Good, in an involuntary election not assumed by the elected one". (Levinas 1991, 15)

Despite Levinas agreeing with Sartre's expression that "existence precedes essence", he provides a different notion of freedom[75] and responsibility from that of Sartre's "sincerity".[76]

---

desires, autonomy, and freedom as well as second-order volitions, something that other animals lack. In Hume, the character of beings is like a container of ideas and expressions expressed in language and self-consciousness. With Husserl, the being is embedded in the world within a noematic-noetic framework explored as intentionality. In Heidegger, this embeddedness in the world is mainly practical and emotional where being's attributes and conditions return to itself. And finally, with Hegel, being is totalized and thematized, taking its power and consciousness to its core depending on its interiority. With Hegel's notion of the self, history ends. "Hegel explicated the progress of reason in history that coincides with God's self-development toward absolute consciousness. Thus, for him, God becomes Absolute Reason or *Geist*, the totality of reality" (Urbano 2012, 66).

75 According to Levinas, freedom is a characteristic that is especially misused in contemporary Western philosophy. It is necessarily connected to human rights and free will. If I have freedom, I am free to express my opinion without any coercion. However, Levinas provides a different view on "Westernized" freedom which is relevant to reason and power alone: "In a civilization which the philosophy of the same reflects, freedom is realized as a wealth. Reason, which reduces the other, is appropriation and power" (Levinas 1987a, 50).

76 Concerning similarities and discrepancies between Levinas and Sartre on God, subjectivity, and politics, see C. Howells, "Sartre and Levinas", in Bernasconi and Wood (eds.) *The Provocation of Levinas* (1988, 91-99). The most profound discrepancy between Levinas and Sartre is that the latter, in his work *Being and Nothingness,* as an atheist, prefers the Greek model of knowing where the encounter between the I and the other person is an event of cognition where selfhood becomes another piece of "furniture" in a mere procedure of intentional objects (Sartre 1956, 344-358). On the contrary, Levinas, as a Jew, is rooted in the Biblical tradition where the other is quite relevant and important to the ethical subjectivity of the pace of my life. The other appears as a "naked image" where she eternally seeks me to heal her wounds. As G. L. Bruns correctly puts it, "for Levinas, the

Levinas contends that responsibility matters only if it goes beyond my commitment to the "Other", before being devoted to myself, even before being. In short, for Levinas, ethics precedes ontology[77], and transcendence[78] precedes immanence.[79] In contrast to Sartre, responsibility, for Levinas, "stem[s] from a time before my freedom" (ibid.). It is the

---

ethical subject is defined by a responsibility that is *prior* to any rational deliberation executive decision; it is an anarchic responsibility prior to the kind of commitments that rational subjects […] know how to contract or refuse or hedge with loopholes and provisos" (Bruns 2004, 34).

[77] As M. Rutin correctly states, "this [relational] way of envisioning subjectivity is one reason that Levinasian phenomenology has played such a crucial role in recent ethical theory, for Levinas sought to understand precisely what it means to proceed from ethics to ontology rather than the other way around" (Ruti 2015, 2).

[78] According to Levinas, "the transcendence of God is his actual effacement, but this obligates us to men" (Levinas 2007, 125).

[79] At this point, I raise objections to those who believe that there are two different meanings of the "Other" in Levinas' *Totality and Infinity*. For instance, W. Large insists that immanence is related to transcendence in his article *The Two Meanings of the Other*, and that there would not have been transcendence without first analyzing immanence, and this is a necessary and sufficient condition to understand both God and human beings (Large 2011, 243-254). Large claims that "the other meaning, which is much less well-known, but which I believe is its true meaning, is the Other of immanence and interiority" (ibid., 243). Levinas, however, makes it clear in his work *Entre Nous* (1998a) what he means by asymmetrical relationship: "The relationship from me to the other is thus asymmetrical, without noematic correlation of any thematizable presence. An awakening to the other man, which is not knowledge" (Levinas 1998a, 168). Thus, from my point of view, immanence has nothing to do with ethical transcendence as the former is about rational beings and knowledge, and the latter about infinite God. They cannot be related to or reconsidered together. Immanence as an ontological term deals with beings qua beings and knowledge of beings. Transcendence as an ethical term deals with or is God. I agree with A. Kin, who notes that for Levinas, "it is especially the encounter of a particular kind of Other, the hungry, that shakes up our ordinary ontotheological consciousness in its complacency, closure, and arrogance, break[s] the circle of immanence that imprisons us in mystification, deception, and ideology, and open[s] a break or fissure in the epic of being in the direction of the beyond where another mode of transcendence can appear" (Kin 2006, 101). I also agree with Grondin's statement that for Levinas, all ontological thought of immanence, of the same present in all individuals, leveling over differences. But [on the other hand metaphysical [ethical] thought is one that discovers the transcendence of the Other which exceeds all my effort to understand it" (Grondin 2012, 244).

excellence of ethical proximity[80] — before any present. The most crucial and vital difference between Levinas and Sartre (and the above Christian dictum) is that, for Levinas, "responsibility for my neighbor dates from before my freedom in an immemorial past [...] to which nothing in the rigorously ontological order binds me [...] an immemorial freedom that is even older than being" (ibid., 131-132).[81]

Furthermore, Levinas contends that the phrase "to be or not to be" is not the principal question of human life. Instead, Levinas states that what really matters, as the principal abstraction of human life, is the bad conscience (mauvaise conscience) (ibid., 130, 133-34). According to Levinas, "the right to be, does not depend on the abstraction to the universal rules of the Laws, or to death" (ibid., 134). Rather, for Levinas, the crucial issue of the implication of being is "not the ontology of the understanding of that extraordinary verb, but the *ethics* of its justice", that is, "how being justifies itself" (ibid.).

Though Levinas started his philosophical thought from phenomenology, he abandoned the Husserlian observation of beings and focused mainly on a metaphysical transcendence of what he calls "Ethics as first philosophy" (Kearney [ed.] 2003, loc. 4718). For Levinas, the philosophy of the other echoes to infinity and the idea of the divine other, whether or

---

[80] Proximity is a crucial term in Levinas's thought. It is related to sensibility in accord with the matter of surprise. It has nothing to do with knowledge and cognition since it strives to get to know the other not through experience but mainly as a trace. Levinas states that sensibility "is itself exposed to alterity [...], is the *for-the-other* of one's own materiality; it is the immediacy or the proximity of the other [...] a relation not of knowing but of proximity" (Levinas 1991, xxvi, 74, 100) where the latter is defined as an "anarchic relationship with a singularity without the mediation of any principle, any ideality" (ibid., 100).

[81] Two articles of immense importance concerning immemorial time are those by M. Dimitrova (2011, 37-48) and M. Newman (2000, 90-129).

not this "Other" is God or another person. However, Levinas insists that we can only see God and communicate with Him through his trace, that is, the promise of openness to the other. R. Urbano correctly states that for Levinas, "God is disclosed to man at the moment the person responds to the call of the Other. This responsibility for the Other attests to the presence of God" (Urbano 2012, 59). However, I would add that this "presence" must be considered an indirect presence as God's presence to our finite minds is impossible. "This is why the face, in contrast to Hegel, is primordial and irreducible and it cannot be totalized, as the infinite, i.e. God comes to epiphany there" (Kearney 2003, loc. 4902). What matters for Levinas is not ontotheology but "the vulnerability of the eye of the other" (ibid.) who commands "Thou shalt not kill".

> "The first word of the face is 'Thou shalt not kill'. It is an order. There is a commandment in the appearance of the face, as if a master spoke to me. However, at the same time, the face of the Other is destitute; it is the poor for whom I can do all and to whom I owe all. And me, whoever I may be, but as a 'first person' I am he who finds the resources to respond to the call" (Levinas 1985, 89).
>
> "Responsibility for the other — the face signifying to me 'thou shalt not kill', and consequently also you are responsible for the life of this absolutely other — is responsibility for the one and only. The one and only means the loved one, love being the condition of the very possibility of uniqueness [...] The alterity of the other is the extreme point of the 'thou shalt not kill' and, in me, the fear of all the violence and usurpation that my existing, despite the innocence of its intentions, risks committing" (Levinas 1998a, 168-169).

According to Levinas, "to separate God from onto-theology" is to reexamine the notion of meaning (Levinas 2000, 127). As Levinas (as well as several postmodernist French thinkers such as Derrida[82] and Jean-Luc Marion)[83] states, in order to escape from ontotheology and its quasi-immanent characteristics, we need to decenter the subject from fundamental ontology and take into consideration "forms of thought different from intentionality" (ibid., 149). Levinas highlights that "to think God outside of onto-theology [is] to think no longer on the basis of positivity" (ibid., 167). "Otherness" must be separated from "Sameness". The former has to be detached from the latter, not be continuously absorbed by "Sameness". In this way, the ethical relationship ceases to be subjugated by ontotheology or "the thinking of being" (ibid., 127). For Levinas, knowledge and the manifestation of thinking beings need to be reconsidered not in the manner of the Greeks, who categorized knowledge within a tautological framework.

---

[82] Concerning similarities and discrepancies between Levinas and Derrida, see J. D. Caputo, "Adieu-sans Dieu: Derrida and Levinas" (2000, 276-312). A variety of secondary literature is dedicated to discussions on God, infinity, metaphysics and selfhood between Levinas and Derrida (Baird 2007, 423-437; Bernasconi 1995, 3-19, idem. 1986, 181-202, idem. 1985, 17-44; Boothroyd 2011, 41-59; Min 2006, 99-116; Papastephanou 2005, 461-485; Zaborowski 2000, 147-165).

[83] Derrida and Marion also raise several objections concerning the God of ontotheology. For instance, Marion claims that "the God of ontotheology is only an idol". See J.-L. Marion, *God without being: Hors-Texte* (1991) and *The idol and distance: Five studies* (2001). However, Marion expressed a different theoretical framework of the philosophy of the other and selfhood, criticizing that Levinas did not escape from ontology (and ontotheology) even if he provided an alternative voice to the phenomenology of Husserl's egology and Heidegger's ontotheology. On this issue see C. M. Gschwandtner, "The neighbor and the infinite: Marion and Levinas on the encounter between self, human other, and God" (2007, 231-249), especially regarding Marion vehement critique of Levinas's endeavor to destroy the self by giving absolute dominance to the other. Gschwandtner on page 234 cites Marion's phrase that Levinas's "[insistent] sincerity phenomenologically destroys the terms of the ontological difference", imposing a dramatic reduction to the self and putting it in danger of elimination. Therefore, for Marion, this "obedience to the ethical infinite would identify, in the new phenomenological reduction, he who oversteps the ontological difference" (ibid.). Thus, for Marion, this insistence in Levinasian ethics where "the self is defined by its responsibility to the neighbor who is always prior to the self" (ibid., 243) increases the danger of the self's elimination.

Meaning, in Levinas's theology, does not need the manifestation of being, i.e. to be, but to become. Levinas raises objections to the ontotheology that gives priority to power of the being who invites God to come to our minds through logic and comprehension. Levinas opposes this with a metaphysics of the good and the face-to-face intersubjective relationship[84] "wherein a nameless universal Being does not have final sway" (Kearney 2003, loc. 4737). Levinas sees Heideggerian ontology as an "ontology of power which is tempted to relate to the other by murder" (ibid., loc. 4759). Instead, Levinas proposes a different dialectic focused on defending the ethical community of the other. Levinas insists on the phrase "thou shalt not commit no murder":

> "To kill is not to dominate but to annihilate; it is to renounce comprehension absolutely. Murder exercises a power over what escapes power. It is still a power, for the face expresses itself in the sensible, but already impotency, because the face rends the sensible. The alterity that is expressed in the face provides the unique 'matter' possible for total negation. I can wish to kill only an existent absolutely independent, which exceeds my powers infinitely, and therefore does not oppose them but paralyzes the very power of power. The Other is the sole being I can wish to kill." (Levinas 1969, 198).

However, killing in Levinas's work is not real or pragmatic but ethical. We are not speaking of criminology or about facts

---

[84] For Levinas, the face-to-face relationship, even though it is derived from Husserl and Heidegger (his predecessors and mentors), has nothing to do with reciprocal and symmetrical intersubjectivity (Dimitrova 2011, 27). We may assume that Husserl's phenomenology is an ontology, and Heidegger's fundamental ontology is a phenomenology, both trying to thoroughly analyze the Greek term "physical". From his perspective, Levinas contends that he has made a step forward by proposing that the main topic of his thinking is metaphysical. As J. Llewellyn correctly infers in his article "Levinas, Derrida and Others Vis-à-vis", in R. Bernasconi and D. Wood (eds.) *The Provocation of Levinas* (1988, 136): "It is metaphysical because it is ethical. And it is ethical not because he aims to present a code or a metaphysics of ethics". He also adds that the "ethical is older than justice… [and] prior to all structures of being-with" (ibid., 137).

related to the penal system. The ethical crime of the "Other" is what Levinas endeavors to point out.

> "If the resistance to murder were not ethical but real, we would have a perception of it, with all that reverts to the subjective in perception. We would remain within the idealism of a consciousness of struggle, and not in relationship with the Other, a relationship that can turn into struggle, but already overflows the consciousness of struggle. The epiphany of the face is ethical. The struggle this face can threaten presupposes the transcendence of expression." (Levinas 1969, 199).

Ethically speaking, Levinas claims that we need to escape ontotheology by reconsidering meaning. However, the question that needs further discussion is this: How can we approach meaning without infringing on it in order to speak of God outside of ontotheology? In analytic philosophy several thinkers give priority to immanence where meaning seems to be *doxic*, expressing a logical exposition. In the Western tradition, the "being" is fundamental and it is characterized by the verb "to be". Everything which is logical, thetic, and analytical posits itself reflecting immanence and is presence. Therefore, it reveals ontotheology. This tradition is derived from the Greeks, who give priority to profound and fundamental experiences where God is attached to ontotheology through a logic of being *qua* being. The meaning of philosophical thought is drawn from the cosmos. In Heidegger, the "Same", which is the rational and the meaningful, is what really matters (Levinas 2000, 135).

Levinas, on the other hand, tries to determine whether ethics is a necessary and sufficient condition to justify God outside ontotheology. The answer is yes only if we find a method to speak about meaning "without reference to the world, to being, to knowledge, to the Same" (ibid., 137). This method can be followed through ethics: to signify a transcendence that would not be interpreted with analytical, thetic, and doxic arguments in presence. As Levinas states, "to transcend oneself toward the other, to go from the Same to the Other (ibid.) without the Other being absorbed and adopted by the Same. If the same can contain the Other then the Same has triumphed over the Other" (ibid., 141). However, Levinas contends that if transcendence is focused on appropriation (as Husserl claimed), it remains phenomenological immanence. The in-itself indicates the triumphant truth of the "Same" over the "Other", suppressing all ethical transcendence.[85] For Levinas, the phenomenon of transcendence

---

[85] It is worth noting that, for Levinas, there are two different views of subjective truth: (a) the triumphant truth and (b) the persecuted truth. Both terms were invented and discussed by Kierkegaard, as Levinas notes in his work *Proper Names*, ch. 8: "Kierkegaard: Existence and Ethics" (1996b, 66-74). Levinas explains that the triumphant truth, as Kierkegaard calls it, derives from Idealism, and especially from the Hegelian dialectic of the egocentric orientation of the subject. Truth triumphs, as Hegel explains, by "letting the human subject be absorbed by the Being that this subject uncovered. Idealism claimed that the unfolding of Being by thought allowed the subject to rise above itself and hand over its last secrets to Reason" (ibid., 66). This line of thought, in brief, culminates the triumph of absolute Being and Reason which empowers the self to be nominated as the core center of meaning and all reality. The self is universal and alone controls and commands everything through the totalization and apprehension of Being: "Being was the correlate of thought" (ibid., 67). On the other hand, Levinas immensely credits Kierkegaard's contribution to presenting a counter-argument against the above idealistic proposition. He proposes that subjectivity is irreducible to objective being (ibid., 68). Hence, truth must not be considered as a triumphant perfect realization of Being which totalizes experience, but as a "belief linked to a truth that suffers" (ibid., 69): as truth persecuted. By persecution Kierkegaard means that "it is through suffering truth that one can describe the very manifestation of the divine: simultaneity of All and Nothingness, Relation to a Person both present and absent-to a humiliated God who suffers, dies and leaves those whom he saves in despair. A certainty that coexists with an absolute uncertainty — to the point that one may wonder whether that Revelation itself is not contrary to the essence of that crucified truth, whether God's suffering and the lack of recognition of the truth would not reach their highest degree in a total *incognito*" (ibid. 69). However, Levinas observes an errant point in Kierkegaard's discussion of triumphant and persecuted truth. He contends that Kierkegaard's contribution to existential

(the infinite) is based on "the responsibility of the neighbor", an aimless meaning without vision (ibid., 142).

Levinasian ethics gives priority not to doxic but to paradoxical transcendence toward the "Other" and not toward itself. Levinas strongly favors the subversion of phenomenological immanence, turning to the phenomenon of enjoyment which does not credit "self-constituting or the primacy of the same over the other" but "the privilege of the other over the self" (Kearney 2003, loc. 4815, 4819). For Levinas, "paradox inscribes the glory of the infinite in the relationship called intersubjective" (Levinas 2000, 162). Hence, Levinas states that we can speak of God escaping ontotheology only if the "Other" as a nonthematizable, invisible interlocutor reveals in our intersubjective self prior freedom and essence. Ethics cannot be interpreted as knowledge of being and comprehension. Ethics rather is the relationship between me and the other, the neighbor. However, in contrast to the Christian Trinity,[86] the neighbor comes to me first without having any

---

philosophy and his correct critique of Hegel and Idealism leaves something crucial behind: responsibility. Levinas underlines that "[True] Subjectivity is in that responsibility and only irreducible subjectivity can assume a responsibility. That is what constitutes the ethical. To be myself means, then, to be unable to escape responsibility" (ibid., 73), something that Kierkegaard puts in the margins. Thus, persecuted truth for Levinas starts from Kierkegaard but ends with responsibility for the "Other" who chases me eternally, driving me into infinity. And the "Other" "is the poor, the destitute, and nothing about that Stranger can be indifferent to it [...and] I am responsible for the very one who commands me." (ibid., 74).

[86] Levinas would strongly reject views such as: "the clearest personal expression of religion and the view of God as Trinity (Τριάς) exists in the relations that make us persons [...] The search for meaning in Christian spirituality is enacted primarily by entering relationship with Christ and the Blessed Trinity [...] God the Father corresponds to our carbon relations because the Father is the creator of the carbon universe" (Bryson 2017, 11). Such a direct communication with God reduces God to our minds and therefore we then speak of ontotheology. For Levinas, the "face of God" is irreducible to finite human beings. The structure of spirituality depends neither on rational theology (such as those of

specific criteria or conditions. It is beyond freedom and essence. It is about responsibility and reciprocal authenticity. Ethical relationship is a responsibility for the other. "It is not a disclosure of something given but the exposure of the me to another, prior to any decision" (ibid., 187). Likewise, Levinas states that the ethical relationship, in contrast to ontotheology, is "a responsibility that obsesses, one that is an obsession, for the other besieges me, to the point where he puts in question my for-me, my in-itself, to the point where he makes me a hostage" (ibid., 138).[87] Thus, we can infer that autonomy, in Levinas's view, can be marginalized. What matters in this sense is heteronomy.[88] The latter is more ultimate than

---

several Christian doctrines such as the Catholic and the Protestant) nor on ascetic contemplation (i.e. Orthodoxy). For Levinas, when the holy is reduced to the sacred, there are idolatry and rational theology, which are both unacceptable. See E. Levinas, Part II: "Transcendence, Idolatry and Secularization", in his work *God, Death and Time* (2000, 163-166).

[87] The term "hostage" sometimes is mistakenly construed by several thinkers as they confuse it with being a prisoner or being taken by someone violently, i.e. slavery or servitude. Levinas, by saying that I am eternally hostage to the "Other", means that responsibility precedes freedom and autonomy: "a responsibility that obsesses, one that is an obsession, for the other besieges me, to the point he makes me a hostage" (Levinas 2000, 138). As M. Saracino underlines, "as hostage for-the-Other, the subject is called to care for the Other in non-totalizing ways, that is, by the way of gestures of justice, generosity and sacrifice" (Saracino 2003, 96).

[88] Concerning the difference between autonomy and heteronomy, Levinas gives priority to heteronomy: he states that "subjectivity, as responsible, is a subjectivity which is commanded at the outset; heteronomy is somehow stronger than autonomy here, except that this heteronomy is not slavery, is not bondage [...] The responsibility for the other comes from the hither side of my freedom" (Levinas 1998a, 111, 114). See further comments in A. Strhan, *Levinas, Subjectivity, Education* (2012, 73-94). J. Raz, in addition, defines autonomy by claiming that "the autonomous person is a (part) author of his own life. The ideal of personal autonomy is the vision of people controlling, to some degree, their own destiny, fashioning it through successive decisions throughout their lives" (Raz 1986, 369). For Levinas, this statement would be correct to define autonomy, but lacks ethical content. If an autonomous person is the author of their life, controlling their own destiny, egology and ontology appear to a high degree. If all my thought is about how to build and maintain a personal pursuit of happiness first, this is, for Levinas, ontology. Autonomy produces an equal-to-thought

the former, where a heteronomous ethics assumes an infinite responsibility. In parallel, eros and *agape* (love)[89] are "breaking out of monadism and the egocentric predicament, where the self *agapeically* goes towards the other as other" (Kearney 2003, loc. 4924, 4932).[90] The self is for the other and not the other for the self. In this sense, the difference or *différance*[91] of the other as hostage[92] gives priority to religion and ethics to speak of God outside ontotheology since the I (ὁ ὤν) depends on the "Other" as an interlocutor and not the "Other" on the

---

status (Levinas 1998a, 180) whereas the "Other" is inevitably marginalized for the sake of self-interest and "Sameness". Levinas develops his thought concerning autonomy and its integration with reason in his work *Entre Nous*, ch. 15: "Uniqueness", 190-191.

89   When Levinas was asked what the difference between eros/love and agape was, he confessed: "I do not think that Agape comes from Eros […] Eros is definitely not Agape, that Agape is neither a derivative nor the extinction of love-Eros. Before Eros there was the Face; Eros itself is possible only between Faces. The problem of Eros is philosophical and concerns otherness […] I have a grave view of Agape in terms of responsibility for the other" (Levinas 1998a, 113). Eros has a dramatic nostalgia which remains in presence. Levinas contends that love as agape has more ethical and metaphysical repercussions. For Levinas, "love [as agape] desires not a nostalgic return to stasis but reaches out instead towards the other and ultimately towards a future: the impossibility or failure of fusion is the very positivity of love" (Sandford 2000, 97).

90   Concerning the phenomenology of eros, see P. Moyaert, "The Phenomenology of Eros: A Reading of Totality and Infinity" (2000, 30-42).

91   The term *différance* is developed by J. Derrida and is adopted also by Levinas in order to explain the importance of transcendence over immanence. In deconstruction and postmodern philosophy, according to Derrida, the subject must be decentered and replaced by intersubjective conditions beyond knowledge and logic. To differ, according to Derrida, means to differ from itself. For Derrida, *différance* is not an analytical concept or even a word. It is not what we represent to ourselves as beings. "It is the nonfull, nonsimple origin: it is the structured and differing origin of differences" (Kearney and Rainwater [eds.] 1996, 449). "It is a trace of something that can never present itself; It is a trace that lies beyond what profoundly ties fundamental ontology to phenomenology" (ibid., 459). Levinas insists that in this way we can speak of God outside ontotheology.

92   As Levinas states, "for all eternity, the *I* were the first one called to this responsibility; non-transferable and thus unique, thus *I*, the chosen hostage, the chosen one. An ethics of the meeting — sociality. For all eternity, one man is answerable for another" (Levinas 1998, 227).

I. Thus, the I, according to Levinas, must be used in the accusative case: "me". "Me" needs someone to exist. It cannot be alone. "Me" (in the accusative case)[93] needs the "Other" as an equal interlocutor[94] (Levinas 1998a, 4-9) in order to be meaningful. According to Levinas, "pre-reflective, non-intentional consciousness would never be able to return to a moral realization of this passivity. The non-intentional is from the start passivity and the accusative [is] its first case (me and not I)" (Kearney and Rainwater [eds.] 1996, 129). One must speak in me and not in I, as Blaise Pascal says the I is hateful; "one has to respond to one's right to be" (ibid., 130). We can assume that Levinas is in favor of a transcendence in the notion of "the awaiting without something awaited" (Levinas 2000, 139). A transcendence "without aiming and without vision" tends to speak of God or to see God outside ontotheology (ibid.).

In this chapter, I do not intend to get involved with ontological aspects. However, through the criticism of fundamental ontology and ontotheology, I intend to explain Levinas's ethics. In ethics, as Levinas points out, there is an urgent need for the concept of the ontological "I" to be changed to the accusative case "me"; no one could replace

---

[93] Levinas writes, "Everything is from the start in the accusative. Such is the exceptional condition or unconditionality of the self, the signification of the pronoun self for which our Latin grammars themselves know no nominative form." (Levinas 1991, 112).

[94] By saying ethical interlocutor, I do not mean a procedure where the other will be absorbed by sameness. Dialogue and equal response in Levinasian ethics is not the same as *parole* and *langue* in connection to language. In Levinas's ethics, by saying that the other must be an equal interlocutor, we mean that the "Same" allows the "Other" to show her otherness in an equal procedure without coercion, (Hegelian) power, or (Husserlian) noematic-horizontal intentionality. The otherness of the other's equal deliberation never returns to the "Same" but, in contrast, echoes a heteronomy which is never strands of presence but in an immemorial time.

"me" (ibid., 152). The ethical "I-Thou" relationship as well as the relation between individuals and God needs not to be systematized but to have relations through responsibility. However, the former is a direct relation and the latter indirect. According to Levinas, "the absolutely other is the Other (*Autrui*). He and I do not form a number. The collectivity in which I say *you* or *we* is not a plural of the *I*. I, you — these are not individuals of a common concept [...] Alterity is possible only starting from me" and not from "I" or ego (Levinas 1969, 39-40).

1.4 Transcendence in Levinasian Thought as a Departure from Ontology

"The neutralization of the other who becomes a theme or an object-appearing, that is, taking its place in the light — is precisely his reduction to the same. To know ontologically [or just] .... to know, amounts to grasping being out of nothing or reducing it to nothing, removing from it its alterity...As for man, it can be obtained by the terror that brings a free man under the domination of another. For the things the work of ontology consists in apprehending the individual (which alone exists) not in its individuality but in its generality (of which alone there is science). The relation with the other is here accomplished only through a third term which I find in myself." (Levinas 1969, 43-44).

Levinas in the above statement tries to show us the difference between ontology and metaphysical ethics or ethical transcendence whereby "opposing ontology's totalitarianism, which attempts to reduce the Other to the same, the primacy given to ethics or metaphysics has its own ground in the irreducibility of the other or the immediate inescapable demand that emanates from it" (Grondin 2012, 244). First, since Levinas seems to admire apophatic or negative theology (only if it is enacted in ethical relations)[95], I will discuss what transcendence is not.[96] For Levinas, there are two different types of transcendence. On the one hand, there is an ontological-idolatrous transcendence which rests on rationality and on "the reign of the kingdom of being as immanence" (Levinas 2000, 165). This transcendence is not what Levinas tries to present since "the emphasis of being as being is Ontology" (ibid.). On the other hand, Levinas supports a different type of transcendence that has nothing to do with ontology. In contrast, he attempts to describe thoughts concerning God that "cannot be reduced to containing what is thought by them, but which should allow us to think properly what the word transcendence means" (ibid., 163). Only ethics can make this attempt possible.

To achieve this, we need to find a non-spatial exteriority, that is, a "movement that goes towards the other man and that is from the outset responsibility" (ibid., 169). According to Levinas, this is the semantic implication of ethics: "to shape a non-ontological transcendence that begins in human corpo-reality, in a direction of the beyond where a God that is other than the visible gods would abide" (ibid.). We are seeking a

---

[95] Levinas, like Kierkegaard, strongly opposes traditional theology since it reduces divine transcendence to immanence. However, Levinas would adopt a theology such as negative or apophatic theology only if imbued and integrated with ethical norms. For instance, Levinas underlines that "without the signification they draw from ethics, theological concepts remain empty and formal frameworks" (Levinas 1969, 79).

[96] According to Kant, transcendence, or the transcendental ideal, is thinking without falling into arbitrariness. Transcendence is divided into three conditions of the psyche towards the divine: theological, cosmological, and psychological, where "the given remains the prototype of being" (Levinas 2000, 154). For Kant, in contrast to Levinas, "God is posited as the totality of reality on an experienced basis" (ibid., 154). Taking into account the aforementioned statement, Levinas contends that Kant keeps the idea of empirical knowledge to understand God as "something that is".

transcendence without reason, "neither aiming nor thematization, a departure out of the world" (ibid., 170). We need to investigate a question beyond ontology, a question without a response. Only through "hunger, at a very humble level transcendence progressively appears" (ibid., 171). However, this appearance does not really appear, especially in the "glory of the Infinite", because it cannot apparently appear in itself (Kin 2006, 101). For Levinas, the appearance of something becomes at the same time an object "of representational consciousness" (ibid.) giving priority to totality and thematization. Thus, God as infinite cannot appear in the world directly since He is unable to be thematized synthetically or phenomenologically. The infinite's revelation is witnessed in the world without appearing but only through the responsibility of the neighbor, where the "Other" calls me and teaches me first.

It is an urgent need, according to Levinas, to surpass ontological transcendence until we reach ethical transcendence. Anarchical subjectivity is what matters and not to be reduced to the "transcendental consciousness that thematizes being" (Levinas 2000, 178). How can we achieve this transition from ontological to ethical transcendence? According to Levinas, we can reach ethical transcendence by seeing subjectivity as anarchy. By saying anarchy we do not mean the ideological definition of the term. Nor do we mean the antithesis of constitutional decisions or the vehement disagreement with civil laws upheld by legal systems. Philosophically speaking, by saying anarchy we mean "an idea that signifies with a significance prior to presence" (ibid., 217).[97] We need to see subjectivity as anarchy outside of an ontotheological framework. We need to build up a structure without a reasonable structure. We must approach the idea of God through inter-human, intersubjective relationships that "do not enter the framework of intentionality" (ibid., 172) and that do not give priority to freedom since Levinas states that "to be responsible is to be responsible before any decision" (ibid.). Thus, we can infer that responsibility precedes freedom and intentionality (Levinas 1994d, 127).[98]

> "The responsibility for the neighbor is precisely that which goes beyond legality and obliges beyond the contract. It comes to me prior to my freedom, from a non-present, from an immemorial. Between me and the other there gapes a difference which no unity of transcendental apperception could recover. My responsibility for the other is precisely the non-indifference of this difference: the proximity of the other. An extraordinary relation in the

---

[97]   Anarchy, in Levinasian ethics, is neither a justified responsibility in presence nor a social condition of meriting conditions such as kindness, gentleness, and good manners. It is rather a "responsibility that goes beyond what I may or may not have done to the Other or whatever acts I may or may not have committed (Kearney and Rainwater [eds.] 1996, 131)." Anarchy is an infinite tendency between me and the other whereas "I am responsible for everything and everyone, but no one is responsible for me" (Smith 2016, 98). As Levinas underlines, "it is despite myself that the other concerns me" (Levinas 1987a, 138).

[98]   Levinas clearly explains what he means by saying that responsibility precedes freedom. It is a claim impossible to declare in Greek thought or in contemporary analytical philosophy. For Greeks and then through Thomistic thought (Thomas Aquinas's Theology), freedom comes first as an eternal gift of autonomy, and responsibility is just a second-term attribute, a characteristic of freedom, which distinguishes moral beings from evil and injustice. In analytical philosophy, responsibility is a mere attribute of oneself. An agent, for instance, is a responsible man because he contributes donations and social activities. A lady is a responsible citizen because she obeys laws, pays her taxes, and has no problems with social and fiscal contracts. However, in Levinas, responsibility has an extremely different conception. For Levinas, "responsibility for the neighbor is precisely what goes beyond the legal and obliges beyond contracts, it comes to me from what is prior to my freedom, from a non-present, an immemorial. A difference gapes open between me and the other that no unity of transcendental apperception can undo. My responsibility for the other is precisely the non-indifference of this difference – the proximity of the other" (Hand [ed.] 1989, 180).

76

absolute sense of the term, it does not reestablish the order of representation in which all of the past returns. The proximity of the neighbor remains a diachronic break, or a resistance of time to the synthesis of simultaneity" (Levinas 1998b, 71).

Signification as one-for-the-other[99] and responsibility for another person are two facts quite crucial for Levinas. Autonomy and equalization are characteristics of sameness and they are not too important for Levinas and thus must be replaced by heteronomy and disequilibrium, which give priority to otherness.[100] What matters is the vital role of anachronism: "an assignation of me by another, a responsibility in regard to men we do not even know" (Levinas 2000, 173). Anarchical heteronomy provides a "nonobjective, nonspatial, obsessional, nonthematizable exteriority" (ibid., 174) against the ontological thesis which holds that all that "is in consciousness is posited there by consciousness" (ibid., 173).

The Levinasian transcendence mentioned above is ethical. The subjectivity of a being must detach himself from the "I". For Levinas, the "I", "affected by the infinite, cannot go to an end that it could equal in his desire. "The approach increases the distance and enjoyment is only the increase of hunger. The desired one thus remains transcendent to desire. It is in this reversal of terms that transcendence, or the disinter-restedness of desire, comes to pass" (ibid., 222). Subjectivity must be *otherwise than being*. He should see himself before himself having an eternal infinite responsibility to the

---

[99]   Levinas is trying to find a signification that is prior to any content. This can be achieved through the "Saying" to another, as the one-for-the-self, where the *for* in contrast to ontological thematization would have the ability to make the person approach the neighbor seeing him as an equal interlocutor far from any personal expediencies.

[100] For further discussion on autonomy and heteronomy, see E. Levinas, "Philosophy and the Idea of Infinity", (1987, 47-48).

other who reveals himself as a hostage. According to Levinas, ethics and responsibility precede freedom.[101] They both are revealed prior to any decision. They have an a priori condition which leads the "Good" to choose me first. It is not me who chooses the "Good", but "Good" is prior to any human decision.[102] Thus, presence must be reconsidered. Levinas points out that there is "a relationship with the Good that has invested me in assigning me to responsibility for another" (ibid., 177).

In order to understand what Levinas means by transcendence and what the main difference between ontotheological and ethical transcendence is, we need to discuss the problem of freedom and the major role of responsibility. As Levinas states, responsibility precedes freedom, and the ethical subject is prior to the initiative of the will. The "me" in the accusative is prior to self-affection due to the role of unlimited responsibility towards the other. The "me", in contrast to the Hegelian total "I", is without a return to self. Levinas therefore gives priority to responsibility since it "frees the subject from the gloomy tautology and the monotony of essence" (ibid., 179). Levinas's notion of responsibility must be understood as expiation,[103] encountering the other

---

[101] Responsibility also precedes dialogue and everything that is covered by thematization: "This responsibility is prior to dialogue, to the exchange of questions and answers, to the thematization of the said, which is superposed on my being put into question by the other in proximity" (Levinas 1991, 111).

[102] As F. Smith correctly points out, "the good has chosen me before I have chosen it" (Smith 2016, 97).

[103] As Levinas mentions, "and this, pushed to the limit, is sensibility, sensibility as the subjectivity of the subject. It is a substitution for another, one in the place of another, expiation." (Levinas 1972, 83-101). The "Saying" is of immense importance for language as well. Levinas mentions that "language does not begin with the signs that one gives, with words. Language is above all the fact of being addressed which means the Saying much more than the Said" (Bernasconi and

not with sympathy but as a hostage who suffers eternally. Being responsible for the other as substituted hostage, subjectivity emerges before all things, "even before freedom and being itself" (ibid., 181).

Transcendence, for Levinas, has nothing to do with presence, as Heidegger and Hegel claim. Levinas objects especially to the Hegelian "end of history" where the self has acquainted itself with the total power of being in presence.[104] Levinas is against this presence, contending that presence is defeated by the other. In order to reach ethical transcendence, we need to decenter the subject or shape it from a different perspective. According to Levinas, the "subject's position is his deposition." (ibid., 181). We need to make a "clear space for the hostage-subjectivity by sweeping away the notion of the person" (ibid.) as a self-enclosed unit where "the subject is not an opaque being equipped with the structure of egoity" (ibid., 182). As John Donne emphasizes, personhood is grounded on relational and not on isolated individual properties:

Wood [eds.] 1988, 169-170). On this subject, see also M. Eskin, "A language before words: Levinas's ethics as a semiotic problem" (2000, 29-49). Specifically, Eskin mentions that "Levinas implies that the other human being must have always been already 'pre-created' by yet another other in order to be able to semethically create me." (2000, 41). By this Levinas infers that the one signifies not in me but the "Other" through the already *said* and not the *saying*.

[104] Despite Levinas exploring entirely different dialectics to Hegel's in order to analyze the notion of the self and the priority of the other, we should not ignore that "it is in Hegel's coverall philosophical system that the other occupies an important position. Absolute spirit is exteriorized or alienated into world and this world contrasts with spirit as the other. Without the contrast with the other, spirit would be empty, without content, and unilateral" (Xiushan 2008, 442). What is vehemently criticized by Levinas as regards Hegelian dialectics on the self and his relation to the other is that being's "horizon as to the other is basically constrained to the scope of empirical beings or various beings [...] His variation means more about different from itself than absolute difference. Therefore, it is understandable that his viewpoint that non-being falls easily into the realm of being is criticized by Levinas" (ibid., 443).

"All mankind is of one author, and is one volume; when one man dies, one chapter is not torn out of the book, but translated into a better language; and every chapter must be so translated; God employs several translators; some pieces are translated by age, some by sickness, some by war, some by justice; but God's hand is in every translation, and his hand shall bind up all our scattered leaves again for that library where every book shall lie open to one another [...] No man is an island, entire of itself; every man is a piece of the continent, a part of the main. If a clod be washed away by the sea, Europe is the less, as well as if a promontory were, as well as if a manor of thy friend's or of thine own were: any man's death diminishes me, because I am involved in mankind, and therefore never send to know for whom the bell tolls; it tolls for thee" (Alford 1839, 574-575).

Chappell agrees with John Donne that "no man is an island", as she contends that "each of us at least begins as a piece of the continent, a part of the main" (Chappell 2013, 31). The word "begins" is crucial to connect this assertion to Levinasian ethics. By "at least begins as a piece of the continent" it is meant that there is an a priori primordial sense of infinite responsibility for the other, as Levinas would say. We are a "part of the continent", at least to begin with, because we are born with a "beyond" and not a "during". I do not earn my responsibility by being a moral person during my life. I am already responsible toward the other because there is a "must" which comes from the other's proximity to me. But this is neither a gift nor a promise.[105] It is an eternal process that infringes on my egoistic autonomy through the face of the other.[106] Closeness and proximity are what matters

---

[105] Levinas evaluates his thoughts on subjectivity and God as well as the way that responsibility appears against the other without any promises or materialistic requirements. On this topic, see further analysis in P. Marcus, *Being for the other: Emmanuel Levinas, ethical living and psychoanalysis* (2008, 193-217).

[106] By prioritizing the face of the other rather than the I, Levinas achieves "the calling of consciousness into question". Levinas insists that through the face-to-face encounter "the *I* loses its sovereign self-coincidence, its identification, in which consciousness returns triumphantly to itself to rest on itself. Before the exigency of the other the *I* is expelled from this rest" (Levinas 1987a, 97). In this

regarding this issue. But where does this beginning come from? Levinas would allege that this beginning comes from the immemorial. It is a beginning without beginning but is just a trace, a non-reciprocal asymmetrical call which is imbued by transcendence. Every person, John Donne mentions, is a "part of the main" (ibid.). Levinas here would add that this participation "of the main" is relationality, a socialized achievement and not an atomistic implementation. The ontological frame has nothing to do with this procedure. Participation in a socialized frame, according to Levinas, must always "begin" through the other and not through the self.

However, I would raise an objection to Chappell's view that "the experience that Levinas calls face to face" is a "direct and unmediated encounter between persons" (ibid., 31). From my point of view, there is no mention in Levinas's works of a direct and unmediated encounter between persons. The face for Levinas implies a non-direct asymmetrical relation between persons whereas the other calls me to an

---

condition, the face develops an infinite responsibility that "empties the *I* of its imperialism and its egoism" (ibid.). Levinas adds that the face-to-face process is "an experience in the strongest sense of the term: a contact with a reality that does not fit into any *a priori* idea, which overflows all of them [...] No movement of freedom could appropriate a face to itself [...] A face is pure experience, conceptless experience" (ibid., 59).

infinite response beyond any directedness. This response is full of mystery[107] and holiness[108] which surpasses even death.[109]

---

[107] Levinas in several works underlines the notion of mystery concerning the relationship between persons which exceeds even death. Since the face-to-face relation overcomes death, this mystery cannot be grasped in direct knowledge; "it is obvious, outside of all grasp" (Cohen 2006, 29). Thus, the face does not have a direct encounter between persons; rather it is a dialogical indirect asymmetrical non-reciprocal divine "trace" awaiting my response. The other, as Levinas contends, "is not an interlocutor in reciprocity" (Levinas 1998a, 34).

[108] A human seeking the desirable, that is, to develop an ethical dialectic with the "Other", cannot depend on a direct relation with the face of the other because there is a danger of infringing on her personality. In contrast, for Levinas, in order to avoid such a danger and "in order that the desire beyond being not be an absorption, the desirable [the Other] must remain separated [that is indirect] within desire: near, yet different — which is, moreover, the very meaning of the word holy [...] The referral to the other is an awakening to nearness, which is responsibility for the neighbor to the point of substitution, which is the enucleation of the transcendental subject" (Levinas 2000, 223).

[109] It is in a similar manner to the relation between persons and God. To this purpose, T. Chappell alleges that "God is not out there in the way that individualism about persons supposes, as a reality that we can encounter [...] He is already present in the foundations of that consciousness" (Chappell 2013, 43). From my point of view, Levinas would agree with the first argument, that is, "God is not out there", since Levinas contends that God does not interfere in finite beings' situations directly. However, he would strongly reject the latter argument, that is, God "is already present in the foundations of that consciousness", since presence is something that is overcome in Levinasian thought regarding transcendence: God/ the good as the desirable is not placed in presence but in immemorial time.

1.5 Understanding God through Subjectivity: Levinas's Responsibility[110] and Kierkegaard's Repetition[111]

There is no such thing as subjectivity if we do not compare it to responsibility and/or repetition. On the one hand, Levinas insists that responsibility precedes freedom and that the fundamental principle of subjectivity is the responsibility towards the "Other" without any coercion or reciprocal expediencies. On the other hand, for Kierkegaard what matters is repetition, especially through the incarnation of Christ. Repetition is inseparable from incarnation and forgiveness.

In more depth, for Levinas, by saying subjectivity, we mean "the everyday extra-ordinary dimension of my responsibility for other men, for what is not in my power" (Levinas 2000, 185). It is of immense importance to understand how Levinas categorizes human relationships since through human relationship we can understand God as well. One of Levinas's most important declarations about God is that "it is only with other relationships as a basis that God can be manifest" (ibid.). By using the term 'manifest', Levinas means that God, due to his infinite essence, is impossible to be understood by finite beings[112] such as us. Thus, we can reflect God's

---

[110] There is a vast range of secondary literature concerning the notion of responsibility in Levinasian thought (Dimitrova 2011, 37-47, 67-74; idem. 2016, 53-122; Coe 2018, 73-99, 159-186; Strhan 2012, 17-70; Zaborowski 2000, 147-165; D. Boothroyd 2011, 41-59).

[111] Concerning the significant notion of repetition (Gjentagelsen) in Kierkegaard, see the expanded bibliography in M. Dooley, *The Politics of Exodus* (2001 74-75, n. 1).

[112] However, Levinas reassures us that "the relation to God is presented there as a relation to another person. It is not a metaphor: in the other, there is a real presence of God. In my relation to the other, I hear the Word of God. It is not a metaphor; it is not only extremely important; it is literally true. I'm not saying

attributes (if there are any) only through another person as equal interlocutor and as hostage: it is found only through the trace of the other. The subjectivity of responsibility is also of immense importance since it exceeds the materialist cosmic background. It is found not in ordinary time as presence but within an extraordinary, nonspatial immemorial dimension. Thus, the subjectivity of responsibility leads one to speak of God through models other than that of being.

Two alternative conditions of subjectivity that lead us to speak about God beyond ontotheology and otherwise than being are passivity and substitution (Hand 1989, 103-108; Large 2011, 251-252). With passivity persons are unique and irreplaceable, paying particular attention to another's subjectivity without a return towards oneself. In the same manner, substitution "remains a relationship with another, staying in discontinuity" with oneself without absorbing the "Other" into the "Same". Thus, substitution remains otherwise than being. (Levinas 2000, 186). The notion that Levinas gives to responsibility has nothing to do with cognition, experience, and knowledge. Responsibility, for Levinas, is not a psychological term. Rather, responsibility "signifies in the one-for-the-other" (ibid., 187) where "Sameness" is separated form "Otherness".

---

that the other is God, but that in his or her Face I hear the Word of God. [The other] is the way the word of God reverberates" (Levinas 1998a, 110). This is also a valuable paradigm to understand what it is to be a trace of God in Levinasian thought in relation to the "face". As M. Dimitrova explains, "the face leaves a trace behind, withdrawing from the world and heading to what lies beyond. The trace is not an intentionally produced sign, which borrows its meaning from the world's order; the trace calls for the opening, reconstruction, and reconstitution of meanings — by turning upside down the significance of causes and effects, of happenings and events" (Dimitrova 2011, 45).

Related to the subjectivity of responsibility, Levinas also highlights the crucial role of subject-subject correlation. Through this correlation the "Saying" is more of a necessary and sufficient condition than the "Said", since the "Saying" must be understood "not as a dialogue but as a bearing witness to the infinite to the one to whom I open my self infinitely" (ibid., 189).[113] However, it would be a huge mistake to limit the witnessing "by a foregoing cognition" (ibid.) that leads us yet again to ontotheology.

On the other hand, for Kierkegaard, selfhood comes through repetition, which is the main tool for understanding the whole religious philosophy of Kierkegaard. By 'repetition', we mean the appropriate method to approach God as an eternal ethical absolute ideal. This is one of the most important discrepancies between Levinas and Kierkegaard. In Kierkegaard, it is by God that I must find a way to love my neighbor, that is, starting from the ethical and leading to the religious. For instance, individual prayer will reveal to me the path of existential love's direction, and not through the objective doctrines of the established Church.

> "If God's word is for you merely a doctrine, something impersonal and objective, then there is no mirror, an objective doctrine cannot be called a mirror; it is just as impossible to look at yourself in an objective doctrine as to look at yourself in a wall. And If you want to relate impersonally (objectively) to God's word, there can be no question of looking at yourself in the mirror, because it takes a person an 'I', to look at oneself in a mirror; a wall can be seen in a mirror, but a wall cannot see itself or look at itself in a mirror" (Kierkegaard 1976, 13).

---

[113] At this point, A. Kin correctly contends that "the only thing we can do (to escape ontotheology) is to bear witness to the infinity of the Infinite in the only way that does not bring it back to being, that is, in the ethical relationship with the neighbor, the sole manner, in which an otherwise than being can signify" (2006, 121).

Repetition, thus, as M. Dooley states, leads to understanding God as an incarnation and not as a dogma: "an object of knowledge in the sense of the traditional God of Scholastic ontology, or indeed the Old Testament God, but one who calls for each individual to 'respond' to him by bringing to life anew (repetition) his ideals of mercy and forgiveness" (Dooley 2001, xxiii). Responsibility for Kierkegaard is not, as Levinas alleges, something that humans can achieve without God. As has been stated above, Levinas states that responsibility has nothing to do with direct communication with God, but with ethics and God's traces: that is, the face of the other. Kierkegaardian thought is exactly the opposite: "Responsibility is ends not with ethics but with faith to the degree that one consistently hopes for the type of justice the God-man so passionately sought to engender" (ibid.).

God-man's prototype in Kierkegaard is of paramount importance to explain the relation between God and humans and the real opportunity for persons to reach God by the path that Christ opened with His incarnation and crucifixion. Even though Kierkegaard was a Protestant, he seems to have had religious influence from the patristic tradition, that is, thinkers from the eastern part of Christian tradition.[114] The latter

---

[114] By saying patristic tradition, we mean the Christian Orthodox perspective in which self-transcendence depends on Trinitarianism through kenosis and faith. This study sets up an intriguing opposition between the Orthodox conception of human and divine personhood as being grounded in love and the relationship to the other and conceptions of personhood drawn from post-Cartesian philosophy which emphasize such attributes as rationality and self-consciousness (criterialism). Fr. Sophrony of Essex, one of the major defenders of patristic tradition, insists that God is not a mere essence or an absolute being without characteristics. On the contrary, he reminds us that God says "ἐγώ εἰμι ὁ ὤν" (I am who I am) (Exodus, 3:14), which demonstrates that He is a person and human beings need the same personal adjustment to be called persons. Sophrony insisted that if we want to justify personhood we must turn towards the triune

line of thought asserts that persons such as monks in hermetic life can have a direct revelation of God through strict prayer and asceticism. Kierkegaard in *Practice of Christianity* insists that in the modern age the definition of God-man has changed due to the secularism of the established Church:

"In the entire modern age, which so unmistakably bears the mark that it does not even know what the issue is, the confusion is something different and far more dangerous. By way of didacticism, the God-man has been made into that speculative unity of God and man *sub specie aeterni* [under the aspect of eternity] or made visible in that nowhere-to-be-found medium of pure being, rather than that the God-man is the unity of being God and an individual human being in a historically actual situation. Or Christ has been abolished altogether, thrown out and his teaching taken over, and finally he is almost regarded as one regards an anonymous writer: the teaching is the principal thing, is everything. This is why people delude themselves into thinking that all Christianity is nothing but *direct* communication, in its simplicity even more direct than the professor's profound dictations" (Kierkegaard 1991b, XII, 115).

At this point, as Dooley points out, Kierkegaard underlines that "to imitate the God-man is the way to become genuinely responsible, and indeed the way to establish concrete

---

God, the real and perfect personal existence. There is an absolute correlation and symmetry between God and man, as in Kierkegaard. Although God is uncreated and man is created, there is a way to share the same personal measures; thus, an entity can become a person exactly as it happens to the Triune God. Levinas, on the other hand, would reject this argument as God does not (at least in Judaism's theological principles) become a person; there is no becoming in God, least of all essential becoming like that. So God cannot become a person in the same way as humans do because there is no way that God has become a person (or three persons in one substance as in Christian Trinitarianism). Levinas is quite specific in the debate on incarnation as he vehemently rejects any theories that could objectify God's essence. For Levinas, it is all about ethics and how or whether man can realize and understand his power of ethical consent, that is, to seek the trace of God through the face of the other person. Levinas understands kenosis only through man's capabilities and not through God's direct interference in the world (as Orthodox Christians do). For Levinas, "more important than God's omnipotence is the subordination of that power to man's ethical consent. And that, too, is one of the primordial meanings of kenosis" (Levinas 1994d, 126).

relationships with the other" (Dooley 2001, xxiii). However, this argument is different from Levinas's perspective. That is, by considering the other as more valuable than myself, I am not, according to Kierkegaard, a hostage to the face of the other, as Levinas claims:

> "But, in the responsibility for the Other, for another freedom, the negativity of this anarchy, this refusal of the present, of appearing, of the immemorial, commands me and ordains me to the other, to the first one on the scene, and makes me approach him, makes me his neighbor. It thus diverges from nothingness as well as from being. It provokes this responsibility against my will, that is, by substituting me for the other as a hostage [...] A subject is a hostage [...] I am a hostage, a responsibility and a substitution supporting the world in the passivity of assignation, even in an accusing persecution, which is undeclinable" (Levinas 1991, 11, 112, 128).

We might argue that Kierkegaard would agree with all of this except for the last sentence. For Kierkegaard, responsibility is not opposed to free will, as in Levinas. Responsibility is inseparable from freedom and love, and surely, for Kierkegaard, I ought not be a hostage of the other since, for him, love and passion are equal to symmetrical, reciprocal subjectivity. Concerning equality, Kierkegaard underlines in his *Works of Love* that "the neighbor is your equal. [...] With your neighbor you have human equality before God. [...] Loving your neighbor is a matter of equality" (Kierkegaard 1995, 50). The other person is engaged to me with love, forgiveness, and respect because we both are enriched by God's commandments and principle to love each other. God provides us this gift. It is not me or the other who are the playmakers of existential love but God. I am not able to truly love my neighbor if I do not receive grace from above, and this grace is imbued, according to Kierkegaard, by Jesus Christ and his commandments.

Kierkegaard's insistence on repetition, therefore, is similar to the Greeks' and particularly to Hegel's recollection[115] but is dialectically directed and construed from a different standpoint:

"Say what you will, this question will play a very important role in modern philosophy, for repetition is a crucial expression for what 'recollection' was to the Greeks. Just as they taught that all knowing is a recollecting, modern philosophy will teach that life is a repetition [....] Repetition and recollection arc the same movement, except in opposite directions, for what is recollected has been, is repeated backward, whereas genuine repetition is recollected forward. Repetition, therefore, if it is possible, makes a person happy, whereas recollection makes him unhappy" (Kierkegaard 1983, 163).

---

[115] Concerning the Hegelian synthesis of recollection and his objection to Kant and the Enlightenment's modernity, see D. West, *An Introduction to Continental Philosophy* (1996, 34-41). As regards recollection and imagination, see D. P. Verene, *Hegel's Recollection: A Study of Images in the Phenomenology of Spirit* (1985, 1-13, 92-103). Verene's main intention is to present in Hegel's recollection the specific method that is not a method of consciousness, as self-consciousness, in order to reach absolute knowledge. The latter, according to Verene, absolutely differs from all the other forms of knowing. The route of absolute freedom can be found between the space and the gap of the two moments of *Ansich*. The inability of the thought of logic to fully master the "and" between the two moments of *Ansich* makes Hegel's "system of science" a circle that is a circle of circles which is not only a circle of logic but also of phenomenology and/or the science of the experience of consciousness. The new subject that emerges from this circular process attempts to overcome the doubling of the *Ansich* in order to accomplish self-consciousness. By this procedure, absolute knowledge surpasses the epistemology of logic and releases itself into the world of metaphysical thought. Verene sums up his epilogue with one of the most important points of Hegel's *Phenomenology of Spirit*, which is that irony, as well as metaphor and recollection, is the key to Hegel's system. Verene uses a reference from Bertolt Brecht's work *Flüchtlingsgespräche* in order to guide us to understand Hegel's *Phenomenology*: "....everything contradicts itself....concepts can neither live without one another nor with one another....I have never met a person without a sense of humor who has understood Hegel's dialectic". Verene concludes his work by admitting that "metaphor, irony and *Erinnerung* are the keys to Hegel's *Phenomenology of Spirit*. These let us enter the science of the experience of consciousness". Concerning similarities and differences between Kierkegaard and Hegel, see M. Dooley, *The Politics of Exodus* (2001, 24-42). For further secondary literature concerning Hegel and Kierkegaard (ibid., 24, n. 1).

Kierkegaard has adopted several philosophical insights from Greek thinkers, especially Socrates.[116] However, Kierkegaard explains why he rejects Socrates's recollection as insufficient for his own thinking. Kierkegaard, like Levinas, rejects that all knowing is recollection.

> "By holding Socrates to the thesis that all knowing is recollecting, one turns him into a speculative philosopher instead of what he was, an existing thinker who understood existing as the essential. The thesis that all knowing is a recollecting belongs to speculative thought, and recollecting is immanence [...] To emphasize existence, which contains within it the qualification of inwardness, is the Socratic, whereas the Platonic is to pursue recollection and immanence." (Kierkegaard 2009a, 206).

Levinas, like Kierkegaard, explores whether immanence is inseparable from knowledge. Of course, as we have also seen above, for Levinas, immanence has an importance secondary to transcendence.[117]

> "Otherwise than Being. It is a matter of stating the breaking apart of a destiny that reigns in essence whose fragments and modalities — despite their diversity — belong the ones to the others, that is [...] do not escape Order, as though the ends of the thread cut by the Parque were tied up again after being cut [...] It is a matter of thinking the possibility of being torn out of essence. To go where? To go into what region? To stand on what ontological plane? But to be torn out of essence contests the unconditional privilege of the question: where? [...] [This is a] uniqueness [...] for which the out-of-self, the difference relative to self, is non-indifference itself in the extra-ordinary recurrence of the pronominal." (Levinas 1974, 9-10).

---

[116] As P. Muench states, "the [*Concluding Unscientific*] *Postscript* is narrated by a fictional character, Johannes Climacus [...] [who] is best conceived as a Socratic figure" (Muench 2011, 102), and he also reminds us that the only thinker who consoles Kierkegaard is Socrates (ibid., 103).

[117] Concerning Levinas's objection to ontology and immanence, see B. Bettina, "Ontology, Transcendence and Immanence" (2005, 141-180).

1.6 *Here I Am*:
The Saying and Witnessing in Levinasian Ethics

"But each individual of these peoples is virtually a chosen one, called to leave in his turn, or without awaiting his turn, the concept of the ego, its extension in the people, to respond with responsibility: me, that is, here I am for the others, to lose his place radically, or his shelter in being, to enter into ubiquity which is also a utopia. Here I am for the others - an enormous response, whose inordinateness is attenuated with hypocrisy as soon as it enters my ears forewarned of being's essence, that is, the way being carries on. The hypocrisy is from the first denounced. But the norms to which the denunciation refers have been understood in the enormity of meaning and in the full resonance of their statement to be true like unrefrained witness." (Levinas 1991, 185).

As we have seen above, this chapter deals with ethical subjectivity and the tendency to raise questions on God and our subjectivity as a response to God's command beyond "Onto-theo-logy". Though influenced by Heidegger and Kierkegaard, Levinas provides a new perspective on beings and transcendence. He insists on ethics as first philosophy (Bloechl 2000, 130-164). An ethics as closeness is contrasted with intentionality and consciousness as well as with total freedom of the ego.[118] In this subchapter I argue that, as Levinas states, "responsibility cannot be stated in terms of presence" (Levinas 2000, 195) but through the pronouncement "here I am" bearing witness to infinity. By saying "here I am", I do not mean standing alone without the other, but,

---

[118] We need to separate and distinguish responsibility and freedom. For Levinas "responsibility for another [person] is not an accident that happens to a subject, but precedes essence in it, has not awaited freedom, in which a commitment to another would have been made." (Levinas 1991, 114). Or, in a similar manner, "the purpose of responsibility is not mine: I do not agree to it, but I find myself responsible" (Manderson 2005, 700).

on the contrary, I am here due to the other's presence. In contrast to Hegelian logic and totality (a manifestation of being to consciousness toward "Spirit") and against the Heideggerian manifestation of being[119] by way of forgetting and concealment, Levinas states that what matters is the "Saying" bearing witness before consciousness and prior to freedom. Taking into consideration the above argument, I argue that it is the saying and not the said, echoes to infinity, which brings the subject into dialogue with the subject as an equal interlocutor in a relationship called intersubjective. The moment the other becomes a material object through immanence she loses her face. God leaves all human affairs in our hands. My personality as a self-consciousness is secondary and constitutes my "I" in comparison to my moral subjection as "me" which is primary, as mentioned above. With the phrase "here I am", Levinas expresses the experience of the self which is not an experience of the will, but rather a matter of a primordial responsibility prior to any experience and decision (Tajalli and Segal 2019, 75-78). "Here I am" is a phrase that echoes to infinity standing on an eschatological time beyond and above any ontological, psychological states of the self.

Levinas, like the French existentialist thinker Jean-Paul Sartre, pays particular attention to sincerity.[120] However,

---

[119] As M. Dimitrova asserts, "in Heidegger's philosophy, the place of the appealing agency is taken by Being, while, in Levinas', it is occupied by the Other" (Dimitrova 2011, 19).

[120] It is, however, worth noting that this sincerity is not similar to Sartre's moral act. According to Levinas, "to have oneself replaced in a moral act is to renounce a moral act". Therefore, we need to renounce a moral act when this act is preceded by reciprocal debt, as we will be never liberated through a reciprocal procedure between me and the other person (https://www.youtube.com/watch?v=qbGaXEqxSvU: 48:56-48:59).

Levinas gives priority to the sincerity of the "Saying"[121] rather than the "Said". It is therefore crucial to explain what we mean by "Saying". Exploring the importance of the "Saying" in his works (without the accompanying "Said"), Levinas means a continuous face-to-face dialogue as a bearing

---

[121] The terms "Saying" and "Said" are not easily explained (Critchley 2004, 17-19; Schrijvers 2010, 222-233). It is not clear what Levinas exactly means by the "Saying". It is metaphysical terminology which aims at exposing oneself without limit. "Saying" refers to another and not to being *qua* being, and for sure it is not held in consciousness as Hegel claims. The "Saying" in parallel signifies the transcendence of the one who is *for* the other. The psyche or subjectivity through the "Saying" is structured not upon the Kantian triptych that merits cosmological, psychological, and theological attributes but as the one-for-the-other seeking my expiation for the other. For Levinas. the saying can be clearly understood if we clarify the correct definition of culture. He contends that "culture is neither a going beyond nor a neutralization of transcendence; it is, in ethical responsibility and obligation toward the other, a relation to transcendence qua transcendence. It can be called love. It is commanded by the face of the other man, which is not a datum of experience and does not come from the world" (Levinas 1998a, 187). Gadamer, on the other hand, gives especial priority to the "Said", that is, history and memory, which must not be marginalized from the frame of culture. Gadamer raises an objection to Levinas's "abstract Ethics", by claiming that Levinas pays particular (hyperbolic) attention to abstractness as well as to the motto "Ethics as First Philosophy is above and beyond all historical context. Gadamer believes that Levinasian ethics lacks historicity and thus it cannot stand within a humanistic frame. For Gadamer, social action is a necessary and sufficient condition if we want to speak of human beings and their interrelation. Sociality, for Gadamer, cannot forget the past, which is culture. Gadamer criticizes Levinas's allegation that all that matters is immemorial time and the other is the future and not past or presence. Gadamer considers the manifestations of both objectivism and subjectivism as antithetical symptoms of the same underlying disorder of the Western philosophical tradition. Gadamer also rejects transcendental subjectivity that is far from both history and life-world. Thus, truth and subjectivity are founded historically and hermeneutically in the life-world. He also rejects accusations of relativism or subjectivism. Gadamer states that only a discipline of questioning and inquiring (by truthfulness) must achieve what other methods could not achieve — by the universality of hermeneutics. He states that the path to understanding can only be achieved through language and it can never be reduced to the positivistic methodologies of natural scientists. A comprehensive study of Levinas and Gadamer on sociality, the said, and the saying is written by F. Smith, "Gadamer and Levinas on the topic of Sociality" (2016, 95-109). See also G. L. Bruns, "On the Coherence of Hermeneutics and Ethics: An Essay on Gadamer and Levinas" (2004, 30-54). For Gadamer on culture, see H.-G. Gadamer, "Culture and the World," (1998).

witness to the infinite and not to presence. The "Said" can be compared to "Sameness" in the presence and the "Saying" is the infinite sincerity of immemorial time. It is something that does not cease to open — going forwards without thematization, totalization, and representation, as Hegel insists. Thus, we can infer that the infinite, from which "the more the distance is covered, the more there remains to cover" (Levinas 2000, 191) is a necessary and sufficient condition of the sincerity of the "Saying". It is like someone who speaks without saying anything at all.

According to Levinas, the phrase "here I am" is quite significant in ethics since it "bears witness to the infinite without bringing it back to being" (ibid., 193) only if it is construed in the accusative case: It is me who is here — not "here I am". It is the passive form — I am for you; command me! Only then can there be communication with the other (Smith 2016, 96-97). "It is through this witnessing that the Infinite surpasses the finite and comes to pass" (Min 2006, 101), In contrast, the "Said" is something that reveals representation and presence and is acquired by way of presuppositions revealing an ontological God "closing itself up in the immanence of being and in its finitude" (Levinas 2000, 193). Thus, in the phrase "here I am" (in passivity:[122] it is *me* who is awaiting your

---

[122] Levinas underlines that "there is here then a passivity more passive than any passivity: filial, a pre-vious, pre-logical subjection, a one-way subjection which it would be wrong to understand on the basis of a dialogue" (Levinas 1987a, 135). It is through this transcendent passivity that the *here I am* is transformed into *it is me*. I am *here* as a human being not because of me but because of him/her. This passivity is purer than no one else: Pure passivity is "responsibility for the freedom of others. There where I might have remained a spectator, I am responsible, that is, speaking. Nothing is theatre anymore; the drama is no longer a game. Everything is grave" (ibid., 136). Levinas prioritizes the importance of persecution, which is connected to his notion of absolute responsibility. He argues that ethical responsibility, which he supports, goes beyond the

command), a new model of transcendence emerged only through the head of ethics in the relationship with the neighbor as a hunger-suffering hostage, whose personality never ceases to seek our a priori responsibility. Therefore, we can conclude that we do not need ontotheological accounts to understand God, but rather an ethical subject related to the subject through an intersubjective relationship outside the reasonable cosmos of knowledge.

Infinity, according to Levinas, is not explained on ontotheological terms in presence or through consciousness and intentionality. Infinity makes its presence above and beyond presence only as glory. Levinas clearly insists that "the excess over the present is the life of the infinite" (ibid., 195). We can only speak of the infinite when the "Other" escapes from the addiction of the "Same". And this fact can only be understood when the "me" finds the way to substitute itself through substitution and the glory of witnessing. The glory of the infinite, therefore, comes through anarchy and dissymmetry, through a disinterestedness and discontinuity of "Other"ness against the "Same": a witnessing of the glory of the "Saying" which, driven from hiding, declares "here I am". The infinite's revelation to us does not have any direct appearing. It does not show itself directly. Infinity, according to Levinas, "is witnessed only by the voice of the witness, and it is in this sense alone that God needs men. The Infinite commands me by my own voice" (ibid., 197). This last verse is of

---

social question. Responsibility is above and beyond everything and everyone and it is inseparable from persecution: "To bear responsibility for everything and everyone is no being responsible despite oneself. To be responsible despite oneself is to be persecuted. Only the persecuted must answer for everyone, even for his persecutor" (Levinas 1994a, 114-115).

immense importance to Levinasian thought concerning God as it reveals that God has come to mind only through the "Other" and the "Other" is God's traces. According to Levinas, "to know God is to do justice to the neighbor" (ibid., 199).[123]

The fascinating point of infinity is that "it is attested beyond-measure by the accusative of the *Here I am*" (ibid., 203). Following this logic, God is placed neither in presence nor in a memorial past. God escapes objectification and the "I-Thou" relation. God, rather, ethically speaking, is a third person or illeity.[124] God is infinite and we as human beings are

---

[123] See two crucial examples in the Old and New Testament where the infinite reveals its glory through the approach of the neighbor (Jeremiah 22, 15-16; Matthew 25, 31-40).

[124] By illeity we mean the process of "detaching itself within the relationship itself". (Levinas 2000, 198). In the same manner, Levinas insists that the anteriority of responsibility is beyond being and non-being — resistant to thematization and origin: "This anteriority of responsibility must be understood in relation to freedom as the very authority of the Absolute which is 'too great' for the measure or finitude of presence, revelation, order and being, and which consequently, as neither being nor non-being, is the 'excluded third party' of the beyond of being and non-being, a third person that we have called *illeity*" (Levinas 1994d, 127-128). Levinas separates the third party from the Other: "The third party looks at me in the eyes of the Other — language is justice. It is not that there first would be the face, and then the being it manifests, or expresses, would concern himself with justice; the epiphany of the face qua face opens humanity. The face in its nakedness as a face presents to me the destitution of the poor one and the stranger" (Levinas 1969, 213). Hence, the third party can be defined as the whole of humanity (ibid.), that is, "all the others in the world whose nakedness and destitution constitute a call for justice" (Bruns 2004, 49). Likewise, it is worth mentioning that illeity, as a philosophical term, firstly used by Levinas, is related only to God and not to the human dyadic *I-Thou* relation that is defended by several thinkers such as Kierkegaard, Scheler, Buber, Heidegger and Sartre and meant as intersubjectivity (Jodalen and Vetlesen [eds.] 1997, 5). According to Levinas, illeity refers only to infinity, that is, to God: "we have designated this manner for the Infinite, or for God, to refer from the heart of its very desirability, to the undesirable proximity of the others, by the term *illeity*" (Levinas 1998b, 69; Hand [ed.] 1989, 178). See also M. Purcell, *Mystery and Method* (1998, 158-161). Concerning the connection between illeity, love, and intersubjectivity, see B. Bajzek, "Intersubjectivity, Illeity and Being-in-love: Lonergan and Levinas on Self-Transcendence" (2016, 1-11). G. L. Bruns remarks that "It is not an I-Thou relation but a relation to an illeity (*il, elle*) who is outside

96

finite because God stays outside of the structure of the cosmos and signifies an "unrepresentable, without-beginning anarchy" (ibid., 203). To sum up, we can say that Levinas raises some objections to the analytic way that God comes into philosophy, i.e. through the thematization of being. On the contrary, he attempts to find an ethical path to speak of God beyond the intelligibility of immanence and beyond the consciousness of the present: to search for transcendence prior to being and freedom.

In the next subchapter I argue that the aforementioned ethical path that allows us to speak of God outside ontotheology is outside of experience, in the praise of insomnia and transcendence to the point of absence. For Levinas, "God is not simply the first other but other than the other, other otherwise, other with an alterity prior to the alterity of the other person, prior to the ethical compulsion to the neighbor" (Levinas 2000, 224). God is "transcendent to the point of absence, to the point of the confusion in which the substitution for the neighbor grows in nobility and in which the transcendence of the infinite is raised to its glory" (ibid., 224). Concluding this discussion, we can accept Min's statement that for Levinas, "the naming of the unnameable God is not a matter of a direct invocation of a divine *Thou* but a matter of bearing witness to the infinite alterity of God through the mediation of care for the hungry and poor human others of this world. Without this mediation our relation to the

---

every horizon and who calls me into question, that is, summons me out of my house, situating me in my ethical condition as hostage (being one-for-the-other) (Bruns 2004, 40). Illeity overflows both cognition and knowledge and is quite different from being and knowing (Levinas 1991, 162).

unnameable God remains inauthentic" (Min 2006, 113).[125] M. Dimitrova clearly explains that we cannot speak of God directly or through ontotheological metaphysics (and maybe

---

[125] However, I would disagree with Min's statement that "the question of naming the unnameable God is not only a theological but also a political question". From my point of view, Levinas distinguishes ethics from theology and politics especially concerning God. Politics is a discipline that has nothing to do with God, but rather it provides rational and conventional arguments giving priority to language and manifestation of being *qua* being and not to transcendence. If we want to speak of politics in a transcendental way, it might be acceptable for Levinas but strictly not related to God as transcendence. According to M. Dimitrova, Levinas defends "an ethics without law, without concept, without morality, and which precedes its determination in laws, in concepts, and in morals" (Dimitrova 2011, 4). In the same manner, C. Yannaras, a modern Greek philosopher, insists on the importance of the term "relation" but in a metaphysical exegesis. In modernity, he claims that God integrated with nature and politics in an erroneous way. Enlightenment, he adds, either put God in a cosmic framework or it placed Him apart from philosophy. Even though Yannaras agrees with Levinas about the unknowability and absence of God in presence, he explores his thesis on God from an extremely different perspective, an Orthodox-Christian dialectic which gives priority to Trinitarianism and to Jesus's revelation as an intermediary of love incarnate (On *Death of God* see Yannaras, 2005, 39-47; on the *Collapse of Modernity* see idem. 2004, 19-46 and on *Against Religion and the Ecclesial Event* see idem. 2013, 21-48). One of the most crucial differences between Levinas and Yannaras is that the former is a Jew and the latter an Orthodox Christian, which means that they interpret God in extremely different dialectics. It is something like *Ethics vs Faith*. For Levinas, as a Tulmidic specialist, the incarnation of God is impossible. In his article "Judaism and Kenosis" (1994d, 114), Levinas underlines a verse from a Talmudic tractate *Sukkah 5a*: "Never has the 'presence of God' come down to the ground level of the earth". Yannaras, finally, we may say, is philosophically closer to a Heideggerian ontological perspective and integrates ancient Greek philosophical accounts, especially those of Plato and Aristotle. Yannaras, in contrast to Levinas, claims that we can speak of God and politics only through the ancient Greek city-state (Πόλις), where people mutually participated in a constitutional state through intersubjective personal relations and not due to conventional interactions. In favor of this statement of personal intersubjectivity and Levinas in politics, see N. O'Connor, "The Personal Is Political: Discursive Practice of the Face-to-Face", in R. Bernasconi and D. Wood (eds.) *The Provocation of Levinas* (1988, 57-69). Kierkegaard also explores arguments against the modern age and the Enlightenment as well as "false Objective Christianity". See R. L. Hall, *Word and Spirit* (1993, 59-89). See also M. Westphal and M. J. Matustik, *Kierkegaard and Postmodernity* (1995). A valuable primary source concerning Kierkegaard's notion of pure and objective Christianity and self-examination is S. Kierkegaard, *Attack Upon Christendom* (1991, 3-76; idem., 113-171). Concerning secondary literature on Kierkegaard and Christianity, see S. Walsh, *Living Christianly* (2005).

we cannot speak of God at all) as "the otherness of the face is not logical, but meta-logical and meta-physical" (Dimitrova 2011, 19). It is true that Levinas insists on the infinite not as a "*being* absolute infinite" like Spinoza[126] (Spinoza 2000, 3; Mayson 1997, 187-246), but rather it is nonsense to attach the word "being" to God's essence since God's essence is unnameable and unknowable to us.[127]

1.7 The Other Man: Insomnia, Outside of Experience and the Point of Absence

Putting knowledge at the margins, which is the production of being, Levinas provides another condition beyond measure to empower his argument regarding the face-to-face relation: so-called insomnia. Levinas uses this term in order to explain its irreducible character concerning the crucial role of the "Other". Insomnia, we can say, replaces intentionality. It tries to awaken the "Same" without referring to intentionality. Insomnia is not an appeal to presence. It goes beyond any consciousness. Insomnia reminds us that the other is suffering[128], waiting for our responsible act.

---

[126] I refer specifically to Spinoza since there is a tendency in the contemporary philosophical community to compare Levinasian and Spinozist ethics, especially concerning the issue of ethics as first philosophy. See, for instance, E. Wyschogrod, "Ethics as First Philosophy: Levinas reads Spinoza" (1999, 199-202) concerning their view on ethics as first philosophy. Regarding their view on God (ibid., 195-199; E. Levinas 1999, 168-173) regarding Spinoza's ethics and theology related to Talmudic science.

[127] This statement above — explored by M. Dimitrova — can be justified through Levinas's notion of man and his relation to God: "God also has a meaning [...] signifying something that man cannot define, formulate, think, or even name [...] God has no place in the world, it is the world which has a place in God" (Levinas 1994d, 162).

[128] Suffering has a paramount importance in Levinasian thought especially in order to ethically explore subjectivity. Levinas investigates a suffering which "opens upon suffering the ethical perspective of the inter-human". Therefore, for

Insomnia resides outside of experience. Levinas intends to clarify that religious experience as it is established, especially in Western thought, has totally missed what is beyond measure. Religious human beings mistakenly interpret God in terms of beings, confusing infinity and finitude. Therefore, the philosophy of God nowadays, especially in the Western tradition, becomes a philosophy of beings. Levinas strongly disagrees with this thematization of God[129] within a framework of (ontological) religious experience.[130] God cannot be understood by finite methods. What matters is a beyond-measure ethical transcendence which leads us to God (only through a non-ontological but ethical way) who is

---

Levinas, "a radical difference develops between *suffering in the Other*, which for *me* is unpardonable and solicits me and calls me, and suffering *in me* my own adventure of suffering, whose constitutional or congenital uselessness can take on a meaning, the only meaning to which suffering is susceptible, in becoming a suffering for the suffering of someone else". (Bernasconi and Wood [eds.] 1998, 159) Levinas discusses modernity and postmodern suffering along with theodicy (the answer to the question of why God permits evil) which derives from immanence. In contrast, he clarifies that "it is in the inter-human perspective of *my* responsibility for the other person, without concern for reciprocity, in my call to help him gratuitously, in the asymmetry of the relation of *one* to the *other*, that we have tried to analyze the phenomenon of useless suffering" (ibid., 165). See also a detailed definition and explanation of Levinas's view concerning suffering in R. White, "Levinas, the Philosophy of Suffering and the Ethics of Compassion" (2012, 113-119).

[129] According to Levinas, the thematization of God (something that is a flawed point from rational theology as well) is a rotten, unacceptable theory and thus rejected. As he himself underlines, "in thematizing God it brings God into the course of being [...] the God of the Bible signifies the beyond being [...] Rational theology, fundamentally ontological, strives to take account of transcendence in the domain of being by expressing it with adverbs of height applied to the verb being; God is said to exist eminently or par excellence" (Levinas 1987a, 154).

[130] As E. Wyschogrod points out, "Levinas must extricate ethics from the various ontological matrices in which it had been embedded. Because for him God cannot be thought apart from ethics, God too must be freed from the ontological encumbrances of this history. A God, who is beyond ontology, resists cognitive grasp" (Wyschogrod 1999, 196).

transcendence itself.[131] This is the reason we, as finite beings[132], are not able to understand God's essence. It is impossible to directly grasp the idea of the infinite.

> "The only way to hear, realize and respond to Transcendence is the answer I give to the presence of the other human. Transcending as an act of crossing the border, is equal to going beyond the ego-centrism of my own world in order to pay attention to the Other and do something for him. It is the only way for the other to be close to me and for my Self to not be a narrow-minded primitive egoism." (Dimitrova 2016, 126).

What Levinas tries to explain is this: transcendence is not a metaphysical phenomenon of the presence which is grasped in rational logos. It cannot be touchable through Kant's transcendental idealism or universalism. Levinas, on the contrary, suggests that "the desirable (God) must remain separated [from the point of presence] within desire" (ibid., 223). Therefore, transcendence is ethical and not ontological. What matters for Levinas is the non-desirable closeness (Jodalen and Vetlesen [eds.] 1997, 20-26) which is denoted by the term illeity (Purcell 1996, 125-138). It is only the referral of the desirable to the non-desirable that "tears God out of the subjectivity of presence and out of being" (Min 2006, 103).

---

[131] The only model of transcendence, according to Levinas, (that is unnameable to us as humans) is outside this world which cannot be reduced to immanence. Only God is transcendence. However, Levinas implies that we may sketch a model of transcendence in the world only under specific conditions, and this unique condition is through the "Other", the hungriest and the meekest, which teaches me and calls me never in presence but in an immemorial past.

[132] Even though we are human beings and therefore finite, this finitude, according to Levinas, has a valuable meaning: "The human finitude that it determines is not a simple psychological powerlessness, but a new possibility: the possibility of thinking of the Infinite and the Law together, the very possibility of their conjunction. Man would not simply be the admission of an antinomy of reason. Beyond the antinomy, he would signify a new image of the Absolute" (Levinas 1994d, 166-167).

But what does God ultimately mean for Levinas, and how can we find God through "Saying" and witnessing in order to empower Levinas's ethical responsibility to the "Other" person? According to Levinas, the answer to this question emerges only if we regard ethics as first philosophy: A very productive answer is given by Stephan Strasser:

> "In personal contact, in the ardent care for one's neighbor, in unselfish effort for the Other, the Holy reveals Himself. He reveals himself in this way, without becoming the object of intentionality, without becoming the object of comprehension, or being made a theme for a statement. He is unimaginable, not because he is too great, too distant or powerful for imagination, but because he speaks to us from a past, that was never actual presence for us, or ever could be actual presence. [What matters for Levinas is the appearing "Saying" and not the "Said" because the "Saying" echoes to infinity, to asymmetrical non-reciprocal responsibility.] The infinity of the Holy is neither beginning nor end, but anarchy. God as Transcendence reveals himself in basic ethical situations, and not through ontotheological conditions in the presence. As Levinas contends, in our era it is no longer possible to talk of [or to] God in the language of ontology or of theology, but always in the language of Ethics." (Jodalen and Vetlesen [eds.] 1997, 65).

1.8 Holiness as an Alternative to the Sacred in Levinasian Thought

Several times Levinas speaks about the "Other" through the "Ethics of holiness". The holy is an important term in Levinas's thought. Derrida informs us of a short conversation they had where Levinas said: "You know, one often speaks of ethics to describe what I do, but what really interests me in the end is not ethics, not ethics alone, but the holy, the holiness of the holy" (Derrida 1999, 4; Levinas, 2001, 47, 49). The idea of sanctity or holiness has not often been discussed by scholars interested in Levinasian ethics.[133] Levinas insists on distinguishing the holy from the sacred.[134] Holiness is a term similar to desacralization. His intention is to destroy the meaning of the sacred as it is reduced to mystical theology, something that he does not accept.[135] Levinas criticizes

---

[133] Two comprehensive works about Levinas's interest in sanctity can be found in J. Hansel, "Utopia and Reality: The Concept of Sanctity in Kant and Levinas" (1999, 168–75; Caruana 2002, 519–34). For Levinas, sanctity has an allegorical meaning and nothing to do with idolatry. Levinas integrates sanctity with death. He states that sanctity appears metaphysically and ethically when "the death of the other can have priority over my own death", when "the death of the other matters more than my own". And thus, we can call this procedure sanctity, which derives from biblical ethical law (https://www.youtube.com/watch?v=qbGaXEqxSvU: 46:40-47:04).

[134] The reason Levinas rejects the notion of religion as sacred is the same reason he abhors mysticism. Both terms support immanence and ignore the direct separation of God and humans.

[135] For Levinas, God is neither an idea nor a being, not because there is a kind of mystical knowledge that we (as humans) do not have the rational ability to surpass, but mainly because there is a "brick wall" between me as finite human and God as infinite transcendence. Through this wall there is something I cannot think or see, and this is because of my "personal stupidity" (Large 2013, 322). However, W. Large by "stupidity" does not mean that humans are stupid or disabled, but that humans' rational and finite logos cannot explain what it is to be God because they are of different essences. According to Large, there are three possible ways to think of God: as an idea, as a being, or as a word. He then claims that the first two alternatives are impossible for Levinas since God is transcendence and cannot be reduced to immanence. However, Large alleges that Levinas accepts that God can be named as a word. It might be absurd to allege that God is a word. However, what Large means by the phrase "God is a word" is that God is a name and not a description. In Judaism, the word God cannot be described by providing ritual attributes to God. Rather, there is a prohibition on speaking the name of God or trying to understand Him. Thus, we can infer that the allegorical reference that justifies that God is a word can only be construed as a responsibility for the "Other". Levinas points out: "Does not the transcendence of the name of God in comparison to all thematization become effacement and is not this effacement the very commandment that obligates me to the other man?" (Levinas 1994d, 124). What matters in order to express God's name is the "Other". When I address the "Other" — even the meeker — I address God. "As the stranger pass, so too does God" (Large 2103, 331). Therefore, I would strongly agree with Large's implication that "the word 'God' names for Levinas is the ethical responsibility for the Other. It does not name a being with certain properties or attributes, nor an idea necessary for human freedom" (ibid., 332). The terms stranger, meek, humble, and hostage are used several times by Levinas. Specifically, for the crucial role and the encounter of the stranger, see R., Bernet, "The Encounter with the Stranger: Two

several sociologists who were unable to distinguish the notion of *le sacré* from *le saint* (Levinas 2004, 113; idem 1991, 11-14). Also, Levinas refers to Plato[136] in order to show that holiness is of immense importance for ethics not as a theological but an ethical term.[137] Levinas defends the thesis that the sacred as well as mysticism develops immanence and the ego's conditions slip away from transcendence and infinity.

> "The rigorous affirmation of human independence, of its intelligent presence to an intelligible reality, the destruction of the numinous concept of the Sacred, entail the risk of atheism. That risk must be run. Only through it can man be raised to the spiritual notion of the Transcendent. It is a great glory for the Creator to have set up a being who affirms Him after having contested and denied Him in the glamorous areas of myth and enthusiasm; it is a great glory for God to have created a being capable of seeking Him or hearing Him from afar, having experienced separation and atheism" (Levinas 1990, 15-16).

Levinas shares with Plato and Kant a distrust of any religious experience for the sake of uniting transcendence. It is nonsense, for Levinas, to reconcile the sacred with the holy as the former relates to ritual concepts and the latter to transcendence. According to the analytic thinker Durkheim, the sacred is a "catchword meant to capture the totality of religious experience" (Caruana 2006, 563). Another analytic thinker, Bataille, contends that "everything leads us to the conclusion that in essence the sacramental quality of primitive sacrifices is analogous to the comparable element in contemporary religions" (Bataille 1962, 22). On the contrary, Levinas reproves

---

Interpretations of the Vulnerability of the Skin" (2000, 43-61) and R. Bernasconi, "The Alterity of the Stranger and the Experience of the Alien" (2000, 62-89).

[136] It is worth noting that Levinas is a great admirer of Plato's philosophy and shows his gratefulness for how he developed the history of philosophy, theology, and ethics by saying that "Philosophy is Platonic" (Levinas 1999, ix).

[137] See comments on Plato in Levinas, *Collected Philosophical Papers* (1987a, 23).

both scholars by supporting a more ethical intuition. He explains that Judaism "consists in understanding this holiness of God in a [different] sense [than analytic thinkers] that stands in sharp contrast to the numinous meaning of this term, as it appears in the primitive religions wherein the moderns have often wished to see the source of all religion" (Levinas 1990, 14). Ordinarily speaking, the meaning of sacred, according to Levinas and Buber,[138] is imbued with power and cosmic religious experience that is not welcomed by God (Buber 1968, 15). It is only with sanctification as holiness that religion can find a genuine expression. Rational individuation must be transformed into moral separateness through the holiness which can only be found in ethics. Levinas hence insists on the transformation of the sacred through an ethical perspective into holiness or sanctification:

> "The numinous or the sacred envelops and transports man beyond his powers and wishes [...] The numinous annuls the links between persons by making beings participate, albeit ecstatically, in a drama not brought about willingly by them, an order in which they lose themselves" (Levinas 1990, 14).

---

[138] A comprehensive article concerning Buber and Levinas is by R. Bernasconi, "'Failure of Communication' as a Surplus: Dialogue and Lack of Dialogue between Buber and Levinas", in Bernasconi and Wood (eds.) *The Provocation of Levinas* (1988, 100-135). It is obvious that Levinas enthusiastically disagrees with Buber's intention to imbue reciprocity to the "I-Thou" relation. Levinas links heteronomy and transcendence, claiming that autonomy is linked mostly to ontology, isolating the subject to itself, and absorbing otherness, and the face of the other is being subordinated to Hegelian totalization. See E. Levinas, *Of God Who Comes to Mind* (1998b, 150): "[...] in Buber, the I-Thou relationship is frequently also described as the pure face-to-face of the encounter, as a harmonious co-presence as an eye to eye [...] In this extreme formalization the Relation empties itself of its 'heteronomy' and of its transcendence of as-sociation [...] There would be an inequality, a dissymmetry, in the Relation, contrary to the reciprocity upon which Buber insists, no doubt in error".

By this, Levinas tries to admit that what matters is not a ritual sacred experience which is merely actual in the world, but rather an ethical holiness which exceeds ontological practices. On the one hand, holiness, for Levinas, is the only way to access (genuine) religion. On the other hand, the sacred consists of "a seething subjective mass of forces, passions and imaginings" (Levinas 1990, 102). Once the sacred separates the finite self from the divine, there is no possibility for the self to be called from the other, as she loses her identity. This dissolution affects the relationship between the "me" and the other, and thus the ego/being returns into itself.

What we need is a massive return to desacralization through ethics. For Levinas, the ethical character of the holy is the nonrational surplus that emerges not from ontological practices but from anarchy. It is about holiness and ethics, both of which stem from the same anarchic source (Caruana 2006, 569). As Levinas points out, "To say of God that he is the God of the poor of the God of justice, involves a claim not on his attributes but on his essence" (Levinas 2004, 116). Levinas means that the sacred is combined with the attributes of God and the holy with His essence. That is, it is the holy that is transcendent and not the sacred. As Levinas states, through the Torah we can assume that the sacred is equal to idolatry while, in contrast, holiness represents "the absolute opposite to idolatry" (1994b, 58). For Levinas, idolatry has not increased because of the intervention of other gods but due to moral indifference as well as the worship of being itself. The reason that in Judaism monotheism is so strict is that God in the Old Testament "does not give Himself over to human fantasies" (Levinas 1990, 102).

"From the Old Testament, however, we also learn that people become moral objects, not through their response and obedience to God's commandments, but by violating them. Man became a moral being after eating the fruit from the tree of knowledge and began to distinguish good from evil. Since then, he began imitating God and wanted to become the master of human fate. Levinas blames both Christianity and paganism for one and the same sin of idolatry. As paganism created its gods according to the norms of the time and began to pray to the forces of nature as gods, so Christianity created an image of God to befit human representations and began to pray in front of icons that replaced God or the Absolute Other. While in Christianity, man is the image and likeness of God and prayers begin with 'my God', the Hebrew God retains his position of exteriority — God is the Absolute Other, God is Transcendence that even could not be named. Levinas insisted that Transcendence could not be contained within the ideas of it, nor could it be embodied. For Levinas, true monotheism is not compatible with my belief in myths or with idolatry" (Dimitrova 2016, 79).

Does holiness affect our selves in terms of contact with the divine? In short, is holiness a direct condition between the human and God? The answer, according to Levinas, comes through negation[139] — neither/nor (Braine 1998). Levinas states that "the infinite who orders me is neither a cause acting straight on, nor a theme, already dominated, if only retrospectively, by freedom" (Levinas 1991, 12). He adds that "this detour is the enigma[140] of a trace we have called *illeity*"

---

[139] Negation for Levinas plays a decisive role in understanding the subjectivity of persons not as Hegel understands negation, that is, as power and totalization through the dialectic of master and slave, but as "total negation, which spans the infinity of that attempt and its impossibility — is the presence of the face. To be in relation with the other face to face — is to be unable to kill" (Levinas 1998a, 10). This inability to deny the other, the incapacity to negate her "noumenal glory [...] makes the face to face situation possible. The face to face situation is thus an impossibility of denying, a negation of negation" (ibid., 34-35).

[140] Levinas prefers the term enigma to Kierkegaard's silence to explore his argument on God's trace in the world. For Levinas, the interconnection between God and humans is an enigma, that is, God's trace which can be found only through the face of the other: "The semantics of the enigma breaks out of the order of autonomous thought, whereby the enigmatic as such becomes visible only as a trace — which means that it cannot be expressed by a direct representation of language (i. e. the sign or the signifier). The enigma is, according to Levinas, always older than, it is presupposed by, the intellectual cognition; but it cannot

(ibid.). *Illeity* is a neologism created by Levinas to indicate a special symbolic allegory. It contains three parts: il (he), ille (she) and -ty (it, as an object). Levinas's *illeity* aims at indicating "a way of concerning me (and not *I*) without entering into conjunction with me" (ibid.). From my point of view, Levinas "invented" the term in order to show his disagreement with the Buberian "I-Thou" dyadic scheme[141] since, as he says, "*illeity* lies outside the 'thou' and the thematization of objects" (ibid.). Levinas continues by saying that "the *illeity* in the beyond-being is the fact that its coming toward me is a departure which lets me accomplish a movement toward a neighbor" (ibid., 13). Likewise, Levinas contends that *illeity* "is excluded from being, but orders it in relation to a responsibility, in relation to its pure passivity, a pure 'susceptibility': an obligation to answer preceding any questioning which would recall a prior commitment, extending beyond any question, any problem and any representation, and where obedience precedes the order that has furtively infiltrated the soul that obeys" (Levinas 1994d, 128).

---

be reduced to a coherent system" (Mjaaland 2008, 127). Concerning Levinas's view on enigma as an ethical phenomenon, see E. Levinas (1987, 61-73).

141 From my point of view, A. K. Min correctly points out that "the true Infinite is revealed and accessible only as *illeity*, neither as a [Buberian] *Thou* of unmediated dialogue nor as an [Husserlian horizon] object of thematization" (Min 2006, 102). Concerning the notion of Husserl's concept of horizon, see J. Mensch, "Life and Horizon" (2018, 7-18). Min, borrowing two phrases from Levinas's work *God, Death and Time*, asserts that the true infinite is revealed only as "a way of concerning me without entering into conjunction with me" (Levinas 2000, 285) or as "the non-phenomenality of the Other who affects me beyond representation, unbeknownst to me and like a thief" (ibid., 201), clearly separating his thesis from Husserl's ontology. In parallel, contrary to Buber's *I-Thou*, Levinas stresses that "there is no initial equality […] Ethical inequality: subordination to the other, original diacony: the first person accusative and not nominative" (Jodalen and Vetlesen [eds.] 1997, 48, 52, n. 2). Another reason that Levinas reproaches the Buberian I-Thou relationship is that it seems quite symmetrical and reciprocal; those two qualities are unacceptable in Levinas's philosophical vision.

What is ultimately the connection between holiness and illeity? Levinas clearly claims that "*illeity* overflows both cognition and the enigma through which the Infinite leaves a trace in cognition. Its distance from a theme, its reclusion, its holiness, is not its way to effect its being (since its past is anachronous and anarchic, leaving a trace which is not the trace of any presence), but is its glory, quite different from being and knowing" (Levinas 2000, 183).

The call of the other is holy and dramatic. The drama of being can be overcome by holiness through the face of the other. Levinas tries to present a "battle" between me, the "Other", and God outside ontotheology,[142] between an ontological and eschatological drama where both dramas can only be surpassed through an ethical "intrigue" — and not an ethical experience (Caruana 2007, 251-173) where holiness (as ethical sanctification) tries to escape from the ritual-cosmic sacred. As to the holiness of the other, we can say that it is not me who knocks at the door of the other human, but the other already finds me before freedom and autonomy. The other's presence "hits me straight on with the straightest, shortest, and most direct movement" (Levinas 1999, 95). Levinas connects the prohibition of the sacred with the directedness of the face of the other as proximity and closeness:

> "The comprehension of God taken as participation in his sacred life, an allegedly direct comprehension, is impossible, because participation is a denial of the divine and because nothing is more direct than the face to face,

---

142 Levinas, as a Jewish thinker, draws from Talmudic views. Levinas underlines that "monotheism would thus be asserted in its absolute vigour without it being from the onto-theological perspective" (Levinas 1994d, 164), but the essence of God (*En-Sof* in Talmudic writings, which means infinity, God) "is hidden away more than any secret, and no name must name it" [...] "not even the end of the smallest letter" (ibid.). For Levinas, only the "act of thinking of the Absolute which never reaches the Absolute is infinite and never-ending" (ibid.).

which is straightforwardness itself [....] There can be no 'knowledge' of God separated from the relationship with men" (Levinas, 1969, 78).

"The straight line between me and the Other's uprightness forbids me to participate in the sacred; it sobers me" (Levinas 1994c, 94).

In conclusion, we can infer that holiness is an ethical tool for Levinas to shape his ethical intuition about the indirect connections between humans and God and humans and the "Other". In contrast to the materialistic experience of the sacred, holiness awakens the self, outside of the subject, in a process of ethical individuation. One of the most difficult things for the self is to make himself aware of his holiness as regards God and the "Other". Meeting the challenge is approached only through the progressive paradox of ethics.

CHAPTER 2:
LEVINAS AND KIERKEGAARD ON THE GOD-PERSON RELATION

2.1 Introduction

Another crucial area which is examined in this work is the positions of Levinas and Kierkegaard on subjectivity and what it means to be a person. How can personhood be defined? Below, I briefly present some remarks on the analytical line of thought concerning personhood which briefly provides epistemological and metaphysical arguments from philosophy of mind about what being a person is by using thought experiments.[143] After that, I argue that Levinas is not

---

[143] By thought experiment in analytic philosophy, we mean "a made-up or imagined situation that is supposed to show something about the limits of a concept" (Martinich 2005, 197). However, the majority of analytical thinkers who endeavor to speak about the concept of personhood compare human beings with other creatures such as animals, angels, aliens, and God. For instance, they raise questions as to whether a chimpanzee or a dolphin are considered as persons as well as questions such as which criteria can be listed for personhood, whether all human beings count as persons, and whether there are non-humans that can be counted as persons. On the other hand, in continental philosophy, it is more important to explore human's subjectivity as it is and not compare it with other creatures using an experimental-psychological methodology. Rather, the only comparison which can be made regards humans and their relation to God, not to other creatures. However, Levinas discusses the distinction between the human and animal face in an interview by a group of students from the University of Warwick which took place at his house in France in 1986. After a question concerning the distinction between the human and the animal face, Levinas answers that "one cannot entirely refuse the face of an animal. It is via the face that one understands, for example, a dog. Yet the priority here is not found in the animal, but in the human face. We understand the animal, the face of an animal, in accordance with *Dasein*. The phenomenon of the face is not in its purest form in the dog. In the dog, in the animal, there are other phenomena. For example, the force of nature is pure vitality. It is more this which characterizes the dog. But it also has a face. There are these two strange things in the face: its extreme frailty — the fact of being without means and, on the other

interested in Western metaphysics or in ontological criteria for exploring his arguments on subjectivity. Rather, as is also mentioned above, he insists that subjectivity can be understood through ethics and the ethical metaphysics that precedes ontology. On the other hand, Kierkegaard provides arguments that prioritize the notion of faith. Even though Kierkegaard started with aesthetics, he then searched for the definition of subjectivity in terms of Christological criteria. I can find my subjectivity as a human by myself: I do not need any established Church[144] or others to assist my mission toward God, but rather a commitment to "Socratic inquiry and to the inflections of a Christian faith" (Mooney 2008a, 2). If we want to speak about subjectivity and its relation to God (and the good), we need — according to Kierkegaard — to consider both a Socratic and a Christian source of self. The established Church must be replaced by a Socratic dialectic far from the manipulation and coercion of the human's spiritual freedom. Of course, as is seen in his *Postscript*, Kierkegaard gives priority to Christian religion over skeptical Socratic dialogical interrogation. However, he confesses that his task is to promote a combination of Socratic and Christian dialectics distracting from the "virtues of questioning the solitude of inwardness" (ibid., 6).

---

hand, there is authority. It is as if God spoke through the face" (Bernasconi and Wood [eds.] 1988, 169). Concerning the approach of the other as a rational animal, see further discussion in P. Atterton, "Face-to-Face with the Other Animal?" (2004, 262-81).

[144] Kierkegaard opposes the secularization of established (Danish) church, especially in the modern age since, as he believes, it develops a falsely objective truth. He adds that "objectively Christianity has absolutely no existence [...] It is subjectivity that Christianity is concerned with and it is only in subjectivity that its truth exists" (Watts 2014, loc. 1595).

2.2 The Notion of the Self in Analytical Thinking

In analytic thought, in my view, there is a confusion between the philosophical and psychological accounts of what being a person is due to the integration of philosophy of mind (Putnam 2004b, 15-85), and there is a danger of "losing ourselves" in psychology instead of seeking what a self is in philosophy. It worth briefly pointing out that in English-language analytical philosophy, several thinkers give priority to ontology, metaphysics, neuro-philosophy, and philosophy of mind (Churchland 1999, 7-51) in order to answer the question of what it is to be a person. They start their question with the word "how", providing epistemological and not ethical criteria for the conception of personhood.

One of the most prominent analytical philosophers, Harry Frankfurt, argues that "one essential difference between persons and other creatures is to be found in the structure of a person's will" (Frankfurt 1971, 6). "Second-order volitions" are necessary conditions for regarding someone as a person (ibid., 10).[145] Another renowned analytical thinker,

---

[145] A very fruitful work written by J. Davenport, *Narrative Identity and Autonomy*, 2012, explores arguments concerning Frankfurt's and Kierkegaard's notion of autonomy and selfhood. See esp. ch. 4.1: "Kierkegaard's Ethically Grounded Wholeheartedness" (2012, 121-127, 131-149). At the conclusion of this study, the author stresses that "there is a narrative dimension to personal autonomy that builds on the narrative structure of personal identity in general, and that the kinds of narrative unity involved in autonomy are especially strong on Kierkegaard's conception of wholeheartedness. For purity of heart involves not just coherence among our cares, but also coherence through commitment to *agapic* ideals to govern our cares, willed to the point of infinite resignation" (ibid., 166). On this matter, see also S. Kierkegaard, *Two Ages: the age of revolution and the present age* (2009b, 68-112). As regards volitions, second-order volitions, freedom, determinism, free will, sin, and despair in Kierkegaardian philosophy see S. Kierkegaard, *Sickness unto death* (1983a, 11-67; Jackson 1998). Another

Peter Strawson, states that "a person or human being, as a subject of discourse, typically collects predicates of all these kinds: [...] actions, intentions, sensations, thoughts, feelings, perceptions, memories, physical position, corporeal characteristics, skills or abilities, traits of character and so on" (Strawson 2008, 187). In addition, Garry Watson strongly argues that volitions cannot be the source of identification (as the main difference between persons and other creatures), claiming that a second-order desire seems to be special not for volitions but for values (Watson 1975, 216). For Watson, a person is a human when she is capable of making first-order decisions and can continue her life according to these

---

valuable monography regarding Kierkegaard's freedom and its relation, or opposition, to reason is by M. Kosch: *Freedom and Reason* (2006, 139-216). See also J. Davenport et al., *Kierkegaard after MacIntyre* (2001), especially on freedom, virtue, and narrative. In the branch of analytic philosophy of the so-called incompatibilists, priority is given to determinism and not to free will. Determinism means "the doctrine that every event has a cause and only events are causes. [It] is often understood to exclude the possibility of free will, when free will is understood as a faculty or ability to choose or act in ways that are not determined or constrained by prior causal events" (Martinich 2005, 191). There is therefore a view – a pessimistic one – claiming that free will is an illusion and human beings cannot freely plan their future at all. This theory, which was distilled by the French mathematician and astronomer Pierre-Simon Marquis de Laplace (1749-1827) and named BOCN (Blind Operation of Causal Necessity), argues that the universe is fully determined by causal necessity, and, therefore, all events are subject to the laws of nature and thus happen of necessity. So, especially in analytic philosophy of mind and psychoanalysis, our mind is determined and thus our brain is also determined, and, therefore, we do not have free will at all, which means we are not autonomous which finally entails that no one is a person. In this theory, free will is incompatible with determinism. However, very few people actually go this far. The majority of thinkers such as Frankfurt, Strawson, Watson, and Taylor bring to a light another more optimistic theory: even if we accept that determinism is true, free will and autonomy can be compatible with determinism. Frankfurt persists in asserting that free will can be placed in a deterministic framework because persons have second-order volitions. Similarly, Strawson tries to show that even if determinism were known to be true, we are not able to change the way we regard and treat each other. We would continue to regard one another as persons: that is, as autonomous beings (Matravers 2008, 33).

directions. David Lewis explains thoroughly the notion of valuing, maintaining that it is a mental, attitudinal state (Lewis 1989, 114). He also adds that if I do not want to desire the thing I desire, I cannot value it. Lewis through his research investigates third-order or higher desires and infers that "valuing is just desiring to desire" (ibid., 115). Eric Olson, on the other hand, gives priority not to psychological but to biological and epistemological criteria: he believes that the "Psychological Approach" must be false (Olson 1997, 95). He argues that we are merely animals consisting of the same biological criteria as animals, giving priority to materialism[146] rather than dualism (ibid., 4). This is one of the most important objections to the claim that sophisticated minds are not enough to justify personhood. The evidence provided to support this objection is that a robot or an artifact which has a sophisticated, intelligent mind cannot be regarded as a person since it does not have organic, rational, free-will consciousness. Olson continues his objection to the psychological approach by underlining that being a person does not have any moral significance if we only care about individuality: if persons consist of non-relational psychological properties, they have no differences from material objects. Olson suggests that there is another alternative: the possibility to be functional animals rather than persons. By saying functional animals, he means human animals with "certain psychological capacities" (ibid., 109). Therefore, in brief, analytical thinkers provide some criteria for counting as a person,

---

146   By saying materialism, we mean "the doctrine that only material objects and their relations exist. It denies that mental objects exist or are anything other than material objects or manifestation of the functioning of material objects" (Martinich 2005, 193).

which is called "criterialism" by T. S.-G. Chappell[147] (Chappell 2011, 2-3), focusing mainly on knowledge and (self-) consciousness:[148]

> "I propose to use 'person', in the sense of a rational and self-conscious being, to capture those elements of the popular sense of 'human being' that are not covered by 'member of the species Homo sapiens.'" (Singer 1993, 87).
> "Persons are beings capable of valuing their own lives" (Harris 1985, 16-17).
> "An organism possesses a serious right to life only if it possesses the concept of a self as a continuing subject of experiences and other mental states and believes that it is itself such an entity." (Tooley 1972, 82).
> "[The six key markers of personhood are] (1) sentience . . . (2) emotionality . . . (3) reason . . . (4) the capacity to communicate . . . (5) self-awareness . . . [and] (6) moral agency." (Warren 1997, 83-84).

2.3 Subjectivity[149] and Selfhood in Levinas and Kierkegaard

On the contrary, in continental philosophy and especially in the field of ethics, psychological, epistemological, and experimental accounts are omitted. This is the main reason that this study insists on ethical (Levinasian) and religious (Kierkegaardian)[150] perspectives rather than the psychological-

---

[147] By criterialism we mean the "actual possession of the criterial properties is necessary and sufficient for membership of the Primary Moral Constituency (PMC)" (Chappell 2011, 2, n. 4).

[148] However, Levinas would raise several objections to this line of thought, replying that "knowledge only comprehends itself in its own essence, starting from consciousness, whose specificity eludes us when we define it with the aid of the concept of knowledge which itself supposes consciousness" (Levinas 1998b, 58).

[149] For Levinas, "to undergo from the other is an absolute patience only if by this from-the-other is already for-the-other. This transfer [...] 'other than essence' is subjectivity itself" (Levinas 1991: 111).

[150] One of the most fruitful works on continental philosophy and Kierkegaard in my view is that of M. Weston in *Kierkegaard and Modern Continental Philosophy* (1994, 11-32, 156-174).

epistemological (analytical) positions explored mainly by analytic philosophy.[151]

Despite the partial truth of the Buberian "I-Thou" statement[152] that S.-G. Chappell analyzes,[153] it needs further analysis to understand Levinas's thoughts about the relation between human and divine, "me" (not "I") and others from an ethical, not ontological, standpoint. Levinas explains that even though his thinking on subjectivity was influenced by Husserl, Heidegger, Maurice Blanchot, Martin Buber, and Gabriel Marcel, his ethics takes a step forward in order to differentiate his position as clarifying the priority of responsibility over phenomenological instruments such as intentionality and consciousness. This is a very important issue, as Levinas

---

[151] It is obvious that Kierkegaard's dialectics are quite far from any epistemological-theoretical framework. It is common knowledge that Kierkegaard never used any epistemological methods in his philosophical writings. As he points out, "the fact of the matter is that we must acknowledge that in the last resort there is no theory". (Kierkegaard 1970, entry 2509).

[152] As Levinas states, "to Buber, the Thou that the I solicits is already, in that appeal, heard as an I who says Thou to me. The appeal to the Thou by the I would thus be, for the I, the institution of reciprocity, an equality or equity from the start [...] The idea of the I or of a Myself in general is immediately derived from that relation: a total reflection on myself would be possible and thus the elevation of the Myself to the level of the concept, to Subjectivity above the lived centrality of the I". See Levinas's article "Apropos of Buber: Some Notes", in H. Jodalen, J. and Vetlesen (eds.), Closeness: An Ethics (1997, 47-48).

[153] S.-G. Chappell argues that in analytic thinking, it is necessary to treat other human beings as equal interlocutors even if they are skilled or fully interlocutors (Chappell 2012, 2). What really matters is to share common values and intersubjective properties as you deserve. In addition, Chappell's thought also favors (together with the argument of equal deliberators) Levinas's "Divine Command" ethics (DCE), that is, "the person above all to whom I have to second-personally justify myself is God. Ethics is a matter of divine commands because ethics is a second personal affair, and relative to every person. God is super-eminently second-personal" (ibid, 6). Thus, we can infer that if we take ourselves as co-deliberators and the second-personal is necessary for personhood, we could easily compare this with the theological phrase "loving my neighbor as myself" (ibid., 7), building bridges for a future reconciliation between (a part of) philosophy and theology.

encapsulates his philosophical and religious standpoint on subjectivity[154] in this argument below:

"The approach of others is not [as Buber and Marcel allege] originally in my speaking out to the other, but in my *responsibility* for him or her. That is the original ethical relations. That responsibility is elicited, brought about by the face of the other person, described as a breaking of the plastic forms of the phenomenality of appearance: straightforwardness of the exposure to death, and an order issued to me not to abandon the other (the Word of God) [...] The ineradicable centrality of the I — of the I not leaving its first person — signifies the unlimited nature of that responsibility for the neighbor: I am never absolved with respect to others. Responsibility for the other person is responsibility neither conditioned nor measured [intentional or conscious] by any free acts of which it would be the consequence; it is gratuitous responsibility resembling that of a hostage, and going as far as taking the other's place, without requiring reciprocity". (Jodalen and Vetlesen [eds.] 1997, 48).

Dimitrova comprehensively sketches the Levinasian ethical overview (and purview) against the Heideggerian fundamental ontology[155] of what it is to be a person, its attributes as well as its connection with other humans and the divine.

"For Levinas, if everything human is reduced to ontology, to be a man is to be in service of Being. And to be a part of Being's adventure is to obey

---

[154] Concerning several views on the modern and postmodern subject and how Levinas evaluates the notion of the subject, see L. Batnitzky, "Encountering the Modern Subject in Levinas", *Encounters with Levinas* (2004, 6-21), especially page 14, where she states that "for Levinas, the self is not one who represents itself to itself through thought (the view that Husserl and Heidegger both attribute to Descartes)". In contrast, Levinas infers that the subject begins by conversing with the other beyond language.

[155] Levinas defines ontology clearly and sufficiently by stating that "the relation with Being that is enacted as ontology consists in neutralizing the existent in order to comprehend or grasp it. It is hence not relation with the other as such but the reduction of the other to the same. Such is the definition of freedom: to maintain oneself against the other, despite every relation with the other to ensure the autarky of an *I*. Thematization and conceptualization, which moreover are inseparable, are not peace with the other but suppression or possession of the other. For possession affirms the other, but within a negation of its independence. *I think* comes down to *I can* — to an appropriation of what is, to an exploitation of reality. Ontology as first philosophy is a philosophy of power" (Levinas 1969, 45-46).

something like the 'faceless' fate. Fundamental ontology is a philosophy of power supporting obedience to the Neutral. Levinas thinks that the humanness of *homo humanus* constitutes itself first of all in the face-to-face relationship with the Other as a real and quite tangible person. The whole Self as *me* is in service not to the system of Being (available only through *mineness*), but in service to a concrete, here and now existing neighbor, whereby the *conatus essendi* of mine-ness is surmounted. Most often Levinas' philosophy is considered to be devoted to the problem of the Other or the otherness of the Other. But in fact, Levinas' thought is concerned not with the Other as such but with my relation to him or her. The main issue is my responsibility for the Other and it can be extended to the substitution of the Other by me, wherein I am transformed into a hostage of the Other. The focus of Levinas' philosophy is the moral subject: the 'I' in accusative case, that is, 'me', who has no chance to hide behind a mask of a Third one" (Dimitrova 2006, 17).

For Levinas, the humanity of the human leads to the very crisis of being *qua* being (Jodalen and Vetlesen [eds] 1997, 47). The fragment above is an implication of a Levinasian line of thought which contrasts not only ontological perspectives of the self but also Christian perspectives concerning the relation of humans to each other and to divinity. Levinas, like Sartre, contends that "me" encounters the "Other" by inventing or constituting her. However, Levinas goes a step further, alleging that I do not encounter the "Other" merely as a "Thou" but as a face which is asymmetrical and non-reciprocal to "me" because, contrary to Kierkegaard, if I expect the other to be merely a "Thou", it would be only an empirical event without transcendence, only facing immanence. However, for Levinas, transcendence of the alter ego is crucial for subjectivity. As Dimitrova points out, "I am summoned to enter into a relation with the other in his or her dimension of Transcendence" (ibid., 18).

Subjectivity for Levinas is based—as we have also seen above—on the asymmetrical non-reciprocal relation between me and the other. As A. J. Veltlesen correctly notes, "I am always one step behind the other. I will never catch up with the other. There is absence of balance, symmetry, reciprocity both as far as the ground and as far as the aim of Levinasian responsibility is concerned", where the latter will be always "dissociated from reciprocity" (Jodalen and Vetlesen [eds.] 1997, 160). Subjectivity, according to Levinas, is "not of the subject's own making, [nor] a product of socialization", a performance of a process of interdependent interaction among equal interlocutors. By contrast, Levinas insists that we need to escape from Hegel's scenario of recognition. If an agent plans to gain advantage through the face of the other, that is, to sacrifice the face for the sake of self-interest, then the other is automatically absorbed by the "Same". Levinas's purpose is to achieve selflessness, which is a primordial ethical ideal and can be attained by giving priority to the other's face, which, according to Levinas, "is the absolute ethical primacy of the other over the *I*" where "the further one moves away from the viewpoint of the acting *I*, the better" (ibid., 162). However, several thinkers raise an objection to Levinas's insistence on the one-way affair. They claim that although Levinas is right in alleging that ethical subjectivity is prior to any personal expediencies and reciprocity, interdependence and intersubjectivity on equal footing as well as vulnerability and responsibility must be shared and not undertaken only through the face of the other.

"To receive, there must be interaction. I grow up, I turn into a human in the full sense of the word, thanks to others who interact with me. [...] They assume responsibility for me—like others did for them—lest I die for want of nourishment, shelter, love. In this way responsibility as received, as enjoyed, indeed as needed for life to be sustained, is prior to responsibility as taken up and assumed for the other, for my other. What is given to the other was originally received from another [...] It is this precious experience of having been at the receiving end of responsibility that is neglected in Levinas's account" (Jodalen and Vetlesen [eds.] 1997, 163).

Subjectivity, however, is not related only to human beings but to God as well. The human-divine relation, therefore, is a trivial and hard issue to get involved in. However, Levinas stresses that God cannot directly be known and understood by humans. God's attributes (if God has attributes understandable to human beings) cannot be explained or revealed by finite thinkers. As Dimitrova mentions, "God is Transcendence and Transcendence cannot be possessed" (ibid., 23). Especially people in modern Western societies have been trapped by anthropomorphism, that is, they, mistakenly, according to Levinas, transmit God from exteriority to interiority,[156] from "outside to inside",[157] from transcendence to immanence. Dimitrova raises an objection to Western culture,

---

[156] In short, we can argue, as P. Rigby does, that for Levinas, "we can find an authentic trace of God only in the moral passage from interiority to exteriority". See P. Rigby, *"Levinas and Christian Mysticism after Auschwitz"* (2011, 310). It is worth noting at this point that Kierkegaard provides an extremely different view concerning the exteriority-interiority debate. He insists that the absolute paradox, that is, God, can be only understood, seen, or explained in secrecy, in a mystical but active silence whereas interiority plays a crucial and decisive role. Derrida provides a quite useful passage in which he praises Kierkegaard's sense of God, subjectivity, and the way of being-with-oneself approaching the divine absolute: "God is the name of the possibility I have of keeping a secret that is visible from the interior but not from the exterior. Once such a structure of conscience exists, of being-with-oneself, of speaking, that is, of producing an invisible sense, once I have within me, thanks to the invisible word as such, a witness that others cannot see, and who is therefore at the same time other than me and more intimate with me than myself, once I can have a secret relationship with myself and not tell everything, once there is secrecy and secret witnessing within me, then what I call God exists what I call God in me, I call myself God" (Derrida 1995, 109)

[157] P. Rigby notes that "Levinas rejects all forms of internalization, whether internalization takes the form either of the evangelical call to forgive one's enemy or of the interior journey to God in prayer. According to Levinas, internalization/interiority is a submoral and sterile exercise in self-absorption and the endless repetition of the same. It is possible to know God only as a moral trace in the stranger, "the widow and the orphan," the other as other" (ibid., 310).

alleging that it falsely creates a secular/cosmic ontotheological God (ibid.). In the same vein, she explains that the human-
divine relation still stands in a mistaken position as modernity promotes the medieval Christian tradition "endowing
man with being a co-creator of the Creation" (ibid.).

For Levinas, what matters most is responsibility[158] to the
"Other". Our finitude transcends into infinity by our show-
ing our responsibility to the other face to face. In contrast to
Heidegger, Levinas underlines the care of myself[159] for the
other's being not ontologically but ethically. I mean that responsibility must sustain "Other"ness in a transcendental
way where the response to the other must be asymmetrical

---

[158] In Kierkegaard, the ethics of responsibility has a direct communication to both
humans and God. I can love and provide my eternal assistance to my neighbor
but before I have a direct communication to God and God shows me the way
to love and respect my neighbor. This existential progression starts from aesthetics, continues to ethics, and is culminated in religion (existential faith).
Responsibility in Kierkegaard does not precede freedom as in Levinas. The
"suffering truth" with which Kierkegaard explores his religious aspects, according to Levinas, provides a theistic and isolated responsibility as "it does not
open out to others, but to God in isolation" (Rée and Chamberlain [eds.] 1998,
30). This is one of the main reasons that Kierkegaard was considered one of the
most renowned Protestant thinkers in Europe. For Kierkegaard's ethics of
responsibility in general, see M. Dooley, *The Politics of Exodus* (2001, 143):
"Responsibility is a matter, according to Kierkegaard, of deciding in fear and
trembling whether one will affirm the God-man—whether, that is, one will
have faith and believe in him in his lowliness, or whether one will hold fast to
the securities of Christendom or the state". Concerning Kierkegaard's selfhood
and personal identity, see (idem, 74-114; Stokes 2015, 1-21). On Kierkegaard's
notion of God-man, see (idem. 115-143). Regarding the subject and the neighbor, see M. Andic, in G. Pattison and S. Shakespeare (eds.), *Kierkegaard: The Self
in Society* (1998, 112-124). For Kierkegaard's view on the self before God, see S.
D. Podmore, *Kierkegaard and the Self before God* (2011a, 10-49).

[159] As G. L. Bruns puts it, "Heidegger's interest is nevertheless in the ontological
rather than ethical meaning of care, and *Dasein's care* is always ultimately for
itself, not for others" (Bruns 2004, 31). For a complete discussion on Heidegger's
view of care and being, see his subchapter 64: "Care and Selfhood", in *Being and
Time* (1962, 364-370). In contrast, Levinas's care is essentially for the sake of
"Others", which derives from the eternal call to me always from the other as a
commandment that I cannot ignore or avoid. Levinas insists that Heidegger's
care is for-itself alone.

and indirect (ibid., 19). However, the main understanding of Levinas's thought is not too much the otherness of the other *par excellence* but rather "me" as a moral subject. It is me and not I that matters in a non-reciprocal condition.

> "The Word, the conversation according to Levinas' model, cannot be properly understood as a reciprocal relation between equal partners, i.e., dialogue (as it is for Buber, for example). The conversation is not a partnership since the Other is in a position of superiority: he or she questions me. But this does not mean that I am in a position of inferiority. I am the Single One who is responsible for responding, for giving to another because he or she is one in need. As a moral subject, I am called to pay attention to the Other and thus feel myself chosen, unique, and irreplaceable. I can't avoid the responsibility because my failure to respond is already a kind of response" (Dimitrova 2006, 26).

Levinas's subjectivity consists in several neologisms and newness. I mean that despite the great influence of Husserl and Heidegger, whose works were presented and scrutinized by Levinas in the French context, Levinas's purpose was to expand an innovation across continental philosophy: "he seeks a meaning beyond the *esse* of being, meaning that no longer states itself in terms of Being and is prior to Being" (ibid., 25). For Levinas, subjectivity depends on the face of the other, but through indirect ethics. If the human face is taken either as too sublime or too real he loses its bewilderment and thus he is unable to clearly present its self through the other.[160] Thus if we consider ethics phenomenologically, approaching the other in such a way, ethics becomes moralism, which would be a fatal mistake, according to Levinas. "Similar to Merleau-Ponty[161] [for whom] ontology can approach

---

[160] Concerning the sublime and sublation in Kierkegaard and his objections to Hegel, see J. Milbank, "The Sublime in Kierkegaard" (1996, 298-321; Pattison 1998).

[161] A valuable comparative study of Levinas and Merleau-Ponty has been written by T. W. Busch, "Ethics and Ontology: Levinas and Merleau-Ponty" (1992, 195-

Being only in terms of an indirect ontology, we can assume that [Levinas's] ethics can approach the other only in terms of an indirect ethics" (Waldenfels 2004, 64). Subjectivity, according to Levinas, can only be understood *via negationis* and *via eminentiae*. Similar to apophatic theology, it is meaningless and misguided to designate human attributes to God. As Levinas underlines, we are living in the face of the other, "seeking or fleeing [from] it, running the risk of losing our own face"; it is a continuous hunting of traces that we will never find; our selves can only be identified, ethically speaking, when "the common face turns into the uncommon, into the unfamiliar, even into the uncanny" (ibid., 65). There is no "me" (rather than "I") without the response of the other. Levinas underlines that "whether he regards me or not, he regards me [...] This is the question of the meaning of being: not the ontology of the understanding of that extraordinary verb, but the ethics of its justice" (Kearney and Rainwater [eds.] 1996, 134).

Levinas underlines that in contrast to fundamental ontology, (moral) subjectivity is devoted to the sustaining other's presence but "the excess over the presence is the life of the infinite" where the moral subject is even responsible for the responsibility of the other (ibid., 27). Kierkegaard. on the other hand, has some similarities with Levinas regarding subjectivity, but he clearly stresses his view antithetical to

---

202). Concerning Levinas's and Merleau-Ponty's views of responsibility and its nonreductive unity to reason, see an interesting work by D. M. Kleinberg-Levin, *Before the Voice of Reason: Echoes of Responsibility* (2008, 147-240). See also S. Mackinlay, "Hermeneutic Perspectives on Ontology, After Metaphysics Has Been Overcome: From Levinas to Merleau-Ponty" (2017, 115-124). Concerning Merleau-Ponty's conception of phenomenology and the self as well as perception and representation, see his article "Preface to Phenomenology of Perception", in R. Kearney et al. (eds.) *The Continental Philosophy Reader* (1996, 79-92).

Levinas's that human beings can reach God's commandments and essence directly with reciprocity and contemplation and that there is a symmetrical relation between individuals and the divine.[162] Kierkegaard as a Protestant advocates
a "leap of faith (Tsakiri 2009, 58) in his writings, which is rejected by both Heidegger and Levinas. However, he agrees
with the latter that it is subjectivity and not objectivity that
matters most.

Several continental and analytical thinkers express their
great interest in exploring philosophical accounts in order to
construe sound and valid propositions on subjectivity and
the conception of the "Self" as well as to compare (if it is possible) Levinas's phenomenology, metaphysics, and ethics
with Kierkegaardian Christian existentialism. Taking into
consideration the aforementioned discussion about Levinas's
and Kierkegaard's views on subjectivity and the "Self", I argue in the next paragraphs that although they both object to
fundamental ontology (mainly derived from Heidegger's
Dasein) and give priority to subjectivity, metaphysics, and
ethics, they consider the concept of the "Self" from different
philosophical perspectives.

For example, if we want to note some similarities between Levinas and Kierkegaard, we may underline that they
both consider the duty of love and sacrifice, which are characteristics of the "Self", as subjects of individual experience
rather than having objective validity and universality (Tsakiri
2009, 61). However, the two thinkers explore their views in
different ways. For instance, Levinas, believes that the ethical

---

[162] See a brief implication in favor of this thesis in M. Dimitrova, "Levinas: How to
think *Humanitas* of *Homo Humanus*" (2006, 29, n. 10).

realm regards us as unique individuals, as "Selves", only when we prioritize the "Other". In contrast, Kierkegaard seeks to generalize the subject by providing theological perspectives on the so-called second ethics (*den anden Etik*)[163], or Christian ethics (ibid., 61-62). Another similarity is that, according to V. Tsakiri, "it seems plausible to suggest that they both delineate a transcendent state-of-affairs, irreducible to universality and the totalizing powers of reason" (ibid., 62). However, one of the most important discrepancies between the two thinkers which emerges from a theological aspect of the above similarity is that Kierkegaard, on the one hand, claims that "the love of one's neighbor is mediated by the love of God, whereas for Levinas on the other hand the love of God is reached through the path that opens up as consequence of the love of one's neighbor" (Westphal 2008a, 70-71). Another crucial difference between the two thinkers concerning the theological/ethical issue of the "Self" and its relation to divinity and the other is that for Levinas, "a face is of itself a visitation and a transcendence [...] To be in the image of God does not mean to be an icon of God but to find oneself in his trace [...] To go toward Him is not to follow this trace, which is not a sign; it is to go toward the Others who stand in the trace of illeity" (Tsakiri 2009, 66).

Levinas, although he agrees with Kierkegaard concerning the pitfalls and errant points in totalitarian ontology,

---

[163] L. Llevadot provides a comprehensive definition of Kierkegaard's second ethics by saying that, according to Kierkegaard, "the second ethics is not established between communicative subjects, but rather between particularities that are irreducible to language. It is in the silence of entrenched inwardness where we can establish our relationship with the dead, irreducible by any aspiration of reasoning or any demand to account for oneself or what is real. In the depths of this silence" (Llevadot 2011, 215).

expresses skepticism (and even suspicion) regarding the Protestant element of Kierkegaard's thought (ibid., 62). This might seem logical and to be expected since Kierkegaard openly accepted the Protestant label. However, Levinas, despite his acute criticism of Kierkegaard's allegation of adopting God directly attributing theological historicism, supports Kierkegaard's theological view that "the Kierkegaardian God is revealed only by being persecuted and unrecognized, reveals only in the measure that he is hunted. God remaining with the contrite and humble on the margin, a 'persecuted truth' is not only a religious consolation but the original form of transcendence" (ibid., 65). The objection that Levinas raises on this matter is that Kierkegaard mistakenly insists on humans' direct connection to God, that is, "it does not open us out to others but to God in isolation" (ibid.).

It important to note that Levinas and Kierkegaard agree that unselfish concern for others is what matters regarding morality.[164] They agree that subjectivity underlies the neighbor and the striving to recognize the other's face. However, they explore this argument using different dialectics. Kierkegaard gives priority to the I, not the intentional I, as was explored by Husserl and Heidegger or the total I of Hegel, but the I in the nominative case which is reflected first by God. The interconnection with and relation to God comes first.

---

[164] At this point, morality has the same meaning as ethics. Ordinarily speaking, morality is an ethical code of moral standards in daily life and ethics is the study of researching these morals. According to Levinas, "Ethics", with a capital E, is not merely a deontological issue, but mainly the procedure of finite human "beings" progressively transcending to the infinite, always indirectly through the face of the other, in the form and context of non-reciprocal responsibility. In Kierkegaard, the "highest expression of that concern – that is the unselfish concern for others – is the unselfish love for the Other regardless of her merits and attraction of lack of such; this is moral love" (Jodalen and Vetlesen [eds.] 1997, 11).

God is always the commander from which I take strength and directions through prayer and conversation with Him in order to understand how to negotiate with and love my neighbor. We may say that God, according to Kierkegaard, is always the middle term between me and my neighbor (Kierkegaard 1995, 57, 58, 67, 77, 107, 119, 121, 142). My relation to others must first be seen through the relation with and the commandments of God, and this is the main reason God, for Kierkegaard, "is the middle term between me and my neighbor" (Stern 2020, 87).[165]

On the other hand, in Levinasian ethics, the direction of revealing and accepting the subjectivity of the other and its relation to the me, instead of the I, is quite reversed. It is not the I who has the greatest importance but the "Other". Even though several thinkers insist that in Levinas "the human Other is the middle term between me and God" (Simmons and Wood [eds.] 2008, 24), I argue that there is not such a thing in Levinasian thought; for Levinas, neither God nor the other is the middle term in terms of justifying subjectivity and my relation to God or the other person. I simply cannot speak of a middle term because I cannot define God.[166] Thus, once it is impossible for human mind to speak of God using mental or human properties, a middle term does not exist. If we suppose that the middle term does not exist, how can we clarify the human's relation to the other or to God? Levinas's answer is not so simple on this matter. He claims that the first

---

[165] For Kierkegaard's subjectivity and God's commandment of asceticism, see C. Hamilton, "Kierkegaard on Truth as Subjectivity" (1998, 61-79).
[166] However, Levinas stresses that the only way to understanding God's traces on earth (if we ever say so) is through the face of the other; the face of the last of my neighbors.

movement comes from outside and never from inside. As A. J. Vetlesen states, for Levinas, "the relation with the Other is one neither of knowledge nor of being since the relation comes to the *I* instead of flowing from it" (Jodalen and Vetlesen [eds.] 1997, 14) Inwardness and intentionality have little importance in Levinas's analysis of otherness. Against the Hegelian totalitarianism of the I, Levinas objects to the primacy of the universal in the name of the "Other", and this is why he prefers not to give priority to the "egoism" of ontology.

Kierkegaard, even though he agrees with Levinas in objecting to the primacy of the universal, gives priority to the individualization of the individual and not the face of the other. He insists that it would be nonsense to fear being an individual. Being uniquely me is the way of finding and accepting the "Other". Understanding myself — through God's commandments — is the key to learning and accepting my neighbor as well.

Kierkegaard's dialectic can be characterized as a three-dimensional progression of existential stages: "from the aesthetic to the ethical and from the ethical to the religious" (Fink

2000, 79-91).[167] The aesthetic stage[168] is a starting point for knowing oneself, integrating the presupposition of the immersion of sensuous experience as well as the flight of boredom where the individual must get to know herself in the highest sense. This approach can be achieved only by the total "fragmentation of the subject of experience", and the main task for the aesthetic is "the transformation of the boring into the interesting" (McDonald 2017, ch. 3). This skeptical approach can be compared to the religious framework as well. Kierkegaard, as a Protestant, insists that the believer must be activated far from secular, political, and psychological coercion in order to proceed to the divine. A very cogent

---

[167] Concerning the transition from the aesthetic to the religious, see G. Pattison, *The Aesthetic and the Religious* (1992, 63-94, 155-188). However, Levinas criticizes this peculiar transition from aesthetics to the ethical and from the ethical to the religious by saying that "Kierkegaard's violence begins when existence, having moved beyond the aesthetic stage, is forced to abandon the ethical stage (or rather, what it took to be the ethical stage) in order to embark on the religious stage, the domain of belief" (Levinas 1998c, 31), and that "violence emerges in Kierkegaard at the precise moment when, moving beyond the esthetic stage, existence can no longer limit itself to what it takes to be an ethical stage and enters the religious one, the domain of belief. This latter is no longer justified in the outer world" (Levinas 1996b, 72). Levinas states that Kierkegaard's reverse on religion abandoned the meeting with the "Other" who has priority over the self, who, in rational and mystical theology, gives priority to the individual's seeking God through prayer rather than the responsibility of the "Other"'s otherness. Levinas alleges that Kierkegaard "philosophizes with a hammer", introducing an irrational and violent dialect to philosophy, especially after abandoning ethics for the sake of religion. Specifically, Levinas contends that "it is Kierkegaard's violence that shocks me. The manner of the strong and the violent, who fear neither scandal nor destruction, has become, since Kierkegaard and before Nietzsche, a manner of philosophy. One philosophizes with a hammer. In that permanent scandal, in that opposition to everything, I perceive by anticipation the echoes of certain cases of verbal violence that claimed to be schools of thought, and pure ones at that. I am thinking not only of National Socialism, but of all the sorts of thought it exalted. That harshness of Kierkegaard emerges at the exact moment when he transcends ethics" (Levinas 1996b, 76).

[168] The most comprehensive secondary literature on Kierkegaard's aesthetics from my point of view appears in T. Adorno, *Construction of the Aesthetic* (1989; Pattison 1992; Walsh 1994; Jothen, 2014; Berry, 1981, 20–41; Schiller, 1954).

paradigm to reflect Kierkegaard's critique of the secularization of modern faith is deduced by M. Watts, who underlines that "Kierkegaard was convinced that in order to realize our true significance, we need to free ourselves completely from the influence of social, cultural and religious values and expectations. Instead, each person needs to develop a clear awareness of their life situation so that they can determine their own path by making conscious, responsible choices from among the alternatives that life offers them" (Watts 2014, loc. 250). In contrast, boredom develops passivity, making persons react without energy or interest in creating ethical relations with other agents, or seeking God. Extremely opposed to secularism and the totalization of the Catholic Church, Kierkegaard criticizes the higher clergy for manipulating believers by leading them into a sociopolitical framework which has nothing to do with pure faith in God. One of the most crucial views of Kierkegaard regarding his vehement criticism of the modern Church was his acute rhetoric on Catholic doctrine, characterizing it as "Objective Christianity".

Kierkegaard's aesthetics is full of irony and arbitrariness.[169] However, Kierkegaard does not want to isolate aesthetics from ethics and religion. In contrast, for Kierkegaard, aesthetics is a basic and compulsory stage in the existential progression of the self. It is basic since aesthetics is the main tool of transiting from finitude to infinity. "Aesthetic irony is transformed into religious humor, and the aesthetic transfiguration of the actual world into the ideal is transformed into

---

169   Concerning Kierkegaard's ethics of irony see M. Dooley, *The politics of Exodus* (2001, 43-73; Rasmussen 2005, 15-42). Regarding humor and irony in Kierkegaard's works, see J. Lippitt (2000, 47-71, 135-157, 158-174).

the religious transubstantiation of the finite world into an actual reconciliation with the infinite" (ibid).

Kierkegaard, as seen in several of his works, gives more attention and importance to the I than Levinas. For instance, he provides a definition of what it is to be a self through the speech of Anti-Climacus: "a human being is a synthesis of the infinite and the finite, of the temporal and the eternal, of freedom and necessity" (Kierkegaard 1980, 13). To recall, a synthesis, being "a relation between two," is still not a self. A self, rather, is an "established relation," or "a relation that relates itself to itself and in relating itself to itself relates itself to another" (ibid., 13-14). Levinas would certainly raise objections to the phrase "a relation that relates itself to itself" since that statement echoes mainly in ontology and not transcendence. For Levinas — who several times ignores and omits the term "being", as persons for Levinas are not beings but humans — persons are not connected necessarily in a relation that relates itself to itself but a "face-to-face relation" where the starting point is always the other (Hofmeyr 2005, 126, 138, 141). For Levinas, there is not I but me, and the me comes only after someone is calling, and I am eternally responsible to this call before freedom emerges.

> "But for this I must encounter the indiscreet face of the Other that calls me into question. The Other — the absolutely other — paralyzes possession, which he contests by his epiphany in the face. He can contest my possession only because he approaches me not from the outside but from above [...] I welcome the Other who presents himself in my home by opening my home to him. [...] The other is not opposed to me as a freedom other than, but similar to my own, and consequently hostile to my own. The Other is not another freedom as arbitrary as my own, in which case it would traverse the infinity that separates me from him and enter under the same concept." (Levinas 1969, 171).

In parallel, Kierkegaard sees "oneself as an individual who has the potential to transform her life according to certain guiding ethical ideas". Also, "becoming self-conscious is the most fundamental requirement Kierkegaardian ethics makes upon the individual" (Dooley 2001, 86). From Levinas's point of view, these statements lack sufficient support and fail to address the central questions of personhood. Subjectivity, for Levinas, is not thematized. Starting from oneself, what really matters is the fact that self-consciousness needs otherness through exteriority to be developed.

> "Self-consciousness is not a dialectical rejoinder of the metaphysical consciousness that I have of the other. Nor is its relation with itself a representation of itself. Prior to every vision of self it is accomplished by holding oneself up; it is implanted in itself as a body and it keeps itself in its interiority, in its home. It thus accomplishes separation positively, without being reducible to a negation of the being from which it separates. But thus, precisely it can welcome that being. The subject is a host, [...] subjectivity is accomplished as service and as hospitality" (Levinas 1969, 299-300).

Even though Levinas gives priority to exteriority, sometimes, as he mentions, interiority has an ethical meaning of paramount importance, especially regarding mother-child love and the role of the woman in the house.

> "And the other whose presence is discreetly an absence, with which is accomplished the primary hospitable welcome which describes the field of intimacy, is the Woman. The woman is the condition for recollection, the interiority of the Home, and inhabitation [...] It is comprehensible and exercises its function of interiorization only on the ground of the full human personality, which, however, in the woman, can be reserved so as to open up the dimension of interiority" (Levinas, 1969 155).

Scholars of the 20th century were divided on whether Kierkegaardian thought is misread as regards the notion of the I. For instance, Levinas mentions that "it is not *I* who resist the system, as Kierkegaard thought, it is the other" (Levinas, 1969,

40). On the one hand, Levinas compares Kierkegaard's notion of subjectivity and his insistence on the decisive role of the I with Heidegger's ontology, which is similar to Kierkegaard's thought in that the ontological task reduces the relationship with the "Other" to the relation with "Being" in general.[170] Here we are not sure whether Kierkegaard is referring to God or to other persons in general by writing "Being" with a capital B. For Levinas, it is obvious that he is referring neither to God nor to persons since he usually omits the terms being or "Being" from his works. For Levinas, neither God nor humans are beings. Perhaps Kierkegaard presents a similar reference closed to the Heideggerian notion of human beings and their relation to God (if any) as analyzed in *Being and Time* (Heidegger 1962).[171]

Several thinkers claim that there is a misconception as to whether Kierkegaard insists on the isolated power of the subject as I, or if what really matters to Kierkegaard is the God relationship. For instance, B. Prosser argues that Kierkegaard's notion of the self was never ontological because what matters is not the I as a thematized, isolated, egocentric self-enclosed unit but the God relationship. Similar to M. Westphal, who claims that Kierkegaard's starting point is the God relation (Simmons and Wood [eds.] 2008, 23), B. Prosser

---

[170] "A philosophy of power, ontology is, as first philosophy which does not call into question the same, a philosophy of injustice. Even though it opposes the technological passion issued forth from the forgetting of Being hidden by existents, Heideggerian ontology [...] subordinates the relationship with the Other to the relation with Being in general..." (Levinas 1969, 46). However, even though there are several similarities in Kierkegaardian and Heideggerian ontology, we can infer that the main discrepancy is that former insists on Christological criteria and the latter provides atheistic, phenomenological criteria.

[171] Heidegger rarely refers to God as a supreme being interconnected to human beings. Concerning a literal and metaphoric reference to God, see M. Wheeler, "Martin Heidegger: 3.5. Only a God can Save Us", (Zalta [ed] 2011).

underlines that it all begins with the God relationship which "breaks through the sphere of immanence and disturbs the system" (Prosser 2002, 397). "It is clear", Prosser suggests, "that Kierkegaard locates our most legitimate source of heteronomy in the relationship to God" (ibid., 400). However, in Levinas's ethical responsibility, as we have seen, such heteronomy occurs in interhuman relations. Such a contradiction is quite crucial to understand the main difference between Levinas and Kierkegaard's views on what it is to be a person through conscientious subjectivity.[172]

---

[172] In analytic philosophy, especially throughout the English-language tradition, the above statement is errant and therefore rejected since several thinkers such as T. (C.S-G) Chappell insist that personhood has nothing to do with subjectivity or a list of properties as presuppositions for an agent to be counted as a person. She argues that "I thoroughly examine the familiar criterial view of personhood, on whether the possession of personal properties such as consciousness, self-consciousness, subjectivity, emotionality, sentience, and so forth is necessary and sufficient for the status of a person. I argue that this view confuses criteria for personhood with parts of an ideal of personhood. In normal cases, we have already identified a creature as a person before we start looking for it to manifest the personal properties [...] It is all human animals (even non-humans: angels, extraterrestrial creatures, spirits) that we identify as persons", including also the very young (infants), the very senile, and the very disable (humans who suffer a persistent vegetative state). That is, persons are everyone (humans and non-humans, and mixed humans, like Christ who were God-man) who have the *potentiality* (even if they do not have it due to biological-healthy problems or theistic properties, like Holy Spirit — that might be counted as God-person) of Primary Moral Constituency (PMC)". (Chappell 2011, 1-2). Concerning Levinas's view on animals and especially on the category of humans who face mental or psychical disabilities, see E. Levinas, *Entre Nous* (1998a, 91-102; idem. 1991, 84-85, 109; Atterton, 2004, 277-279). By focusing on this discussion, I would like to stress that the notions of personhood, selfhood, subjectivity, and intersubjectivity are vast and expanded on throughout the continental and analytical lines of thought and are explored and discussed not only in philosophy and ethics but also in philosophy of mind, neuroscience, anthropology, theology, psychology, and cognitive studies. This study is focused on Levinas and Kierkegaard's insights especially on the points on which they agree and disagree concerning the concept of the self from the perspective of religion, ethics, and theology.

On the other hand, Levinas, as a postmodern, post-structuralist thinker,[173] makes an attempt to decenter the subject[174], claiming that what matters is not the total thematization of the subject but the call of the "Other" that precedes the subject. Levinas's intention is not to infringe on the subject but to explore its passivity. From the beginning of its existence, the subject is passive, not active, "because it is responsible before anything else" (Morgan 2007, 143). In contrast to analytic philosophy, where the subject is an autonomous and rational agent, in Levinas's thought the subject is heteronomous, accusation and hostage. However, even though he vehemently raises objections to the analytic line of thought regarding the locus of the subject and its primacy over the "Other", he has no intention of replacing anthropocentrism. This is the reason that Levinas prefers to speak about persons and their relation rather than about God. His intention is not to infringe on the subject but to decenter it, giving priority to the other.

For Levinas, each of us is a subject, but what gives our subjectivity real existence is not the real notion of "Being" as

---

173   One of the most renowned post-structural thinkers, Derrida, influenced Levinas on decentering the subject, but he himself was influenced by Levinas, especially on the matter of exteriority and heteronomous intersubjectivity. For instance, Derrida agrees with Levinas's claims that "the absolute experience is not disclosure but a revelation [...] which is the privileged manifestation of the Other, the manifestation of a face over and beyond form [...] [and] the manifestation of the face is already discourse" (Levinas, 1969, 66). Concerning heteronomous intersubjectivity and transcendence, see M. Westphal, *Levinas and Kierkegaard in Dialogue*, part 3, ch. 5: *The Trauma of Transcendence and the Heteronomous Intersubjectivity* (2008, 81, 165, n. 30).

174   Or at least, to defend the priority of otherness, "a radical alterity that demands our ethical response (Kearney and Rainwater [eds.], 1996, 122). M. Dimitrova adds that by decentering (the egoistic, self-enclosed unity of) the subject and giving priority to the other (which can be achieved through ethics), there is a possibility of transcending the subject beyond being. "Ethics is concerned with the possibility of transcending (one's own) being, that is, the possibility of obtaining the meaning of being by subjecting myself to beyond being" (Dimitrova 2016, 56).

being but the fact that we are encountered by another person. Levinas's technical word "ipseity" plays a decisive and crucial role in understanding the interconnection between me and the other person because "there is no self *prior* to the encounter with the other" (ibid.). The latter argument is also integrated with the view that responsibility precedes freedom. That is, I am summoned and called into question by the other even before freedom and autonomy have taken place.[175] Levinas, in his work *Time and the Other*, underlines the importance of ethical transcendence as a necessary and sufficient condition of decentering the subject (from itself).

> "(Ethical) transcendence offers the subject a liberation from itself. The world offers the subject participation in existing in the form of enjoyment and consequently permits it to exist at a distance from itself. The subject is absorbed in the object it absorbs [...] It is not just the disappearance of the self but self-forgetfulness, as a first abnegation" (Levinas 1987b, 67).

It is also worth noting that Kierkegaard was immensely influenced by Pascal.[176] Kierkegaard several times praised

---

[175] Levinas underlines that "responsibility for another comes from what is prior to my freedom. It does not come from the time made up of presences, nor presences that have sunk into the past and are representable, the time of beginnings or assumings. It does not allow me to constitute myself into an *I think*, substantial like a stone, or, like a heart of stone, existing in and for oneself [...] Before the neighbour I am summoned and do not just appear; from the first I am answering to an assignation" (Hand [ed.] 1989, 180).

[176] Concerning Pascal's philosophy and its impact on Kierkegaard's existentialism on subjectivity and the self, see L. Pareyson, *Kierkegaard e Pascal* (1998); H. L. Dreyfus, "'What a monster then is man': Pascal and Kierkegaard on being a contradictory self and what to do about it" (2012, 96-110); J. R. M. Neto, *The Christianization of Pyrrhonism: Scepticism and Faith in Pascal, Kierkegaard and Shestov* (1995, 83-89); A. Clair, *Pseudonymie Et Paradoxe: La Pensee Dialectique De Kierkegaard*, (1976, 80); R. Grimsley, *Søren Kierkegaard and French Literature: Eight Comparative Studies* (1966, 73-88); H. Höffding, "Pascal and Kierkegaard" (1923, 221-246); D. Patrick, in his work *Pascal and Kierkegaard* (1947, 316) in order to underline their (Kierkegaard and Pascal's) common opposition to rationalism, notes that both thinkers "challenged the whole anthropology of Renaissance, with its enthronement of self-sufficient reason, its affirmation that man is the measure of all things". In parallel, A. Buben states that Pascal "is so similar in

137

Pascal's existential philosophy, opposing Hegel, asserting that "human beings have no essence, but rather define themselves through their cultural practices" (Dreyfus 2008, 11). Subjectivity, as Kierkegaard underlines, is beyond objective reasoning. Selfhood does not rely merely on itself. Kierkegaard admits that the self is a spirit, a relation, insisting that it is a relation not only to oneself alone but to another (Kierkegaard 1989, 16). The self, in analytical thinking, derives from objective reasoning and consciousness. For Kierkegaard, we need to escape from this model of self-sufficient rationalism. Kierkegaard argues that it is impossible to talk about metaphysical or ethical properties such as happiness, the idea of God, good, and evil by relying on objective reasoning (Adams 1977, 229). For Kierkegaard, in the same manner as Levinas, it would be absurd to try to rationalize the subject, as Hegel unsuccessfully endeavored to do. However, Kierkegaard, in contrast to Levinas, separates Christianity from the Judeo-Greek tradition. He insists that Christian ethics is a step forward for speaking about the subjectivity of oneself.

In *Works of Love*, Kierkegaard claims that love is a necessary and sufficient condition of subjectivity. He explains that love is a task, a duty, in contrast to Levinas, who alleges that love is prior to any sentimental feelings. As Kierkegaard puts it, "only when love is a duty, only then love is eternally secured [...] The love which underwent the change of eternity through becoming duty, knows no jealousy; it loves, not only

other ways to Kierkegaard" (Buben 2011, 65). However, "Kierkegaard has shown that he is focused, at least in his description of Christianity, on precisely this extreme sort of dying to the world, but it would seem that Pascal is not ready to deny all worldly comfort to the Christian" (ibid., 75).

as it is loved, but it loves" (Kierkegaard 1949, 27, 30). According to Kierkegaard, love starts from the religious and not from the ethical, as Levinas claims. These thinkers, however, raise an objection to the analytical model of listing properties of personhood and love in different ways. For instance, Kierkegaard notes that "when it is a duty to love, there no test is needed and the insulting stupidity of wishing to test is superfluous" (ibid., 28). For Levinas, it is not because of our duty to love that we need to reject criteria. Love, for Levinas, is "a pre-established harmony with what is yet to come to us [...] [Love] does not love Being, but loves the happiness of being [...] [Love] is neither a representation of life nor a reflection on life [...] I love fully only if the Other loves me, not because I need the recognition of the Other" (Levinas 1969, 145, 266). Therefore, we can infer that they both reject the analytical methodology of assessing love by criteria, though their arguments use different frameworks. Levinas prefers ethics and Kierkegaard Christian religious ethics.

2.4 Subjectivity and God in Levinas

By decentering the subject, Levinas develops his argument that God cannot be an equal and direct interlocutor with humans.[177] Several thinkers misunderstood, however, what Levinas expresses when he says that "revelation is discourse [and] in order to welcome revelation a being apt for [the] role of interlocutor, a separated being, is required" (Levinas 1969, 77). In contrast to that statement, Levinas contends that "the

---

[177] In Levinasian ethics, "God is pulled out of objectivity, out of presence, and out of being. He is neither object nor interlocutor. His absolute remoteness, his transcendence, turns into my responsibility for the other" (Levinas 1998b, 69).

absolutely foreign alone can instruct us [...] and it is only man who could be absolutely foreign to me" (ibid., 73). Prosser, taking into consideration the above passages in Levinas's *Totality and Infinity*, mistakenly infers that "for Levinas it becomes problematic to talk about the God-relationship as distinct from the interhuman relationship" (Prosser 2002, 398). From my point of view, Dimitrova provides a better explanation of this matter by asserting that Levinas vehemently rejects God having a relationship with humans. God is not an immediate interlocutor in the subject-subject or in the subject-object relations of mankind. God has nothing to do with inter-human relations. Humans, and not beings, can only feel God's trace if they get involved with each other without any coerced intervention. That is, the I is eternally responsible to the "Other", as a hostage, and the "Other" is eternally asymmetrical and heteronymous to the I, without infringing on the subject's uniqueness.

> "God is present for us, precisely when he is absent, when he withdraws, such that, everything becomes dependent on us; it is up to us whether we will read His Word and follow His Trace. Our definitions, symbols, and ideas reduce God to something we possess. However, Transcendence (God) cannot be possessed [...] Transcendence (God) shines (to us, as finite persons only) in the face of the other human, and is not anymore omnipotence of God, but weakness, vulnerability, being-towards-death of the Other and an appeal to me not to leave the other alone in his suffering and in his rebellion against the nothingness of death." (Dimitrova 2016, 79, 126).

Levinas, as an "a-theist",[178] does not begin with God (Simmons and Wood [eds.] 2008, 24), which does not mean that

---

[178] It is quite hard to provide an exact definition of an atheist for Levinas. I insist, however, on Levinas's definition: "The atheism of the metaphysician means, positively, that our relation with the Metaphysical is an ethical behavior and not theology, not a thematization, be it a knowledge by analogy, of the attributes of God" (Levinas 1969, 77). Levinas, by using the term atheism, intends to

he rejects God. According to Levinas, atheism is not the rejection of God but rather "conditions a veritable relationship with a true God καθ' αυτό" (Levinas 1969, 78). Levinas's position on atheism is of paramount importance to his philosophy as a whole:[179] "Atheism is a distinct relationship with true God, far away from objectification and participation" (ibid.). There is truly a divine word from above but there is no need for a knowing object. According to Levinas, humans are all atheists before facing the other. "In face of the other's destitution the words 'I believe in God' are to be conceived of as a waste of time" (Levinas, 1991, 149). Atheism, for Levinas, is integrated with human's finitude: "finitude, means, among other things, the fact that people eat and drink to maintain their being, or even that they are 'capable of atheism'" (Levinas 1969, 58).

> "One can call atheism this separation so complete that the separated being maintains itself in existence all by itself, without participating in the Being from which it is separated — eventually capable of adhering to it by belief. The break with participation is implied in this capability. One lives outside of God, at home with oneself; one is an *I*, an egoism. The soul, the dimension of the psychic, being an accomplishment of separation, is naturally atheist. By atheism we thus understand a position prior to both the negation and the affirmation of the divine, the breaking with participation by which the *I* posits itself as the same and as *I*. It is certainly a great glory for the creator to have set up a being capable of atheism." (Levinas 1969, 58).

---

explain that God must be excluded from thematization, something that happens in theology. Levinas contends that theism signifies God as a theme, and this is a crucial mistake because it infringes on God's infinity and transcendence. By thematizing God, (as Descartes did) we automatically think of God as an eminent being, and this is another huge error in the theistic position.

[179] Levinas insists that atheism starts with the being-for-itself. This means that ordinarily speaking every cosmic proposition "as being of finitude as given in creation is atheist; it is atheist in the most literal sense that it is non-God [...] atheism is the precondition of a different relativity between the human and divine" (Kearney 2003, loc 4838, 4846).

It is noteworthy to mention that Levinas insists that humans must start knowing themselves in terms of otherness and their relation to others first in order to find God's trace. Interpretation of human beings as humans is the best and unique presupposition and the first stage of atheism. Levinas speaks very little about God and His essence because he simply prefers to emphasize humans and their face-to-face relation to others. A theoretical affair is something that can be only shaped to immanence and not to transcendence. Because transcendence (God) is not a theoretical affair, God is not "the answer to the problems that finitude poses" (Schrijvers 2011, 13). Thus, we can infer that the a priori atheism of the creature gives her the opportunity to free herself from the immanent process to relate God with the subject. On the other hand, someone might ask whether there is a transcendental alternative for a person to open the divine dimension in order to get to know God. Levinas answers that "to posit the transcendent as stranger and poor one is to prohibit the metaphysical relation with God from being accomplished in the ignorance of men and things. The dimension of the divine opens forth from the human face. A relation with the Transcendent—free from all captivation by the Transcendent—is a social relation". (Levinas 1969, 78). Therefore, for Levinas, God never comes to mind directly but through the face of the other:

> "The face is a way of being present which it manifests itself. And it is a nakedness, and it expresses a weakness, that is to say, an effort to be which for it is difficult to support. And consequently, in the face there is as a solitude and as a demand. This demand is elsewhere expressed in the simple fact, that by approaching somebody you ask them 'how does it go?' [...] There is therefore in the face a weakness that I support and accept. I have in this weakness a responsibility. It is about a responsibility that is not formulated. It is the responsibility of abandoning someone who is there without greeting

them. It is this relation with the face that I call the 'response' to the misery of the face. The face speaks a special language. It is always the other who demands of me. [And finally] it is God who speaks in these circumstances [always through the face of the other]. It is God who speaks, and my election is the election of God who speaks". (https://www.youtube.com/watch?v=wBk4nlPd_24: 16:26-19:28)

As far as concerns the above excerpt, Levinas clearly notes that God is present in the world through His absence — through His death, where the self emerges out of the "there is" — *il y a*[180] — which responds to the moral call of the "Other".

---

[180] In order to explain the symbolic meaning of *il y a* (English translation: *there is*), Levinas provides a fascinating cosmological paradigm: "*il y a*: in the absolute emptiness imaginable before creation, *il y a*. There is nothing. But it cannot be called nothingness [as in Heidegger]. An event that is neither being nor nothingness. All I do is an attempt to exit this *il y a*. (https://www.youtube.com/watch?v=qbGaXEqxSvU: 35:07-35:52)". As Urbano underlines, *il y a* is a Levinasian technical term concerning the "anonymous existence or Being in general that is devoid of beings or contents. He likens it to nothingness that menaces the ego and from which the ego desires to escape" (Urbano 2012, 79, n. 46). However, from my point of view, it would be more sufficient to replace the term "Being" with the term "Human", as for Levinas, humans or persons must be preferred in order to refer to the face-to-face relation. Humans are echoes to infinity; beings are not. In parallel, S. Critchley, citing P. Davies, mentions that "the *il y a* is a contribution to ontology that ruins ontology" (Critchley 1993, 111). With the term *il y a* Levinas intends to show the impersonality and the neutrality of Being, aiming at raising questions against fundamental ontology by claiming that what matters is the radical alterity of the absolute relation to the other and not the notion of "Being" as impersonal neutral reality (Levinas 1978, 57). For Levinas, if we consider *il y a* as an impersonal experience that must be overcome for the sake of the face of the "Other", this procedure can be achieved only "through a certain retrieval of philosophy, ultimately of ethics as first philosophy" (Critchley 1993, 114). Levinas does not forget his mission to decenter the subject from being, something that can be achieved if we "look beyond freedom" (Levinas 1991, 8). Here, thus, there is through the *il y a* an allegoric endeavor to hide consciousness and the subject behind the veil of darkness. Levinas states that: "we could say that the night is the very experience of the *il y a*" (Levinas 1978, 58). "The *il y a* is the experience of consciousness without a subject" (ibid., 60). Concerning the notion and definition of *il y a* as well as its comparison to other phenomenologists and existential aspects such as Heidegger's "Being-in-the-world", see M. Fagenblat, "*Il y a* du quotidien: Levinas and Heidegger on the self" (2002, 599-600, n. 22).

143

"A-theism" for Levinas has two different meanings. First is the natural presupposition of the self as separated from the world (from society and justice) living as a solitary ego apart from any relation to others. Sameness and beings as self-enclosed units are synonymous with atheism. "To be I, a-theist, at home with oneself, separated, happy, created — these are synonyms" (Levinas 1969, 148). When being is egoistic and separated from "Other"ness, it becomes atheistic, enslaved to its interiority. It forgets and abandons the *il y a*, and the more the self becomes isolated, the more it creates an atheistic standpoint.

> "One can call atheism this separation so complete that the separated being maintains itself in existence all by itself, without participating in the Being from which it is separated — eventually capable of adhering to it by belief. The break with participation is implied in this capability. One lives outside of God, at home with oneself; one is an I, an egoism. The soul, the dimension of the psychic, being an accomplishment of separation, is naturally atheist. By atheism we thus understand a position prior to both the negation and the affirmation of the divine, the breaking with participation by which the *I* posits itself as the same and as I." (Levinas 1969, 58).

It is very dangerous for Levinas to accept theology when it promotes the "sacred" or mysticism. Modern theology sometimes can be characterized as "atheistic" by adopting ontological concepts such as that "the image or concept of God gradually becomes more important than God himself" (Urbano 2012, 64). This makes Levinas raise several vehement objections to Christianity. Levinas contends that Christianity's errant point on God is that it dramatically exceeds God's presence through incarnation. Logos is only eternally accepted and not through cosmic or doxic procedures. Humans start always from atheism and then the only way "to get to know" God is through the face of the other person whose face is always infinite and transcendent. When the face becomes real in presence, God's traces vanish.

The second meaning of atheism, according to Levinas, starts from philosophy. For Levinas, philosophical logic and totality derive from atheism. The self's sovereignty and egoism are nothing but atheistic conditions of sameness. The more selfhood is enclosed in itself, the more it becomes atheistic. For Levinas, both ancient and modern philosophy are atheistic. On the one hand, from Socrates's maieutic method to Aristotle's definition that human beings are living beings or animals that have *logos*,[181] and on the other hand, from Descartes's *cogito* and Hegel's totality of being, Levinas argues that philosophy always starts from and is atheism. This atheism starts with freedom, autonomy, and self-development.

> "Philosophy is atheism, or rather unreligion, negation of a God that reveals himself and puts truths into us. This is Socrates' teaching when he leaves to the master only the exercise of maieutics: every lesson introduced into the soul was already in it. The I's identification, its marvelous autarchy, is the natural crucible of this transmutation of the Other into the Same. Every philosophy is — to use Husserl's neologism — an egology. And when Descartes comes to discern an acquiescence of the will in even the most rational truth, he not only explains the possibility of error but sets up reason as an ego and truth as dependent on a movement that is free, and thus sovereign and justified". (Peperzak 1993, 96-97).

---

181 Aristotle (like Plato and Plotinus) influenced several contemporary analytic thinkers with his argument that human beings are merely animals who merit specific presuppositions in order to be counted as persons, paying particular attention to logos and self-awareness. Aristotle mentions in his *Nicomachean Ethics* that "οἷον τὸ μέν ἄλογον αὐτῆς εἶναι, τὸ δέ λόγον εἶχον" which means "soul is divided into two parts; the thinking and the non-thinking part". It is because of the thinking part that human beings are more advanced than non-thinking animals (Aristotle 2006, 202-203). Concerning a generic conclusion about Aristotle's conception of human beings in philosophy, see M. Knoll, "To Philosophize or not to Philosophize" (2014, 96-105).

2.5 Kierkegaard on God as a Scandalous Paradox

"Kierkegaard's thought has contributed to this [philosophy], by its intransigent vehemence, by its taste for scandal." (Levinas, 1996, 72)

It has been claimed by contemporary scholars that Kierkegaard's controversial and sometimes divergent religious works push research to be split into two lines of thought: (a) scholars who admiringly defend his thesis and (b) those who raise several objections against the peculiar and confusing dialectics he used to explain God's essence in Christ incarnate. He himself during his academic career cut short by his unexpected death vehemently criticized the Western philosophical tradition, denouncing reason and knowledge as inefficient to speak about God. He tried to show that the established Church cemented a false doctrine in the Danish and European societies where the relation between the high clergy and individuals was bureaucratic exploitation and not a spiritual way of being.

Kierkegaard's works can be divided into aesthetics, which were written under pseudonyms and explore the indirect communication between God and man, and religious texts written under his own name that develop direct communication between God and man. Kierkegaard, admiring and drawing from Socratic maieutic dialectics, intended to penetrate into the reader's soul so she would think more deeply about her relation to God. Human existentialism and its relation to God was the main topic of his religious works.

Kierkegaard does not aim to provide a strict holistic definition of God or explore the question "what is God?" He has

146

no interest in cosmology or quantum mechanics like Newton, Pascal, and Copernicus. His insistent question is whether and how man can relate to God in this world. Also, Kierkegaard contends that what really matters is not preaching or ethical advice from high clergy but the need to change our hearts from inside: to modify the way of being and of seeing ourselves. He also claims that man relates to God through honest faith, but no one can define what God is epistemologically. For him, no ontological or psychological syllogisms can define God. By trying to define God, we merely understand that our failure is due to our weak and inefficient mind. Kierkegaard, like Kant, infers that human and practical reason will neither define God nor prove or reveal God's essence through experimental criteria. Even though Kierkegaard agrees to some extent with Kant's position that we cannot define God, he disagrees with the Kantian position that God must be understood as an ethical teacher. In Kant, God is viewed as an ethical lawgiver or a punisher for those who deviate from legal-ethical norms. In contrast, Kierkegaard contends that ethical duty has nothing to do with faith.

Kierkegaard during his attendance at Schelling's lectures in 1841–42 had started to explore the relation between God and humans in more depth, but he also wrote many texts concerning the subject-object relation. His conclusion is that subjectivity is infinity in truth and truth is subjectivity in infinity. That is, subjectivity does not necessarily entail knowledge or the "I-it" diptych, but in contrast, it cultivates inner faith in God.

Kierkegaard speaks about a scandalous paradox in God's essence in relation to people: human beings mistakenly try to prove something that is outside of the human conscience. According to Kierkegaard, the only way to approach God is to sacrifice knowledge and reason for the sake of faith, or, in similar way, when mental states are annihilated, a fortunate passion emerges: faith. The very difficult part in understanding God is to reconcile ontological and transcendental attributes in God's essence. That is, how can we reflect an absolute divine infinite God who is outside of our finite thinking? How does God reveal His face to mankind? Kierkegaard contends that there is a hidden place between God and persons which can be only unveiled through faith.

However, Kierkegaard underlines that we need to be very careful not to consider God as a mere divine subject who speaks and relates to people, attributing to Him human characteristics, since there is a danger of falling into idolatry. Kierkegaard rejects both Catholicism and Orthodoxy because, he claims, both doctrines provide icons and idols (saints and patristic fathers) before God. However, in *Fear and Trembling*, Kierkegaard characterizes God as the absolute "Other" and as a person as well in order to show that God is ready to be revealed to people but only through honest prayer and faith. Kierkegaard underlines that it is not logos that expresses the communication between God and persons but exactly the opposite: silence. It is transcendental faith through a paradox and not ontological reason that justifies the importance of silence in approaching God. The more we abandon ourselves as narcissistic, self-enclosed units, the more we understand how God can be approached. The more we understand ourselves in depth, the more God directs our way of being. Inner comprehension of the self assists persons to find God through individual prayer and faith.

One of the most crucial examples of God as a scandalous paradox is the incarnation of the *logos* in Jesus Christ. The incarnation of Christ as a God-man has a major importance in Kierkegaard's works. For Kierkegaard, God's choice to get involved with people in history as a humble carpenter is one of the most scandalous actions we have seen in the history of mankind. Through this absolute paradox, infinite God meets the finite human being in order to invite him to transcend to God's essence through love and forgiveness. Christ's appearance in history was incognito[182] in order to preserve his hiddenness. This procedure of hiddenness was of immense importance because God did not want to infringe on humans' free will. Mankind must have the personal choice to believe this paradox or not without any divine coercion through a face-to-face meeting with God's power. This is why Christ appeared as a modest servant and not as a king, not to be served but to serve. Incarnation, thus, for Kierkegaard, presents a scandalous paradox: It historicizes infinity, and it transcends history into infinity while every human being can be transformed into a *microtheos* through true and authentic faith.

In summary, for Kierkegaard, faith is a necessary and sufficient condition for persons to approach God. Faith hence can be achieved neither through a passive procedure of apprehension nor as a magic gift given by God only to high clergy. The gift of faith is granted to every single individual as the presence of the persecuted Christ in our hearts and as

---

[182] See footnote 85.

a persecuted truth[183], something that would have been supported by Levinas as well. Finally, human beings are invited by God to participate in this absolute and scandalous paradox of incarnation through an agapeic and self-denying relation, in contrast to Heidegger's notion of God: a philosophical, strict God who is isolated and foreign to humans. Kierkegaard's God is a direct I-thou relation where God awaits persons to transcend and approach him in faith, love, and forgiveness.

2.6 Conclusion

To sum up this discussion concerning the comparison between Levinas and Kierkegaard regarding subjectivity and the self, we can infer that for Levinas's ethics the point of departure in order to conceive the self and its relation to divinity and to others is that "my Self, becoming 'me', can be elevated and inspired to fly beyond its attachment to the totality of cosmic interests. For Levinas, this happens only when the "Self" is not merely *for-itself*, but for-the-Other" (Dimitrova 2009, 51).[184] Several continental thinkers present the issue of

---

[183] Ibid.
[184] The above debate is also related to the issues of morality, responsibility, and freedom as *for-itself*, *in-itself*, and *for-the-other* are terms which are discussed by several ancient and contemporary thinkers in both analytical and continental philosophy. The first thinker who systematizes the question of morality "Is a man a moral being" was Aristotle, who contended that man is inseparable from ethics. Man is born as a moral being and if not, he has the opportunity to change. He also admits that man as a moral being is "endowed with the gift of ἀρετή (virtue), which is accompanied by πρᾶξις (actions) and φρόνησις (practical virtue) (Flyvbjerg 1993, 11-27), and τέχνη (Art)" (Dunne 1993, 104-167). What makes man a moral being is, according to Aristotle, his being a social (and political) animal/being: "man is by nature an animal fit for a state" (Aristotle 1995, 1253a, 2-3). Through his capacity of reason, man, Aristotle claims, has the opportunity to cultivate virtue through interaction with others. However, this interaction is problematic for Levinas since it is based on consciousness, self-consciousness, reason, and cognition. It is a kind of phenomenological ethics

subjectivity and the self as an eternal combat between ontology and ethical transcendence. Levinas, however, seems to overcome the primacy of ontology by offering an ethical reconciliation of the ontological I with the "Other" (Drossev 2012, 56). As Darin Drossev points out, "the *I* of Levinas enters into heteronymous relationship with the Other and the *I* who has met the Other passes grammatically and ethically from the imperative to the accusative case, thus the *I* becomes 'me'. The activity of the Other is through the *I* towards the accusative, towards the 'me'. That is how the active approach to the philosophy of Levinas is preserved" (ibid., 61).[185] As

---

based on immanence as it is the I who seeks salvation and not the other. In Hobbes, man is not born a moral being. There are no positive presuppositions on achieving an a priori morality as a human being. It is possible to become a moral being throughout the stages of my life. For Hobbes, it is a matter of choice. I am free to decide to be a moral or immoral person. We may say that for Hobbes, man starts as an egoistic agent who gives priority to being-for-himself and not being-with- or being-for-others. There is an apparent distrust between the I and the other. The other for Hobbes is "an enemy" who seeks to exploit my weakness for his/her self-interested advantage (Levinas 1987a, 94). On the other hand, Sartre opposes any social interaction with morality. The latter is incommensurable with morality. I need to be far from from society to gain my freedom on my own: "the more it is chosen by way of opposing and questioning what is expected by socially upheld conventions, the more authentic [it] will be" (Jodalen and Vetlesen [eds.] 1997, 145). So, whereas in Aristotle my being as a moral human is sustained and assisted by others (gaining self-interest), and in Sartre and Hobbes my being faces a serious threat of being undermined by the other, Levinas develops a very different dialectic. He gives priority to responsibility — not within a materialistic framework but a primordial one. For Levinas, we are moral beings because of the responsibility for the other, but not as in the Aristotelian one-dimensional dialectic. It is not me whom I strive for but the other. I do not sacrifice the other's heteronomy for my own sake, that is, to gain virtue. For Levinas, responsibility "does not come in degrees" (ibid., 153), that is, as a list of properties that I must fulfill in order to merit responsibility for the other. Responsibility is a beyond and not a *given*. I hold in my hand the other's fate.

185   D. Drossev's statement is also justified by Levinas, who contends that what matters is the accusative *me* rather than the *I*. "The *I* is a passivity more passive still than any passivity because it is from the first in the accusative — oneself (*soi*) — and never was in the nominative; it is under the accusation of the other, even though it be faultless. It is a hostage for the other, obeying a command before having heard it, faithful to a commitment that it never made to a past that has never been present" (Hand [ed.] 1989, 178).

Chappell remarks, "selfhood is not something I achieve on my own, it is a gift, the gift to *me* (and not *I*) of others" (Chappell 2013, 3-28). Chappell also supports the Levinas who "speaks of the individual soul as living in the Other" (ibid.). Finally, as Simon Critchley concludes, for Levinas, "ethics is first philosophy where it is understood as a radically *asymmetrical* relation of infinite responsibility to the other person" (Critchley et al 2002, 6). We may add that ethics must be defined as the infinite condition of possibility for the revelation of God.

CHAPTER 3:
LEVINAS AND KIERKEGAARD ON DEATH AND TIME

"To study Philosophy is nothing but to prepare one's self to die"
(Cicero 2005, 1.30.74)
"A free man thinks of death least of all"
(Spinoza 1992, 162)

3.1 Introduction

It is impossible to analyze the conception of death in a chapter. The intention of this chapter is to compare and interpret Levinas's and Kierkegaard's views on what it is to be death and how and whether it might be overcome. Can an afterlife be justified? Is there any middle way between finitude and infinity? Can we — as finite beings — have knowledge of death beyond death? All these questions emerged thousands of years ago during the pre-Socratic philosophers and even now continue to be posed. Religions such as Christianity, Hinduism, and Judaism, both monotheistic and polytheistic, present their doctrines regarding death and whether it can be overcome through faith or a certain way of life. Scientific fields such as medical studies, anatomy, and biology which are grounded on epistemological and rational criteria raise objections to the possibility of death being surpassed. They only admit that neurons continue to function only some minutes after death. However, the death of the body means the death of the whole entity as an individual. Death is the complete interruption of organic human life. According to medical studies, there is no evidence of an afterlife based on scientific and clinical evidence. Therefore, death is the end of existence.

On the other hand, the philosophy of religion has something more to say. It is not crucial to explain the process of dying, but, rather, it is more urgent to start our question on death by asking why. Why did an eternal God decide to create finite beings? Or, for atheists, why did an infinite universe — if we adopt the big bang theory — create finite beings? If we suppose that humans are the wisest animals on earth, meriting mental and rational attributes and capabilities, wouldn't it be illogical to exist to an average of eighty years old?

3.2 Ancient Greek tradition on the notion of Death

Ancient Greek philosophers provide several arguments on death from which contemporary thinkers derive their own views. Parmenides, for instance, argues that "death and self-consciousness are mutually exclusive" (O' Meara 2015, 284), while Plato in *Phaedo* explains how the true philosopher relates to death (Plato 1914, 222, 235).[186] Plato contends that "the

---

[186] Plato, in *Phaedo*, describes the conversation between Socrates and Simmias concerning the immortality of soul. By asking rhetorical questions — the Socratic maieutic method — Socrates aims to answer whether the soul is immortal and what death is. Socrates asks Simmias "ἡγούμεθά τι τὸν θάνατον εἶναι;" (Do we think there is such a thing as a death?). Once Simmias does not raise any objection to this statement, Socrates replies that "Ἆρα μὴ ἄλλο τι ἢ τὴν τῆς ψυχῆς ἀπὸ τοῦ σώματος ἀπαλλαγήν; καὶ εἶναι τοῦτο τὸ τεθνάναι χωρὶς μὲν ἀπὸ τῆς ψυχῆς ἀπαλλαγὲν αὐτὸ καθ' αὑτὸ τὸ σῶμα γεγονέναι, χωρὶς δὲ τὴν ψυχὴν ἀπὸ τοῦ σώματος ἀπαλλαγεῖσαν αὐτὴν καθ' αὑτὴν εἶναι;" ("We believe, do we not, that death is the separation of the soul from the body, and that the state of being dead is the state in which the body is separated from the soul and exists alone by itself and the soul is separated from the body and exists alone by itself?") (Plato 1914, 223-225). Socrates, then, explains how the true philosophers

philosopher seeks knowledge; that the body is an obstacle to this search; and that death, as the freeing of soul from the body, gives access to the knowledge which the philosopher has been seeking." (ibid., 286) Philosophy, as both Parmenides and Plato assert, must lead us to deathlessness. On the other hand, Epicurus[187] provides a different explanation for death. He asserts that death, even if God exists, is the end of a hedonistic life and therefore inevitable. In Epicurus, death is not merely the gods' punishment for our sins and crimes. It is far from anxiety and destiny. Determinism, according to Epicurus, is not accepted, as free will shapes our lives. He also argues that, in contrast to Plato's forms, souls are not eternal. Souls like bodies and mind expire, dissipate, and are dissolved. According to Epicurus, "there is nothing left of us in death." (ibid., 287) So death also includes thinking; knowledge and mental and bodily attributes cease to exist. Epicurus states that:

"Τὸ φρικωδέστατον οὖν τῶν κακῶν ὁ θάνατος οὐθὲν πρὸς ἡμᾶς, ἐπειδήπερ ὅταν μὲν ἡμεῖς ὦμεν, ὁ θάνατος οὐ πάρεστιν, ὅταν δὲ ὁ θάνατος παρῇ, τόθ'

consider death: "Οἱ ὀρθῶς φιλοσοφοῦντες ἀποθνήσκειν μελετῶσι καὶ τὸ τεθνάναι ἥκιστα αὐτοῖς ἀνθρώπων φοβερόν" ("The true philosophers practice dying, and death is less terrible to them than to any other men") (ibid., 235). It is worth noting that Socrates develops a more skeptical dialectic on this matter since, as he claims, we lack philosophical understanding and we need to maintain intuition rather than epistemology in order to elaborate on metaphysical or ethical issues such as death, mortality, and infinity (Wertheimer 1993, 143-163). See also S. Ahbel-Rappe and R. Kamtekar (eds.), *A Companion to Socrates* (2006, 200-213). For Socrates's philosophy in general, see T. I. Bayer, "Socrates' Profession" (2014, 83-92). For his contribution to applied ethics, see B. Richard B., "Socrates and Skepticism" (2006, 298-311; Wertheimer, 1993, 143-163).

[187] Concerning the Epicurean notion of death, see a comprehensive study written by J. Li, *Can Death be a Harm to the Person who Dies?* (2002, 1-31; Warren 2004, 1-56, 109-160; Witt 1954, 197-215). In contrast to Epicurus's motto "when death is, I am not, and when I am, death is not", Kierkegaard advocates "a stance toward death in which one thinks of oneself in death, and thinks of it not as our shared human condition, but as something that is one's own" (Guignon 2011, 189).

ἡμεῖς οὐκ ἐσμέν. οὔτε οὖν πρὸς τοὺς ζῶντάς ἐστιν οὔτε πρὸς τοὺς τετελευτηκότας, ἐπειδήπερ περὶ οὓς μὲν οὐκ ἔστιν, οἳ δ᾽ οὐκέτι εἰσίν" (Ἐπίκουρος 1957, §125).

"Death, the most dreaded of evils, is therefore of no concern to us; for while we exist death is not present, and when death is present, we no longer exist. It is therefore nothing either to the living or to the dead since it is not present to the living, and the dead no longer are." (Bailey [tr.] 1957, §125).

Epicurus advises us to live in presence. In life, presence matters; past and future do not. He means that death is so close to us that it would be nonsense to focus our awareness on the future or recollections of the past.[188] As a hedonistic thinker, Epicurus, in contrast to Kierkegaard, avoids anxiety and suffering, which are both incompatible with real thinking. What matters for Epicurus is what we are going to do today and not tomorrow since death cannot be predicted:

"Μνημονευτέον δὲ ὡς τὸ μέλλον οὔτε πάντως ἡμέτερον οὔτε πάντως οὐχ ἡμέτερον, ἵνα μήτε πάντως προσμένωμεν ὡς ἐσόμενον μήτε ἀπελπίζωμεν ὡς πάντως οὐκ ἐσόμενον." (Ἐπίκουρος 1957, §127).

"And we shall remember that the future is not completely ours, but also not entirely unknown, thus, it is neither prudent to expect it, nor wise to reject it" (Author's translation).

To conclude with the ancient Greek thinkers, it is noteworthy to sketch Plotinus's notion of death since it is crucial to compare it with Plato's immortality of the soul. In contrast to Epicurus and Stoics in general, Plotinus argues that the soul (ψυχή) is a part of divine and eternal God and therefore is eternal (Baracat Jr 2017, 205-245). However, Plotinus does not

---

188 However, Epicurus defends the view that death is not presence nor can it be seized (Levinas similarly says that death "is ungraspable" [Levinas 1987b, 72]) by human beings. Death runs always to the future. Levinas explores a similar argument, since he cites Epicurus several times (ibid., 71, n. 46). On that issue, Levinas agrees with Epicurus on the "eternal futurity of death" (ibid.) by saying that "death is never now; when death is here, I am no longer here. Not because I am nothingness but because I am unable to grasp" (ibid., 72).

connect the soul to ethics or morality but rather to reason. Self-awareness continues in the afterlife, targeting the attachment to the "One", the absolute God (Tὸ Ἕν)[189]. For Plotinus, death can be understood only by "wise individuals" who do not care about mortal, unimportant, secular situations but rather about intellectual divine phenomena. "Plotinus' wise man will know that soul has a natural function in illuminating and caring for the body; that this function is limited in time; that in due course soul will be freed of the body and will be able to live its life, if it is purified, as intellect in the eternal and divine. This life is what Plotinus identifies as happiness." (O'Meara 2015, 290). We can then infer that, according to Plotinus, the more we are intellect, the less death concerns us. Below, I argue that Levinas's and Kierkegaard's methodologies explore arguments derived mostly from Greek thinkers' ideas that death can be transcendent.

3.3 Starting from Heidegger Once Again

It is not easy to determine how Levinas considers death.[190] He starts his propositions with Plato and Augustine.[191] It is

---

[189] Plotinus contends that "in the case of numbers, the unit remains intact while something else produces, and thus number arises in dependence on the unit; much more than does the unit, the One, remain intact in the principle which is before all remains intact, owe their existence to no other, but to its own all-sufficient power [...] in the realm of Being, the trace of the One establishes reality: existence is a trace of the One", (Plotinus 2018, 5:5, 589).

[190] Levinas tries to avoid a clear definition of death as he asserts that "the aporia of death is non-said [...] It is indefinable as such" (Mjaaland 2008, 99). Similarly, Kierkegaard contends that "death is indefinable and inexplicable" (ibid., 100-101). Both thinkers intend (by using different dialectics) to escape the ontological isolation of Heidegger's *Dasein* in which *Being* is static and unable to be represented by someone else.

[191] It is obvious that in secondary literature and especially in analytical thinking, Levinasian thought is compared to Augustine's views on God, subjectivity, and death. A very comprehensive paradigm is T. S-G. Chappell's comparative study

impossible to explore Levinasian thought on death without looking at Heidegger's notion of death in relation to being *qua* being. Heidegger's view is that death is a certitude that initiates itself through being's attributes. This certitude is not allowed to approach the death of the other. It is isolated and enclosed in being and always returns to being. Death, therefore, is a matter of being: a secondhand experience which is related to time and to the phrase "being-toward-death". According to Heidegger, death is related to existential experience and not to any relational ethical repercussions.[192] Death, Heidegger explains, is a reality of stopping behavior where the biological movements "lose all dependence in relation to signification" (Levinas 2000, 11). It worth noting that for Heidegger, death passes through the identity of the "Same" assimilated to itself, which is "the source of all meaning" (ibid., 13). *Gewissheit* — certainty — of oneself is the origin of all conscience even to death. In brief, Heidegger contends, especially in his work *Being and Time*, that the meaning of death is related neither to the death of the other nor to any exterior

---

of Levinas and Augustine on the knowledge of persons and their relation to God (Chappell 2013, 31-56). Chappell claims that Levinas is the greatest thinker of the second person since Augustine. Chappell considers Levinas the first thinker who expressed the motto "relationality precedes individuality and the latter presupposes the former. She defends Levinas's view that "it is by this living in the Other — and not logically, by opposition to the Other — that the soul comes by its identity" (ibid., 50). M. Ruti adds that "Levinas thus privileges relationality over ontology, particularly over consciousness as a structure of being, which is exactly why he [...] seeks to break 'the obstinacy of being' to explode the 'ontological contraction that is expressed by the verb to be,' so as to move beyond the sovereign, self-contained I to the realm of what he calls 'the order of the human, of grace, and of sacrifice'" (Ruti 2015, 5) [phrases in single quotation marks: Levinas 1998a, 202].

192 Levinas strongly disagrees with Heidegger concerning relationality. For Levinas, "if subjectivity is inherently relational — if the presence of the other is constitutive of subjectivity as such — there is no way to envision the subject outside of ethics" (Ruti 2015, 2).

fluctuations. What matters, according to Heidegger, in order to comprehend the origin of death, is to attach the anxiety of being as the source of all affectivity in being-toward-death.[193] Levinas infers that Heidegger focused only on the fact that "the relation with death is thought as an experience in nothingness in time" (ibid., 13).[194]

Though Levinas started thinking about death by considering Heidegger's and Blanchot's arguments in the early stage of his philosophical career, it is apparent that there are several discrepancies between them, especially regarding the questions Levinas raises on the condition of death and its

---

[193] As R. A. Cohen reminds us, Heidegger insists that "it is only in being-toward-death that the temporality of own's own being, and the historical-ontological content within which one's own being, finds its ultimate sense, are disclosed" (Cohen 2006, 23). The core argument of Heidegger's ontological view of death comes from *Being and Time*, where he states that "death is the possibility of the absolute impossibility of *Dasein*. Thus, death reveals itself as that possibility which one's ownmost, which is non-relational and which is not to be outstripped" (Heidegger 1962, 294). However, "Levinas rejects the Heideggerian account of death and its intimate link to ontology" (Cohen 2006, 22). Levinas, with his ethics and the priority of the "Other", tries to supersede temporality and the pure phenomenality of time by developing the theory of an irreducible temporality of alterity where the privilege comes through the "Other"ness of the other. For Levinas's objection to pure phenomenology and temporality, see J. Cohen, "Levinas and the Problem of Phenomenology" (2012, 363-374). Cohen argues on ibid., page 371 that "beyond the ontological determination of the question aiming to explicate itself as and in the deployment of the meaning of being, Levinas retains, by suspending or bracketing its ontological [that is, phenomenological] determination, the dimension which transits all questioning: the Other".

[194] In contrast to Heidegger, who claims that death is related to nothingness and that what matters "is the anxiety for my Being experienced in Being-toward-death" (Critchley 1993, 115), for Levinas "what is most horrible is not the possibility of my own death but much worse the impossibility of my death" (ibid.). This horror and anxiety regarding death, for Levinas, is much more painful when death is not the end of existence but its continuation. If, Levinas asserts, there is a continuation of death in the aftermath, this path would be horrible because existence will continue without an exit. This is the reason, from my point of view, for Levinas's claim that "anything [inside the *il y a* condition] can count for anything else" (Levinas 1978, 59).

relation to ontology and Heidegger's phrase being-toward-death (*Sein zum tod*).[195]

3.4 The Levinasian Argument on Death

Levinas pays particular attention to Socrates's framework of the notion of death in *Phaedo*, presents the last words of Socrates's *Apology* (Cohen 2006, 22)[196] before his death in relation to "Other"ness, and argues that the meaning of death is much more than the Heideggerian conception which is based on certainty of being. Levinas, like Plato, refuses "to treat time and death in relation to being" (Levinas 2000, 8) *qua* being. Death, in contrast to the Heideggerian view, cannot be reduced to the ontological predicament of *Dasein*. Soul, due to its immortality, as Plato explains in the dialogue between Socrates and Simmias in *Phaedo*, needs to merit some ethical

---

[195] Levinas is quite hesitant as to whether death can be defined: "death hides itself by the very effort to describe it, thus introducing a deep rupture even in the ontological analysis of phenomenology" (Mjaaland 2008, 103).

[196] Levinas admires and pays particular attention to Socrates's death because through his death there is an apparent similarity to Levinas's ethical phenomenology. If we want to more deeply examine Levinas's strategic point on how he sees death, we need to "capture" Socrates's indirect confession of his own death. Specifically, Socrates has no intention to speak about the unspeakable, to see the invisible, to provide reason to the unreasonable, or to get to know the unknown. Levinas — in contrast to Heidegger, other phenomenologists such as Husserl and Merleau-Ponty, and other ethicists like Spinoza — insists, that, like for the Epicureans, death is something that can be confessed by and relational to the others and not on behalf of mineness. Thus, his reply during an interview in 1982 concerning the notion and the conception of death (whether it can be seen or understood through the intimate link of ontology): "Spinoza will say, as you know, that philosophers should think of nothing less than of death. Heidegger, by contrast, is the one who pursued philosophical thought's reference to death the farthest. The philosopher's mortality marks his thought as it does his existence. A finite existence. A finite human existence, even if philosophical. Philosophical thought because of that finitude. Heidegger calls the extreme possibility of death possibility of impossibility. Without wishing to play on words, I have always thought that possibility implied a human power, whereas dying is 'unassumable': it is rather 'an impossibility of possibility'." (Levinas 1999, 155)

presuppositions in earthly life in order to be prepared to continue its eternal life in the afterlife.

"[Ψυχὴν] ἀφικομένην δὲ ὅθιπερ αἱ ἄλλαι, τὴν μὲν ἀκάθαρτον καὶ τι πεποιηκυῖαν τοιοῦτον ἢ φόνων ἀδίκων ἡμμένην ἢ ἄλλ᾽ ἄττα τοιαῦτα εἰργασμένην, ἃ τούτων ἀδελφά τε καὶ ἀδελφῶν ψυχῶν ἔργα τυγχάνει ὄντα, ταύτην μὲν ἅπας φεύγει τε καὶ ὑπεκτρέπεται." (Plato 1914, 108 B).

"And when it arrives at the place where the other souls are, the soul which is impure and has done wrong, by committing wicked murders or other deeds akin to those and the works of kindred souls, is avoided and shunned by all." (ibid., Fowler [tr.])

As seen here, the immortality of the soul is quite crucial, not only because it is eternal, but mainly due to its mental and sentimental attributes that continue in the afterlife. Levinas would agree that the soul merits ethical capabilities such as otherness and closeness to the "Other". The soul has a face[197]– a face that still exists after death even if death is decomposition, a non-response. The phrase "τοιοῦτον ἢ φόνων ἀδίκων ἡμμένην" ("by committing wicked murders") can be compared to Levinas's statement "Thou shalt not kill", which is a basic commandment of the Levinasian principle about subjectivity. Death is negativity only if its negativity is in relation with the "Other". Plato, in *Phaedo*, underlines that the soul has an entire consciousness and self-consciousness by

---

[197] In analytic philosophy, views are controversial concerning the notion of the soul. On the one hand, L. Wittgenstein, in his *Philosophical Investigations*, claims that "I am not of the opinion that he has a soul" (Wittgenstein 1958, PII, iv). On the other hand, several analytical thinkers, such as T. S-G. Chappell, insist that the soul has a crucial role in defining and construing selfhood and its relationship with the other persons. Chappell alleges, as a Levinasian ethicist, that "individuality presupposes relationality" (Chappell 2013, 32), that is, humans' existence is justified through the relational status of exteriority prior to any experience or knowledge. For further discussion of Levinas and Wittgenstein, see B. Plant, *Wittgenstein and Levinas: Ethical and Religious thought* (2005, 148-179). Concerning Wittgenstein's view on Kierkegaard, see M. Gallagher, "Wittgenstein's Admiration for Kierkegaard" (1968, 43-49).

contending that "ταύτην [ψυχὴν] μὲν ἅπας φεύγει τε καὶ ὑπεκτρέπεται" ("[soul] is avoided and shunned by all"). Levinas, in contrast to Heidegger regarding the role of death, rejects that death is related to "the identity of the Same with itself" (Levinas 2000, 13). The source of meaning as regards death and the immortality of the soul is integrated with the death of the "Other".[198] My relation with the death of the "Other" affects my psyche as "I", empowering the accusative case of "me" (ibid., 188). Death and its meaning cannot be construed merely as a second-hand experience through interiority within the "Same". Death is not just a certitude that is known by inner self-enclosed attributes. Death, according to Levinas, is not just a matter of anxiety. It is not just an event that took place apparently at a specific time, but it "indicates a meaning that surprises" (ibid., 13; Bergo 1999, 96-104) which manifests dying as an ethical possibility of infinity. Levinas argues that Hegel by totalizing death mistakenly

---

[198] Levinas, in his work "Transcendence and Height" (1996, 13), gives a very brief but valuable definition of what other thinkers believe a soul (or a human, as the incarnate soul) is: "But, in its turn, the Soul and, in our times, the incarnate Soul, man, are interpreted as unavoidable moments in the play of Being itself. For Plato, the Soul is wedded to the Ideas, while for Plotinus it is a hypostasis. For Hegel, subjective spirit—as soul, as consciousness, and finally as subject—is ineluctably part of the History of Spirit or Being. For Heidegger, man is the shepherd of Being." Levinas also uses the term hypostasis in order to explain the difference between the for-one and for-another. Hypostasis (ὑπόστασις) is a Greek term which is often used in theological issues to explain Orthodox Trinitarianism: one God, in three ὑποστάσεις (hypostases), that is, the Father, the Son (the *Logos* incarnated) and the Holy Spirit. For further discussion on Christological and human hypostasis, see N.V. Sakharov, *I Love Therefore I am: the Theological Legacy of Archimandrite Sophrony* (2002, 78-79, 160-163, 174-176; Khrapovitski 1963, 3-24). In Levinasian ethics, hypostasis, as explored in *Otherwise than Being*, is mainly referred to humans and not to God, and it is always in the accusative case prior to any form, knowledge, and apprehension: "The hypostasis is exposed as oneself in the accusative form, before appearing in the said proper to knowing as the bearer of a name [...] Prior to the play of being, before the present, older than the time of consciousness " (Levinas 1991, 106).

contends that "the relationship with death and with the deceased, outside any reference to being and nothingness, is a necessary moment in the logic of the *Phenomenology of Spirit*, that is, of the movement, or the becoming, or the history wherein consciousness attains its full possession of self, wherein its freedom is an absolute thought" (Levinas 2000, 84). Hegel, in brief, explores the idea that death is a matter of knowledge where the spirit is revealed in-itself by isolating the self to get to know its own destiny and, therefore, death can be known only by comprehensive signification.

However, Levinas raises some interesting objections to that statement. He claims that my death — as well as the death of the other — is neither an object of knowledge nor an experience which can be explained through immanent characteristics of a deep comprehension. Death, as Levinas explains, is "an emotion, a movement, a disquietude within the unknown" (ibid., 16). But why is the unknown of immense importance for Levinas? First, the unknown echoes to infinity if and only if it is detached from objectification and thematization. It is impossible, Levinas argues, to see being or to aim at nothingness by objectifying the subject. Levinas, in contract to Husserl, Heidegger, and Sartre, who all give priority to nothingness, argues that it is not nothingness that is significant to consider death in relation to my existence but the radical alterity which surfaces alienating my will by the "Other".[199]

---

[199] For further discussion concerning Levinas's preference of ethics as first philosophy and for several different views on phenomenology in Levinas, Husserl, and Sartre, see a comprehensive work by S. Crowell, "Why is Ethics First Philosophy? Levinas in Phenomenological Context" (2012, 1-25). For divergence and variance on phenomenology and metaphysics between Levinas, Husserl, and Heidegger see A. Peperzak, "Phenomenology — Ontology — Metaphysics:

"In the being for death of fear I am not faced with nothingness, but faced with what is against me, as though murder, rather than being one of the occasions of dying, were inseparable from the essence of death, as though the approach of death remained one of the modalities of the relation with the Other [...] The order of necessity that is carried out in death is not like an implacable law of determinism governing a totality, but is rather like the alienation of my will by the Other". (Levinas 1969, 235)

At the same time, it is nonsense to think of death by trying to make the unknown logical. This is why Levinas explores the argument of immemorial time where disquietude cannot be converted into a response but remains unanswered in an eternal future.

Death does not have a mere ontological structure grounded upon axiological intentional attributes, but it aims at attaching to the infinite through the death of the other. If I am not concerned about what the death of the other means to me, it is impossible to grasp, as Levinas infers, the meaning of death, which does not rest upon knowledge or intentionality, as Husserl claimed.

If not intentionality, then what? Does Levinas provide any alternative to justify the appearance of the immortality of soul and its relation to death beyond knowledge and intentionality? The answer is yes: through the ethics of responsibility for the death of "Other". This statement needs to be clarified, defined, and scrutinized in depth. First, we need to define what time is and its relation to being and death. In ordinary life, time "is the indefinite continued progress of existence and events that occur in an apparently irreversible succession from the past, through the present, into the

---

Levinas' Perspective on Husserl and Heidegger" (1983, 113-127), where the author discusses Levinas's objections to fundamental ontology, "Being *qua* being", *cogito*, and other rational presuppositions in Husserlian and Heideggerian thought.

future" (Fowler 1965, 239-240). Philosophically speaking, starting from Aristotle, who argues that time is relative to movement and a measure of change[200], several theories have been proposed on time.

"Ὅτι μὲν τοίνυν ὁ χρόνος ἀριθμός ἐστιν κινήσεως κατὰ τὸ πρότερον καὶ ὕστερον, καὶ συνεχὴς (συνεχοῦς γάρ), φανερόν [...] ἆρ' οὖν [χρόνος] ὑπολείψει; ἢ οὔ, εἴπερ αἰεὶ ἔστι κίνησις; ἄλλος οὖν ἢ ὁ αὐτὸς πολλάκις; δῆλον ὅτι ὡς ἂν ἡ κίνησις, οὕτω καὶ ὁ χρόνος · εἰ μὲν γὰρ ἡ αὐτὴ καὶ γίγνεταί ποτε, ἔσται καὶ χρόνος εἷς καὶ ὁ αὐτός." (Ἀριστοτέλης 2008, 292, 308)
"It is clear, then, that time is a number of movements in respect of the before and after, and is continuous since it is an attribute of what is continuous" [...] "Will time then fail? Surely not, if motion always exists. Is time then always different or does the same time recur? Clearly time is, in the same way as motion is. For if one and the same motion sometimes recurs, it will be one and the same time" (Aristotle 2006, 61, 64).

In contemporary philosophy, René Descartes in his *Third Meditation* explored a quite different idea concerning the definition of time. He relates time with bodily existence and God, arguing that "a material body has the property of spatial extension but no inherent capacity for temporal endurance and that God by his continual action sustains (or re-creates) the body at each successive instant. Time is a kind of sustenance or re-creation" (Dowden 2020, "time"), while Kant argues that "time and space are forms that the mind projects upon the external things-in-themselves; they are, forms of human sensible intuition" (ibid.).

---

[200] Aristotle provides a *modus tollens* syllogism to infer that time exists and is relative to movement and change:

If time exists, then change exists
Change exists through movement

Therefore, time exists through movement

By considering the above statement as true, we can infer that if change and movement do not exist then time does not exist (Martinich 2005, 28).

3.5 The Notion of Time: Starting from Heidegger Yet Again

Before I analyze Levinas's argument about time and its relation to death, it is worth further discussing Heideggerian thought regarding time and its repercussions on death. First, as Levinas notes, for Heidegger, time cannot be explained or defined because "one then immediately posits time as being" (Levinas 2000, 7). For Heidegger, even if we cannot say what time is with certainty, we can relate it to death through the experience of nothingness in time. We need to aim at nothingness if we want to speak about death and its relation to time, Heidegger says. Emotions, according to Heidegger, must be reduced to the confrontation with nothingness in anxiety. Ontological meaning is necessary and sufficient for Heidegger to discuss death and its relation to time, which is the limitation of being there, being in the world, and being toward death. Heidegger's being is comprehended, apprehended, and appropriate, which means that to be there as a being it must be in the world and not somewhere else. This is the reason that for Heidegger, human existence is described in being-in-the-world and not outside beings. Since beings exist, being-always-already-in-the-world. Heidegger's question of being in time is quite different from Aristotle's metaphysical view that God is interconnected with being's existence. Heidegger's anthropology has nothing to do with a process of "security of an event […] whether absolute or divine" (ibid., 30). Heidegger explains that "the meaning of death is the end of being-in-the-world" (ibid., 36), where ontology remains the core of all meanings for understanding being and death. Only through fundamental ontology is death understandable for me. Even if I am a humanitarian, the death of the other, according to Heidegger, "is an effective final event and cannot provide access to the experience of the totality of *Dasein qua Dasein*" (ibid., 38). Dasein is a being for whom only his own being is at stake and no one else's.[201] To comprehend our death, which is mine, one cannot "take from the other his own death [...] In dying, the ontological structure that is mine-ness, reveals itself" (ibid., 39). From this argument, Levinas begins his own theory of "Other"ness. Below, I intend to explore Levinas's argument as to the priority of ethics over fundamental ontology as regards death and its relation to humans; it is the "Other" who makes me responsible for comprehending my responsibility for his own death, something that leads to the infinite process of escaping from my egoism.

3.6 Immemorial Time: A Step towards Infinity[202]

A long conversation has been had concerning the role of time and the matter of death. On the one hand, several authors

---

[201] However, as M. Mjaaland points out, "the significance of death is not only connected to a possibility of understanding *Dasein* in its totality (Ganzheit), but also to death as a test of what you have understood about life. And further, not only examining what you understand, but even how you act, what you are, and what you believe about life and death" (Mjaaland 2008, 105).

[202] It is worth mentioning that the term infinity, in Levinasian thought, has a two-fold metaphysical sense. S. Hand (ed.), in his introduction to *The Levinas Reader* (1989, 166) underlines that "infinity, which overturns the primordial character of intentionality [...] includes and negates the finite: the *in* of infinity means both *non-finite* and *in-the-finite*. Such a transcendence reveals what is beyond being: the good, and the limitless empirical event of obligation to another. This responsibility is announced by the phrase: *Here I am*". "The *in* of the Infinite were to signify both the *non* and the *within*" (ibid., 174). Levinas adds that the *in* of Infinity "devastates presence and awakens subjectivity to the proximity of the other" (ibid., 179).

specializing in Levinasian ethics claim that memory is inseparable from history and therefore that death must be considered in terms of immanent characteristics. Transcendence, in Levinas's view, they allege, merits cosmic criteria where egocentric discourse cannot be put aside.[203] Memory, for them, cannot be excluded from the sphere of transcendence; that is, transcendence is not a fundamental constituent of the self (and therefore also of death).[204]

On the other hand, there is another line of thought alleging that it is impossible to derive an ethical norm from a historical source. Memory and history, therefore, need to be detached from metaphysical discourse.[205] Memorial time has nothing to do with transcendence. Critical-historical analyses are grounded mostly on *doxa* and cosmic criteria and thus we need to seek an effort beyond ourselves: "to expire my time for the time of the Other" (ibid., 38). Defining the "beyond" is a matter of immemorial time, which has been comprehensively analyzed by M. Dimitrova, who infers that immemorial time is based on a dialogical relationship between me and

---

[203]   J. A. Barash claims that "transcendence which for [Levinas] is the necessary precondition of the ethical injunction, radically opposes the idea of memory and of history inherited from a tradition which, in its refusal of all that cannot be included in the sphere of immanence". (Dimitrova 2011, 33-34)

[204]   Barash continues that "he insists on transcendence, not as a source of faith—a theme which lies beyond what concerns me here—but as fundamentally constitutive of the self, does it not run the risk of forgetting the time of memory and of history in which the identity of the self finds a living source?" (ibid., 34) It is obvious that Barash does not understand the core role of transcendence since he confuses the criteria of immanence which are derived from fundamental ontology and not from metaphysical ethics.

[205]   The Levinasian face-to-face is beyond history and memory. Levinas underlines that through the relation between me and the other "the interlocutor appears as without a history, as outside the system" (Levinas 1998a, 34). It is neither a horizontal pure phenomenological relation, as in Husserl, nor a total system of power as in Hegel. Levinas's face-to-face needs a language prior to any speech. It is a communication where the *saying* appears before the *said*.

the "Other", through the caring for the "Other" and not enslavement by the "Other".

The term "beyond" needs to be defined within an ethical framework where the face must be signified as a trace. Totalization then is in favor of memory and history is focused on the inside-of-oneself via interiority. Levinas, in contrast, develops his argument by claiming that the outside-of-oneself is the exteriority of the beyond. Beyond oneself is not merely the outside-of-the-world presupposition. What is relevant to the subject-object relationship is grounded on the I-it relationship, which, for Levinas, is radically absorbed by itself. The point that Levinas insists on is how the Buberian I-thou model could implement the face of the "Other" as a necessary and sufficient condition — the justification of ethics as first philosophy. Comprehensive and ontological models which adopt the I-it relation cannot be relevant to immemorial time — which appeared as an absolute absence.

But how does Levinas discuss the I-it and the I-Thou relationships? First, he admits that we need to start with the "Other" as the addressor and then continue with the self as the addressee, which is considered in the accusative case (me and not I). He also claims that the self or selfhood is no longer alone on the stage, as Plato alleged. The subject, as me, is not merely a storyteller who is entrapped in the "Self"'s egocentric horizons. It is through language that humans explore their intersubjective criteria from which they communicate as humans and not merely as beings. As Dimitrova correctly points out, someone "speaks" "thanks to the meeting with the otherness of the Other" (ibid., 40).[206] Language, according to Levinas, approaches a relation which is irreducible to a subject-object relation. Language does not intend to make the other agree with the same but to maintain the other without infringing on her personality.

> "Language precisely maintains the other [...] language does not consist in invoking him as a being represented and thought. But this is why language institutes a relation irreducible to the subject-object relation: the revelation of the other. In this revelation only can language as a system of signs be constituted. The other called upon is not something represented, is not a given, is not a particular, through one side already open to generalization. Language, far from presupposing universality and generality, first makes them possible. Language presupposes interlocutors, a plurality [...] Their commerce, as we shall show shortly, is ethical" (Levinas 1969, 73).

---

[206] Levinas states that "man is the only being which I cannot meet without expressing the meeting itself. A meeting differs from cognition exactly in this". By saying being, he means humans and not beings *qua* beings like Heidegger. Levinas throughout his career as a philosopher made clear that humans are something more than beings due to their infinite responsibility against the "Other" (and not merely due to their freedom), This argument is based on expression and the dialogical requirement that is thoroughly discussed by Levinas against the monological classic German line of thought where thinking, knowledge, and cognition are the most important characteristics which revolve around the subject, being self-reflection. By expression and dialogue, Levinas succeeded in defending that the I-thou relationship is incommensurable with knowledge and therefore communication is of immense importance and related to the instrumentality of actions and interactions between me and the "Other". However, this diachronic dialogue passes through danger, suffering, and compassion. The ethics of dialogue that Levinas develops has common ground with Z. Baumann's view that "a postmodern ethics would be one that readmits the Other as a neighbor [...] an ethics that recasts the Other as the crucial character in the process through which the moral self comes into its own" (Baumann 1993, 84). See also a very comprehensive text concerning Levinas's ethics of dialogue written by J. T. Nealon, "The Ethics of Dialogue: Bakhtin and Levinas" (1997, 129-148). The author clearly provides a sufficient exigency of what it is to be a Levinasian ethics far from any ontological and epistemic knowledge or experience. Likewise, M. Gardiner correctly states that the relation between self and other, as Levinas describes it, "cannot [simply] be translated into rational, conceptual thought, for this would destroy the unmotivated, spontaneous character of the encounter" (Gardiner 1996, 131).

Levinas also raises several objections to Platonic argumentation concerning the role of the self in memory and death. For Plato, (in Socrates's conversation with Glauko and Simmias) the otherness of the "Other" cannot be valid. It is just a moral situation that emerges from God/the good. What matters for Plato is to get to know myself as well as I can in order to fulfill some criteria for gaining wisdom which are a requirement in the afterlife. Dimitrova notes that for Plato, "dialogue is not a conversation with the Other, who is part of the crowd, but is a conversation about eternal ideas, reaching as far as God (the Good), and is finally a conversation of the soul with itself" (Dimitrova 2011, 39). Death, for Plato, is the greatest happiness for wise people since the soul achieves its freedom from the sinful and useless body. The self finds its true essence after its release from the body. According to Plato, bodily accounts as well as the relation to the "Other" are merely secondary for the Self and its connection to the "Good". All relational attributes must be left behind for the sake of the teleology of the One, which is interconnected with oneself and its integration with the soul.

For Levinas, Plato's view that my relation to the good/God is a direct one is false since it reduces humans' ethical condition to immanence.[207] Levinas believes that what

---

[207] The notion of Good/God or good has a profound importance in Levinasian ethics. It is a reversal of subjectivity that determines its origin. The Good's attributes are extremely different between Levinasian ethics and ontology. If one considers the being in-or-for-itself, goodness has nothing to share or to merit with oneself. Good, ontologically and metaphysically speaking, is something meaningless and useless in a being; good has nothing to do with representation. It is prior to the unity of apperception and immanence. For Levinas, "to be good [with a lower-case letter, as an adjective and personal characteristic of humans] is a deficit, waste and foolishness in a being; to be good is excellence and elevation beyond being. Ethics is not a moment of being; it is otherwise and better than being, the very possibility of the beyond" (Hand [ed.] 1989, 179). Levinas

really matters is the lowest passage from me to the "Other" and not a direct path that leads immediately to God without a mediator.[208]

Death, therefore, for Levinas, can be understood through the immemorial time above and beyond any historical criticism and secular reminiscence. Thoughtfulness is a basic characteristic of the "Other" in order that it be abandoned by

---

also discusses the notion of the "Good" (with a capital letter, that is God). He contends that "the Good"/God is beyond and above any objectivity, presence, and being. Good, in contrast to Plato and other Greek theories based in an ontological frame, is the desirable of the non-desirable. It is untouchable and even beyond otherness. God is not only "the absolute other but other than the other" (ibid.). Transcendence thus is quite distinct from phenomenological discussions or as Husserl and Heidegger consider it (ibid., 179-186). Levinas stresses that, in contrast to Plato, "the desire for the other, sociality, is born in a being that lacks nothing, or, more exactly, it is born over and beyond all that can be lacking or that can satisfy him" (Levinas 1987a, 94). Levinas was, for sure, concerned about Plato's and Plotinus's "One" and Husserl's pure ego when he admitted that it is urgent to decenter the subject and the good from its egoity. Levinas explains that in order to achieve this, we need to speak beyond history and outside of the egalitarian system. He underlines that "the exceptional, extraordinary, transcendent character of goodness is due to just this break with being and history. To reduce the good to being, to its calculations and its history, is to nullify goodness [...] Goodness gives to subjectivity its irreducible signification" (Levinas 1991, 18).

[208] Plato and classical German Idealism: OTHER <-------------GOD (as direct mediator)-------------> MY SELF
Levinas: ME (My way to God) <----------Face of the Other (as mediator – passage to God)----------> GOD (indirect relation to Humans).
From this scheme it is inferred that Plato theologizes since the conversation of the soul is with itself through the theology of the "Good". Kant. like Levinas, "leaves God aside and does not allow reference to him in discussing and settling human issues" (Dimitrova 2011, 39). At this point, we can deduce that Levinas provides an ethical argument rather than a theological syllogism. Levinas draws from Talmudic writings, especially those of the great Talmudist Rabbi Hayyim Voloshiner, who states that man is the mediator of God's principles on earth: "Man exercises his mastery and responsibility as mediator between *Elohim* [God in Hebrew] and the worlds by ensuring the presence or absence of *Elohim* to the incatenation of beings which never ceases to need its living force in order to be" (Levinas 1994d, 159-160).The "Other", though, as a face, has an eternal task towards me: "the face of the other issues an appeal to me to assume responsibility for his fate" (Jodalen and Vetlesen [eds.] 1997, 148). Therefore, it is the other who calls me in the world following the trace of God outside in heaven.

the "Self"'s totalization. The "Other"'s otherness appears as heteronomy to "One"self since the "Other" has the status of an "Absolute". However, this "Absolute" meaning echoes in mortality, vulnerability, and passiveness. This is the reason Levinas defends immemorial time in terms of asymmetrical, non-reciprocal conditions. Thus, the Heideggerian being-toward-death is for Levinas neither a necessary nor sufficient condition to explore his argument on death and time.[209] Knowledge and comprehension within a historical framework need to be detached from immemorial time.[210] As Dimitrova points out, "the ethical cannot be derived from a historical source, but we need to retain an intermediate space between the Other and me" (ibid., 42). What mostly matters to realize death is to see the "Other" as an expression of heteronomy and via intersubjective communication[211] through a dialogical commandment. I am hostage to the "Other"'s face due to my infinite responsibility to his otherness. There is no choice to respond (to some extent) to the "Other" since, according to Levinas, there is a deterministic procedure where

---

[209] As Levinas states, "Ethics, concern for the being of the other-than-one-self, non-indifference toward the death of the other, and hence, the possibility of dying for the other — a chance for holiness — would be the expansion of that ontological contraction that is expressed by the verb to be, dis-inter-estedness breaking the obstinacy of being, opening the order of the human, of grace, and of sacrifice" (Levinas 1998a, 202).

[210] As Levinas points out, "no memory could follow the traces of this past. It is an immemorial past — and this also is perhaps eternity, whose signifyingness obstinately throws one back to the past. Eternity is the very irreversibility of time, the source and refuge of the past" (Levinas 1987a, 103). For a helpful discussion on memory and Levinas's view of the immemorial, see E. Levinas, *In the Time of the Nations*, ch. 4: "Beyond Memory" (1994b, 76-91).

[211] Levinas underlines that "it is the possibility of communication that underwrites the possibility of there being individual minds, reasoners, or persons at all" (Chappell 2013, 51).

"I am the chosen and hostage because of the Other's freedom" (ibid.).

My death, for Levinas, is tautological to the death of the "Other".[212] Even though the death is mine, it begins with the "Other". There is no equality between me and the "Other" as Christian universalism and Greek philosophy allege. For Levinas, autonomy and social equality absorb "Other"ness into the self-enclosed unit assimilating it. Rather than that, we need to see the "Other"'s heteronomy as a necessary condition for the I-Thou relation.[213] The maxim of my own pleasure-seeking in my social and personal lives is not capable of making me feel or comprehend the real meaning of death. Utilitarianism and universalism, for Levinas, lack an ethical process to justify death and time. Ignoring the otherness of the "Other", which is a main characteristic of utilitarianism, is a fatal mistake that prevents the "Self" from getting to know his death. According to Levinas, I must not love the "Other" due to his similar attributes, but due to his heteronomous attitude. Maximizing the "I" does not mean that I do not violate the otherness of the "Other". Violence to the "Other" starts not only by harming him but by ignoring him as well. The "Other" must always be the mediator of Heidegger's phrase

---

[212] Levinas states that "the very difference between me and the other is non-indifference, is the-one-for-the- other. The-one-for-the-other is the very signifyingness of signification" (Levinas 1991, 178). Levinas depicts the relationship between selfhood and the other as a radical ethical impulse, a rupture of being as nothingness, representing the other as a turning point to understand myself. Thus the death of the other person can give a new ethical horizon to one's own death since the openness of caring for the other even until her death creates an ethical model in me and the other which is a gift, an infinite sacrifice through which the first call comes from the other and not from myself.

[213] M. Ruti, in his text *Between Levinas and Lacan* (2015, 1), provides a characteristic paradigm relevant to the above statement: "Human ontology, in other words, is inherently social so that it makes no sense to talk about the self as an autonomous entity who unilaterally acts on the world".

"being-toward-death". Death must be seen through the death of the "Other" which is sensible to me. I cannot see and realize my death; thus the "Other" is the "being-toward-death" that matters. Dimitrova correctly notes that:

> "When speaking about death, the immediate question is about the death of others because nobody can be a spectator of or witness to his own death; where my own death is concerned, I can judge only indirectly relating to others. Exactly because the Other is a being-toward-death he touches me not in [the] indicative but in the imperative". (Dimitrova 2011, 44)

This is why Levinas does not adopt Hegel's view of historicity, which gives priority to instrumentalization. Hegel argues that a human's deeds (*praxis*) and historical facts are always in front of him, ready to judge his future, even his death. This totalized method is something that Levinas rejects because he understands death as something that is grounded upon ethical, not logical, presuppositions. Experience and memorial time are not sufficient or even necessary to Levinasian thought in order to realize death. Any immanent aspects that infringe on "Other"ness and the possibility of neglecting or abandoning what the "Other" offers us are rejected. We are not in need of the "Other" to instrumentalize her. Rather, we are in need of the "Other" to understand ourselves and to comprehend the understandable, that is, to see beyond my death through the death of the "Other". As M. Dimitrova points out, "Levinas would have added" to Heidegger's phrase that *Dasein* (Being) as a being-toward-death bears the burden of his time from the very moment of birth, "that the moral subject not only cares for his own time [and his own death] but also undertakes to carry the load of the Other's time and because of this double burden, human existence is diachronic" (Dimitrova 2016, 86).

Meaning and the meaning of death start when the self hears the voice of the "Other", not as intellectualism claims: through its reduction to consciousness and intuition.[214] Dimitrova points out that "the abstractness of the face disturbs immanence without settling into the horizons of the world" (ibid., 45). This means that it is not necessary for me to understand the call of the "Other". Rather, I am obliged, before freedom comes, to be responsible before this call. This is the reason, Levinas argues, that responsibility precedes freedom. As Sartre argues that existence precedes essence (Kearney and Rainwater [eds.] 1996, 67), Levinas also gives priority to existential dialectics rather than to immanent[215] criteria of our

---

[214] Levinas mentions that several empiricists and idealists such as Plato and Hume present meaning as inseparable from consciousness and intuition and that "meaning is reducible to contents given to consciousness. Intuition, in the straightforwardness of a consciousness that welcomes data, remains the source of all meaning, whether these data be ideas, relations or sensible qualities" (1987a, 76). For Plato, meaning is "the intelligible, [which] is indeed present in the sensible world, which is characterized by change and becoming; it is in fact only to be discovered via sensible reality, which however, thought must rise over" (ibid., 83, n. 22). Husserl, then, even if he does not adopt the same method concerning meaning and its relation to consciousness, continues to insist that "intuition remains the source of all intelligibility", while Heidegger believes that "experience is reading, the understanding of meaning exegesis, a hermeneutics, and not an intuition" (ibid., 72). For Heidegger, "ontological intelligibility reveals itself as basic to all rationality" (Levinas 1998a, 210). On the contrary, Levinas contends that meaning takes its real meaning through the trace of the "Other". He rejects an ontological procedure where a transcendence (in being) "revealed is inverted into an immanence, the extra-ordinary is inserted into an order, the Other is absorbed into the Same" (ibid., 103).

[215] In ancient Greece immanent criteria of essence are also called "esoteric". The language of dialectics in Greek thought passed through a word which "has gained the privilege of disclosing the concealed territory of the esoteric" (Dimitrova 2013b, 89). The most famous paradigm of Greek esotericism is the phrase from Plato: "the conversation of the Soul with itself" (ibid.), which means that I am obliged to be wise in order to prepare my soul to meet the world of forms in the aftermath. What matters to the majority of Greek thinkers is to use language as a means. However, for Levinas, we need to seek a different dialectics which gives priority to cause and effect. We need to start our research questions using the word *why* or the phrase *ought to be* and not the word *is* or *how*. This is the big difference between metaphysics and epistemology, and between ethics

essence. The meaning of death can be found through the proximity of the "Other". However, for Levinas, the "Other"'s face does not leave any sign.[216] Signification is a criterion of immanence and thus unacceptable in Levinasian ethics — if it is integrated with intentionality.[217] The only way to catch the symbolic utterance of the "Other" is through its trace.[218] Human traces also have a theological impact on me. My death can be considered as something holy and not

---

and ontology. See M.-A. Webb, "Eros and Ethics: Levinas's Reading of Plato's Good beyond Being" (2006), 205-222. Webb contends that "ethics of alterity may allow the human being to refer irrationally to the good *beyond* being" (ibid. 205), as well as "without reducing them to mathematical or logical equations" (ibid. 211).

[216] The face, as a symbolic trace, cannot adopt any immanent procedure. As Levinas explains, "a face is the unique openness in which the signifyingness of the trans-cendent does not nullify the transcendence and make it enter into an immanent order; here on the contrary transcendence refuses immanence precisely as the ever bygone transcendence of the transcendent" (Levinas 1987a, 103). However, by symbolic we do not mean that a trace is merely allegorical or that it can only be grasped in the imagination. A trace is not a product of a magic world. It is a real outcome of [human] being's existence, but not as a being-in-the-world or a being-towards-death. Levinas insists that only [human] being can leave a trace, but under a specific presupposition: "only a being that transcends the world, an ab-solute being, can leave a trace. A trace is a presence of that which properly speaking has never been there, of what is always past" (ibid., 105).

[217] M. Dimitrova in her work *Sociality and Justice* (2016, 99-100), provides a clear distinction between analytic philosophy and Levinasian ethics on the role of signification by saying that "Levinas argues that for people in the West [analytical thinking], it is not approaching the Other through speech that matters; what is more important is communication of information — meaning is attained in what is reported. Signification is considered a representation of being. Levinas however spoke of the relation One-for-the-Other regardless of any content and any communication of content. At the ontological level, [in the analytical thinking] 'for' has the meaning of a break-up with rationality, but on ethics what mostly matters is the one-for-the-Other relation. Therefore, in contrast to the Hegelian *in-itself* and the Sartrean *for-itself*, Levinas develops an ethical, non-narcissistic, term, that is, for-the-other. He states that "it is not through substantiality — through an in-itself and a for-itself — that man and his interiority are defined, but through the 'for the other': for that which is above self, for the worlds" (Levinas 1994d, 161). For Levinas's conception of narcissism and Western thought, see Levinas's arguments (1987a, 49-53).

[218] Concerning the notion of trace in Levinasian thought, see ch. 6, "Meaning and Sense" (1987a, 102-107).

merely sacred[219] when they merit several ethical presuppositions.[220]

3.7 Categories of Time in Levinas

The meaning of death is also grounded in time. However, for Levinas, time[221] needs to be divided into three categories before analyzing its functionality toward death.

(a) Existential Time: Ordinary time which counts time as it exists is past, present, and future. It is the moment that cannot be stopped or changed by anyone. Subjects live in an existential time through materialistic facts and events. Death has the power of time in existential time and not human beings. Death is a direct threat to humans, who await this inevitability without knowing the exact date of its arrival. Nothingness approaches our lives from the opposite side allied

---

[219] See the difference between holiness and the sacred in subchapter 1.9 above. Holiness, as M. Dimitrova claims, starts not from the I or the self's criteria but through the suffering of the suffering of the Other, since suffering is meaningless in front of the ego.

[220] M. Dimitrova, in her article, *In Response to Andrew Jeffrey Barash: The Immemorial Time*, page 37, provides some properties that are relevant to Levinas's perspective on human characteristics with ethical nomenclature such as transcendence, beyond essence, otherwise than being, Otherness, An-archical, ethics, Good [author's view: Closeness and Proximity]. Those attributes are simply against any immanent characteristics such as Essence, Being *qua* being, "I". Ego-centric inwardness, Ontology, cognition, etc. Even though the above model seems to be categorized in two different lines of thought—ethical and ontological—our intention is not to put Levinas's thought in any theoretical framework since he argues that if we want to seek to find the "Other" we must look use asymmetrical, anarchical presuppositions. It is the same as regards God: It is impossible for Levinas to catch the meaning of God by trying to think of goodness or deity *per se*. As is inferred in a previous chapter analyzing arguments on God and ontotheology, Levinas is strongly opposed to any theoretical, direct, ontotheological criteria of God's essence. The only way to possibly understand God is through the trace of the "Other"'s face.

[221] For Levinas's notion of time and its relation to the other, see the chapter "Time and the Other", in S. Hand (ed.) *The Levinas Reader*, 37-58, where he purposes a transition from existence to ethics.

with death against the I. The fear of death emerges in existential time and individuals' consciousness of death arises during the last period of their lives, anility.

> "Death is a menace that approaches me as a mystery; its secrecy determines it — it approaches without being able to be assumed, such that the time that separates me from my death dwindles and dwindles without end, involves a sort of last interval which my consciousness cannot traverse, and where a leap will somehow be produced from death to me. The last part of the route will be crossed without me; the time of death flows upstream; the I in its projection toward the future is overturned by a movement of imminence, pure menace, which comes to me from an absolute alterity." (Levinas 1969, 235)

It is thus inevitable to avoid death as we understand it in existential life. Levinas agrees with ancient Greek thinkers that death is a real mystery and inevitable as well as impossible for us to know exactly when it comes: "Death, the most dreaded of evils, is therefore of no concern to us; for while we exist death is not present, and when death is present, we no longer exist" (Epicurus, 1957, §125). However, Levinas extends this argument by saying that, in contrast to Heidegger (who argues that human being is being-towards-death), being is against (and above) death. Even though it is really hard to speak about death and how to avoid the unavoidable, Levinas develops this argument by claiming that the self can be seen metaphysically through the suffering for others as something that gives the opportunity to the "I" as a self-enclosed unit to escape mine-ness. Levinas does not reject consciousness, but he insists that it always must be combined with ethical and not immanent perspectives. Thus, bringing attention to the suffering of the other opens the moral dimension between human beings since the suffering of the "Other" and not only Myself is the core of the highest level of ethical imperative.

(b) Historical Time: Hegel is the first thinker in contemporary philosophy who speaks about and pays particular attention to history and the historicity of the subject[222] in his work *Phenomenology of Spirit*.[223] He compares and analyzes historical time with politics and the model of Master and Slave in order to show social inequalities and the importance of self-consciousness within a philosophical and not merely an epistemic framework: "if man is nothing but his becoming [merely a conscious entity], if his human existence in space is his existence in [historical] time or as time, if the revealed human reality is nothing but universal history, that history must be the history of the interaction between Master and Slavery: the historical 'dialectic' is the 'dialectic' of Master and Slave" (Kojeve 1980, 9). Alexandre Kojeve intends to show that, for Hegel, history is completed and it cannot be yet again fulfilled in a different tense or period of time (ibid: x). Thus, historical time reflects on "universal laws, embodied in the system of institutions and human interactions, in order to seek

---

[222] E. Demirel criticizes the subject as it has been developed by several thinkers such as Hegel, Nietzsche, Freud, and Butler. Several thinkers, he argues, did not succeed in conceptualizing the subject between the inner and the outer. Demirel provides an alternative argument in terms of the ethical dialectic in which the subject must be decentered from itself as well as from the subject-object relation of cognition, re-cognition, and self-recognition. See E. Demirel, The Subject-Matter: The Subject" (2019, 75-98). Concerning cognition, Levinas mentions that it is inseparable from science and totality when it is integrated with generality and not singularity: "Cognition consists in grasping the individual, which alone exists, not in its singularity which does not count, but in its generality, of which alone there is science" (Levinas 1987a, 50).

[223] The most comprehensive texts on Hegel's *Phenomenology of Spirit* from my point of view are A. Kojeve's *Introduction to the Reading of Hegel* (1980) and D. P. Verene's, *Hegel's Absolute: An Introduction to Reading of Phenomenology of Spirit* (2007; idem. 1985).

protection in its resistance to death and in the hope of receiving an objective judgment of its meaning. Such a verdict is the verdict of history [...] People have meaning in terms of the personification of their historical roles" (Dimitrova 2016, 91). Historical time can be construed through a model of logical time that is past, present, and future with a real and inevitable beginning, middle, and end having a sequential and reasonable course of development. Thus, for Hegel, historical time is a totality deriving from mathematical and physical norms without infringing any normative or epistemological presupposition. The self in a such framework has the right to choose a professional, personal, and individual mode of living without any coercion from ethical or metaphysical intuition. Conventional presuppositions are what matters in a historical time. However, for Levinas, there is an urgent need to escape from the continuity between being and history in order to transit to an eschatological time where death can be surpassed.[224]

---

[224] The above expression, according to Levinas, can be achieved through the power of language. Levinas states that "language accomplishes a relation between terms that breaks up the unity of a genus. The terms, the interlocutors, absolve themselves from the relation, or remain absolute within relationship. Language is perhaps to be defined as the very power to break the continuity of being [and] or of history" (Levinas 1969, 195). Levinas's aim was to present a new dialectic concerning language far from the ancient Greek line of thought. For instance, he rejects that language "expresses the essence of objects because it expresses the reasoning itself" (Dimitrova 2013b, 90). Unfortunately, the dialectics of the ancient Greek *logos* and Latin *ratio*, which both empowered—through the Medieval fathers and Renaissance—practical reasoning and the "Absolute Subject", increased to a tremendous level the power of a new capitalistic-bureaucratic dialectic, which is "the most powerful operation masking and legitimizing power" through the power of logic and sameness, which ignored and absorbed the face of the "Other" and his proximity to exteriority and free will. In order to escape from the dominance of reason, language must cease to be merely *logos*. It must appear as "the human cry and calling of the One summoning the others to respond; this calling ought to be understood as the appeal to the personal responsibility of Me" (ibid., 94). Thus, for Levinas, presence is not

(c) Eschatological Time:[225] This mode of time is grounded on an ethical and metaphysical framework where the "Self" is not at the center of the life's cycle. The "Self" puts aside his egoistic preferences and "cannot be responded to in any ontological, phenomenological, sociological, epistemological or any other logical terms" (ibid., 93). Within an eschatological time, the I goes back to itself, responding to an inquiry from the "Other", while the responsibility of the I is

---

inseparable from time because presence "incorporate[s] a movement of return to itself" (Kanton 1996, 24) and this is rejected by Levinas, who gives priority to diachrony which is irrecuperable of the present. For Levinas, "the face to face founds language" which is beyond words and knowledge. (Chappell 2013, 51). "Intellectual activity" and "reasoning will", Levinas claims, (Kearney [ed.] 1996, 124) are neither necessary nor sufficient conditions of ethical language. In contrast, Levinas contends that the "immanence of the known to the act of knowing is already the embodiment of seizure" (ibid.), which includes the "Other" who is threatened to be absorbed by the "Same" through knowledge which ontologically appears as "presence and adequation" (ibid., 125). Whatever is known by knowledge is reduced to consciousness (and self-consciousness). However, according to Levinas, "this reduced consciousness which in referring upon in self, rediscovers and masters its own masks of perception and science as objects in the world, thereby [affirms] itself as self-consciousness and absolute being" (ibid., 127). For Levinas, beyond any representation and perception, "prior to any knowledge about the self or death, language and mortality lie in the Other" (Hand [ed.] 1989, 83). The "Other" is prior to any language and directs me to speak and to express myself not as a self-enclosed unit but as an interlocutor who needs the "Other" to re-exist without any coercion, marginalization, or absorption of each other. Concerning knowledge as a subject-object relation, as truth and its relation to beings and the "Other", see E. Levinas, "Martin Buber and the Theory of Knowledge" (1989, 59-74), where Levinas discusses ancient Greek thought, from object to being, continues with Husserl and Heidegger's phenomenology of experience, and then evaluates Buber's I-Thou by raising some objections: Even though Levinas prefers the I-Thou scheme to the I-It, he claims that Buber's knowledge mistakenly transits from the I-It to the I-Thou because it "implies a passage to consciousness" and thus it returns again to intentionality and immanence (ibid., 73).

[225] Eschatological time is based on futurity. Death in eschatological time always remains in the future "not because the human subject somehow projectively integrates what is coming, which for Levinas is impossible, but quite the reverse, because the human subject cannot catch up to, cannot embrace, cannot be-toward death [as Heidegger interprets] which is always and ever future" (Cohen 2006, 31). For death and future see also S. Hand (ed.), *Levinas Reader*, part 1, ch. 3 "Time and the Other" (1989, 41-42).

"the fundamental relation with the Other" (ibid., 94). In eschatology, Levinas insists that time has nothing to do with egocentric secularism or with materialistic conceptions but with "Other"ness:

> "In Ethics it is not my rights that are central but the rights of the Other. Being I, says Levinas, is to see beyond universal rights and laws into the insult inflicted by the verdict of history, which does not respect the uniqueness of the Other. What is not seen in historical time is the ignoring of the first person and its rights of defense, which no one else could perform for it. Being myself, and not just the embodiment of universal laws or dialectic movements of the World Spirit, means to be responsible not only for one's own actions, as per the judgment of history and the laws of the State, but to answer first for the Other; to fear for the rights of the Other more than for one's own rights and to foresee my responsibility even before an action has been committed [...] This is to be afraid for the Other, more than the *I* is afraid of death and to take risks to avoid leaving the Other alone and without an answer, i.e. [...] expand my time for the time of the Other." (Dimitrova 2016, 95-96).

It is true that Levinas, during his philosophical career, was declaring ethics as first philosophy. By doing this, he explored a view in favor of the "Other" and her proximity to (a) me and (b) God. Both terms are inseparable and, according to Levinas, are shaped within an eschatological/metaphysical framework construed (not through a theological or ontological frame but) through ethical presuppositions,[226] where finitude has passed through infinity without infringing the holiness of the face of the "Other". Eschatology, of course, derives from theological and messianic conceptions. By

---

[226] For instance, *Levinas* states that "our relation with the Metaphysical is an ethical behavior and not theology, not a thematization, be it a knowledge by analogy, of the attributes of God [...] The Other is the very locus of metaphysical truth, and is indispensable for my relation with God. He does not play the role of a mediator. The Other is not the incarnation of God, but precisely by his face, in which he is disincarnate, is the manifestation of the height in which God is revealed" (Levinas 1969, 78-79).

messianic, we do not only mean Christian messianic principles, as Kierkegaard alleges, but mainly Biblical and ethical
derivations. By eschatology we mean the "end of history [...]
Eschatological time masters the course of the One's existential time, which leads to death, directing it towards the time
of the Other [...] Eschatological time is produced as overcoming *conatus essendi*[227] of the mortal being in the diaconate, in
the vigil for the Other, in the selfness of the Apostles' work,
in the service and lithurgy[228] for him and for the others" (Dimitrova 2016, 97). Eschatology is diachronic because my existential time is important for the existential time of the
"Other". It is built on the asymmetrical and non-reciprocal
relationship with the other without infringing her rights or
absorbing her essence into oneself. Eschatological time must
affect historical and existential time and not vice-versa. Its
main task is not merely to show the way to one's salvation
from death but to save the other as well. Eschatological time
goes beyond being and historical properties such as laws, justice, politics, economics, and fundamental ontology. Rather,
eschatological time is more apologetic and transcendent since
it echoes to infinity. What really matters in eschatology is negation, not a Hegelian negation within a Marxist framework,
where materialism is at stake, but a negation and marginalization of the "Self" in favor of the neighbor, caring for her
salvation and her own eternal prosperity. In this way, death
no longer touches the will.[229]

---

[227] See footnote 12.
[228] Or liturgy.
[229] Levinas on this matter contends that "death marks the subjectivity of the will
not as an end, but as supreme violence and alienation. But in patience, where
the will is transported to a life against someone and for someone, death no longer touches the will" (Levinas 1969, 240).

3.8 "Dying for" vs. "for-itself": Death beyond *My* Death

> "The priority of the other over the *I*, by which the human *being-there* is chosen and unique, is precisely the latter's response to the nakedness of the face and its mortality. It is there that the concern for the other's death is realized, and that 'dying for him' 'dying his death' takes priority over 'authentic' death. Not a post-mortem life, but the excessiveness of sacrifice, holiness in charity and mercy. This future of death in the present of love is probably one of the original secrets of temporality itself and beyond all metaphor". (Levinas 1998a, 217)

As discussed above, Levinas aims to reexamine the notion of death, starting—as a phenomenologist—from pure phenomenology (observation)[230] like Husserl and Heidegger, (but)

---

[230] M. Weimin, for instance, who believes that Levinas was never a phenomenologist, even in his early career (Weimin 2008, 74-77), provides arguments concerning the crisis of the phenomenological subject (Weimin 2008, 61-65), also taking into account some alternatives from the ethical perspective (ibid., 65-69) to support the thesis that the anonymity of (Heideggerian) *Dasein* falsely rests on nothingness and on a "chaotic rustling of an anonymous existing, an existence without existent, that no negation can happen to surmount" (ibid., 66, n. 8). Weimin infers that it is only through the responsibility for the other that the "Subject" (that is human and not a generic being) escapes anonymity and nothingness (ibid., 69-74). I would add something that Weimin ignores or considers secondary: that the "Subject"'s responsibility is an *a priori* condition, prior to any autonomy and freedom. From my point of view, there is not a criterion that a human must fulfill in order to be responsible or irresponsible as regards the other. Levinas's theory of responsibility echoes to infinity; that is, the "Subject" is called from the other, having an eternal duty regarding his salvation first, and then that of caring for himself. This is the reason that Levinas ultimately is based on Dostoyevsky's principles: "We are all guilty of everything and everyone, and I, more so than all the others" (Levinas 1998b, 72; Jodalen and Vetlesen [eds.] 1997, 48). I am a hostage of the other's otherness before any direct call or summons. My existence is already conscious of the other before any knowledge and rational exegesis: "The relation between the same and the other is not always reducible to knowledge of the other by the same, nor even to the revelation of the other to the same, which is already fundamentally different from disclosure" (Levinas 1969, 28). Concerning Dostoevsky's influence on Levinas, see A. Tumayan, "'I more the Others': Dostoevsky and Levinas" (2004, 55-66); V. Vinokurov, "Levinas's Dostoevsky: A Response to 'Dostoevskis Derrida" (2003, 318-340). Levinas informs us of his admiration for Dostoevsky by saying that "I always quote Dostoevsky" (Levinas 2001, 100).

reversing his argument in favor of ethics as first philosophy. For Levinas, Heidegger's *Dasein* was a tremendous "invention" in contemporary philosophy that was the fundamental tool to speak about ontology since Plato. However, for Levinas, it is not enough. Being-toward-death as the self-understanding of being is, for Levinas, a mere hermeneutic-ontological structure without addressing the real issue of death. Levinas provides an alternative vision of ethics as first philosophy. Levinas's argument starts with a main proposition:[231] "care for the other's death takes precedence over care for one's own" (Cohen 2006, 25), which is the core statement to understand (my) death. In ethics, in general, mortality is inseparable from morality, and the latter is not an ontic region of signification (ibid., 26).[232]

---

[231] We need to be very careful when using the term "proposition" for Levinas's thought because, as R. A. Cohen points out, Levinas's notion of proposition is not based primarily on knowledge and/or on epistemological criteria but rather in ethics, which is integrated with the idea of infinity and not totalization: "Nevertheless, because the central claim of Levinas's thought is not ultimately a knowledge claim, and therefore not a thesis or a theme that can be fully represented in propositions, but a moral imperative — the 'idea of infinity' as the irreducible height and transcendence of the other person and self-sensing as the irreducible independence or separation of subjectivity [...] where it encounters the imposition of a non-cognitive significance [...] whereby the imperatives of morality are traced in and overwhelm the very intentional ('consciousness off'...) and constitutional (transcendental consciousness) structures which define phenomenology as a science" (Cohen 2006, 26-27).

[232] However, Levinas makes a step forward, contending that this scheme, that is, mortality, is highly connected and integrated with morality, and must be reconsidered and reexamined by giving priority to the mortality and suffering of the "Other". My mortality and suffering does not come first but always passes through the imperative of the face of the "Other" which "commands me to not remain indifferent to this death, to not let the other die alone, that is, to answer for the life of the other person, at the risk of becoming an accomplice in that person's death [...] through the face of the other, through *his* [and not my] mortality" (Levinas 1987b, 107-108).

186

"I think that the human[233] precisely consists in opening oneself to the death of the other, in being preoccupied with his or her death. What I am saying here may seem like a pious thought, but I am persuaded that around the death of my neighbour what I have been calling the humanity of man is manifested." (Levinas 1999, 157-158)

What does exactly Levinas mean by "opening oneself to the death of the other"? Levinas, characteristically, in several texts, shows that the term for-itself cannot justify or free being from pain. In contrast, Levinas provides the term dying-for (the other) which is linked to suffering. It is thus not enough for someone to live for-itself.[234] By doing this, the

---

[233] Levinas prefers the term *human* and not *Being* contrarily to Heidegger, since he believes that humans merit not only ontological (physical) but also ethical and metaphysical attributes — and Beings do not. Several positivists and empiricists use the term *Being* instead of *human*. At first glance, it would be illogical for an existentialist like Heidegger to use the term *Being* instead of human. However, Heidegger is not so much interested in presenting man as playing the role of transcendental subjectivity. Heidegger is not an ethicist at all. His metaphysics underlines the *how* and not the *why* of the *mode of being*. He is interested in the adventure of being as it *is* and not as it *ought to be*. Levinas gives us an astonishingly hermeneutic scheme of how Heidegger sees the nature of being: "[For Heidegger] Man [...] is expressed in terms of his being there and his being-in-the-world, a modality of the authentic or the event of being. Philosophy is no longer interested in the man of humanism, or an excellence or a dignity that, as a being, he would derive from some non-philosophical tradition or doctrine, or from a partiality of man for 'everything that is human', or from the privileged nature of evidence derived from reflection on the self in the search for certain truths, and in which man already poses himself as a subject of transcendental idealism. It is as being-there in its concern for being that Heideggerian phenomenology brings to the heart of ontology that essential articulation of the event of being, which is also understanding of that event, thought in the strong sense of the term, flanked by science, which extends into techniques that absorb it and that would pervert man" (Levinas 1998a, 210). For a deeper analysis of how Heidegger evaluates humanity, see M. Heidegger, "Letter on Humanism", in *Basic Writings* (1978).

[234] Levinas rejects both terms, *for-itself* and *in-itself*, as he claims that their presence is quite insufficient to justify subjectivity and selfhood and its relation to other subjects (humans). He suggests that the ontological self must be replaced by the ethical one through the term *for-the-other*: "This human inversion of the *in-itself* and the *for-itself* (of every man for himself) into an ethical self, into a priority of the *for-the-other* — this replacement of the *for-itself* of ontological persistence by an *I*, henceforth unique certainly, but unique because of its chosenness for a responsibility for the other man — inescapable and nontransferable, this radical

187

pace toward death will always be insufficient and egocentric. For-itself and being-toward-death always depend on the present. For Levinas, it is not enough to speak about death *qua* (my) death since "the supreme ordeal of freedom is not death but suffering" (Levinas 1969, 239). Levinas adds that "in suffering reality acts on the in itself [and not for-itself] of the will, which turns despairingly into total submission to the will of the Other" (ibid. 238). He integrates suffering not only with death but also with ambiguity, which is of immense importance in Levinasian thought:

> "In suffering the will is defeated by sickness. In fear death is yet future, at a distance from us; whereas suffering realizes in the will the extreme proximity of the being menacing the will [...] Suffering remains ambiguous: it is already the present of the pain acting on the for itself of the will, but, as consciousness, the pain is always yet to come. In suffering the free being ceases to be free, but, while non-free, is yet free. It remains at a distance from this pain by its very consciousness, and consequently can become a heroic will." (Levinas 1969, 238).

Considering this passage, we can infer that Levinas's aim is to decenter the role of consciousness from the will. By suffering for the sake of the face of the other through patience, "dying for" can be justified as a necessary and sufficient condition of understanding the meaning of death. When we consider the will (of being) free, independent, autonomous, and absolute, we inevitably isolate it and enclose in it something

---

turnabout would take place in what I call an encounter with the face of the other" (Levinas 1998a, 202). It is worth noting that the Levinasian "Other" on the one hand, has authority but no force (Jodalen and Vetlesen [eds.] 1997, 48), nor does it threaten my own's selfhood, as Hegel believes. On the other hand (but simultaneously) the "Other" "calls to me and orders me from the depths of his defenseless nakedness, his misery, his mortality. It is in the personal relationship, from me to the other, that the ethical event, charity and mercy, generosity and obedience, lead beyond or rise above being" (Levinas 1998a, 202).

that prevents the will from understanding the mystery[235] of the other's death. There is, therefore, a danger that the consciousness alone could see the other as an "objectifying subject". In contrast, through the suffering and "dying for", Levinas presents an understanding of being [as human] "that would no longer be the objectification of a quiddity or representation of substantives qualified by adjectives and answering the question: What is it?" (Levinas 1998a, 210). Levinas, therefore, gives priority to the phrase "ought to be" or to the question "what ought one do?" rather than to the question "what is good for me?" since the latter question reduces the "Other" to being through knowledge and rationality. In this way knowledge goes to the other, trying to absorb it, but returns inactive. For Levinas, what I am looking for in order not to be but to be what I ought to be is the face-to-face[236] relation with the "Other": an eternal responsibility which comes from

---

[235] Concerning the term "mystery" in Levinasian thought. see in particular M. Purcell, *Mystery and Method* (1998, 335-357).

[236] In addition, it is worth noting that M. Dimitrova contends that responsibility is beyond any egalitarian reason and knowledge. "The Other is neither below me, nor equal to me. Egalitarianism does not respect him enough" (Dimitrova 2011, 17). She opposes J. Rawls's view concerning the importance of rational consensus — if we want to speak about justice. She, in contrast, suggests that ethical responsibility and justice are beyond the intentionality of consciousness that merely initiates cognition through ontological repercussions (Dimitrova 2013a, 5-11). Dimitrova is surely concerned about Rawls's model of a rational plan of life, something that I have called above a list of the criteria of properties of a life-world. Dimitrova, through Levinas's texts, correctly admits that Rawls's ethical theory underlies a starting point which is inseparable from consciousness and self-respect. First, beings for Rawls must defend their self-interest in accord with autonomy and rational choice (Rawls 1971, 433–446). In contrast, Levinas vehemently criticizes the "rational-choice theory" since he considers it a "subject-centered theory that emphasizes thinking and acting in accord with rules, principles, duties, codes, beliefs, teachings, communities, theories of the right and the good" (Bruns 2004, 30). On this matter, Levinas highlights that "Humanity [and therefore human beings] must then not be first understood as consciousness, that is, as the identity of an ego endowed with knowledge" (Levinas 1991, 83).

outside directly to me inevitably from just hearing its voice —
a call and an eternal response (Jodalen and Vetlesen [eds.]
1997, 20-21).

For Levinas, "Dying for..." (the other) through suffering
takes precedence over Heidegger's being, whereas "the human finds himself enslaved in the meaningfulness of meaning *qua* meaning" (Levinas 1998a, 211). For Levinas, the human takes on meaning *beyond-being* and through the "dying
for..." reveals man as transcendental subjectivity. Levinas
tries to reevaluate Heidegger's term being-with-others by escaping the power of being *qua* being. Being-with-others is not
necessarily being-in-the-world. For Levinas, being-for-the-
others must be reconciled with "dying...for". Dying for the
other person is not a characteristic of fundamental ontology
but a characteristic of ethics. For Levinas, it is of paramount
importance to underline that all meaning of death passes
through the death of the other and the care I have in respect
to the "Other"ness.[237] Levinas contends that for "the human,
[...] worry over the death of the other comes before care for
self. The humanness of dying for the other would be the very
meaning of love in its responsibility for one's fellowman and,
perhaps, the primordial inflection of the affective as such"
(ibid., 216).

---

[237] Levinas underlines that putting the self into question and opening the way for
another's alterity is of paramount importance in ethics to realize the meaning
of death: "The epiphany of the Absolutely Other is a face by which the Other
challenges and commands me through his nakedness, through his destitution.
He challenges me from his humility and from his height. He sees but remains
invisible, thus absolving himself from the relation that he enters and remaining
absolute. The absolutely Other is the human Other (*Autrui*). And the putting
into question of the Same by the Other is a summons to respond" (Levinas
1996a, 17).

The Levinasian "dying for" is not only suffering but also sacrifice, love, and self-denial.[238] The priority of being as human being is not to be served as a self-enclosed unit, but to serve. This service is kenotic, non-reciprocal, and asymmetrical.[239] It is a duty and an eternal task from me to the other. Levinas contends that the death of the other is something that is my eternal responsibility and I have to sacrifice myself, to be a hostage, prior to any reservations and presuppositions. By doing this, I am not an autonomous being and yet am free. The "Other" always has "the face of the poor, the stranger, the widow, and the orphan, and, at the same time, of the master called to invest and justify my freedom" (Levinas 1969, 251). Therefore, there is no place for sacrifice in the mineness of being. Considering the above discussion on "dying for",

---

[238] Levinas explains the role of suffering in death and how suffering is connected to death in an ethical way. He contends that "in suffering there is [...] the proximity of death. There is not only the feeling and the knowledge that suffering can end in death. Pain of itself includes it like a paroxysm, as if there were something about to be produced even more rending than suffering, as if despite the entire absence of a dimension of withdrawal that constitutes suffering, it still had some free space for an event, as if it must still get uneasy about something, as if we were on the verge of an event beyond what is revealed to the end in suffering" (Levinas 1987b, 69).

[239] For Levinas, there is not a criterion of morality as a necessary and sufficient condition for counting as a person. Sins, crimes, and bad behavior are nonsense and meaningless for the "face". Levinas explains that his ethical perspective of the other does not infringe religious — especially Jewish — tradition. On the one hand, he does not promote a sinful life, but on the other hand, he insists that sins and crimes do not determine whether someone has a "face" or not. My responsibility regarding the other does not depend on her moral or immoral character (whether, for instance, someone loves her neighbor or shows mercy or kindness to another). Levinas explains that responsibility is asymmetrical and non-reciprocal: "I am in reality the absolute responsible for the other even when he or she commits crimes, even when others commit crimes. This is for me the essence of the Jewish conscience. But I also think that it is the essence of the human conscience: All men are responsible for one another, and I more than anyone else. One of the most important things for me is that asymmetry and that formula: All men are responsible for one another and I more than anyone else" (Levinas 1998a, 107).

Levinas infers that what matters to ethically understand death is neither the "immaculate freedom of Jean-Paul Sartre's for-itself" (Cohen 2006, 28) nor the Heideggerian being-toward-death since both terms are based on an ontological frame.

Levinas concludes that "the relationship to the other in sacrifice, in which the death of the other preoccupies the human *being-there* before his own death, indicate[s] precisely a *beyond* ontology" (McLachlan 2010, 179-196) "– or a *before* ontology – while at the same time also determining – or revealing – a responsibility for the other" (Levinas 1998a, 217). If we further study the notion of kenotic self-denying sacrifice that Levinas suggests, we could infer that there are some similar points in relation to Biblical tradition.[240] The Byzantine

---

[240] This may be related to Christological principles. However, it is better to avoid a direct comparison between Levinas and Christian theology since Levinas insists that his main purpose is to explore the Jewish/Biblical and not the Christian tradition in his philosophical writings.

patristic tradition[241] also pays attention to the kenotic self-denying gesture for the sake of the "Other".[242]

However, Levinas openly raises severe objections to both Heidegger's ontic and ontological[243] consideration of death and Kierkegaard's religious ethics.[244] On the one hand, Levinas criticizes Heidegger's conception of *Dasein*, which

---

[241] The most valuable and comprehensive work concerning kenosis (suffering) in the Byzantine patristic tradition is by N. V. Sakharov, *I Love Therefore I am: the Theological Legacy of Archimandrite Sophrony* (2002, 93-115). See also J.-C. Larchet, "Suffering in Spiritual Life and Teaching of Elder Sophrony (in Greek)" (2007, 455-456). A comparative study of Levinas and the Orthodox patristic tradition on the relation of beings and freedom is by T. A. Ables, "On the Very Idea of an Ontology of Communion: Being, Relation and Freedom in Zizioulas and Levinas" (2011, 676-678). For Levinas's view of suffering, see his chapter "Useless Suffering" in *Entre Nous* (1998a, 91-102; Edelglass 2006, 45-48), where he discusses the notion of suffering along with being and alterity. See also a valuable text on Levinas and kenosis by R. D. N. van Riessen, *Man as a Place of God: Levinas' Hermeneutics of Kenosis* (2007, 101-206), where the author defines and discusses the paramount importance of kenosis in Levinasian thought on ethics and religion in comparison to other philosophical and theological accounts. The terms kenosis and self-emptying sometimes also refer to the God-person relation: for a helpful discussion, see M. L. Baird, "Whose Kenosis? An Analysis of Levinas, Derrida, and Vattimo on God's self-emptying and the Secularization of the West" (2007, 423-437). As Baird correctly points out "Levinas's model of *kenosis*, which he defines (borrowing a Levinas's phrase: 'as subordination of [God's omnipotence] to man's ethical consent" (Levinas 1994b, 126) "is a diachronic and transcendental self-emptying that has no immediate real time analogue" (Baird 2007, 424).

[242] Presumably, Levinas was familiar with the Byzantine theological tradition since in his work *Time and the Other* (1987b, 70, n. 43) he discusses Heidegger's view on death in relation to the Byzantine tradition: Levinas says that "death in Heidegger is not, as Jean Wahl says, the impossibility of possibility, but the possibility of impossibility. This apparently Byzantine distinction has a fundamental importance".

[243] Concerning ontic/ontological definition, especially in Heidegger's *Being and Time*, see C. Guignon, "Heidegger and Kierkegaard on Death: The Existentiell and the Existential" (2011, 186-188).

[244] Not only Levinas, but also Kierkegaard, can be compared to Heidegger's notion of the self in relation to death (ibid., 184-203). In short, Guignon mentions that Heidegger does not accept Kierkegaard as an existential thinker since as a Christian he merely provides an existentiel argument based only on faith and theology. However, according to Guignon, "both thinkers are committed to the idea that the actual termination of life is a crucial aspect of understanding death" (ibid., 194).

pays particular attention to the responsibility for one's own death and not for the death of the "Other". Heidegger, focusing on the ontological perspective of death, insists that what really matters is not the death of the other, who directly threatens me — to the extent that he can kill me — but the ontological reality that "*Dasein* consists of something more than a particular being when it assumes its own death [...] In order to regard *Dasein* ontologically, it is necessary to take 'one's own death' (*der eigene Tod*) into consideration, in an individual and authentic (*eigentlich*) manner. Only in this way can *Dasein* confront its finite nature and discover itself as 'Being-towards-death' (Levadot 2011, 205). Levinas vehemently criticizes the above argument, considering that Heidegger's *Dasein* falsely gives priority to the ego rather than to the other. Isolating subjectivity in one's own death automatically corrals her infinite responsibility into an enclosed egoistic unit: an ontic self that cares only for her own advantage and sees the other as an enemy ready to kill her. Levinas hence contends that Heidegger ignored a very highly esteemed principle of the death of the "Other" in relation to me: "It is for the death of the other that I am responsible to the point of including myself in his death [...] I am responsible for the other in that he is mortal. The death of the other: therein lies the first death" (Levinas 2000, 43). Levinas sees death with its symbolic meaning. The death of the other is not merely the death of a specific someone. He explains:

> "In the death of another, in his face that is exposition to death, it is not the passage from one quiddity to another that is announced; in death is the very event of passing [...] 'he has passed ["*il passe*"]) with its own acuteness that is its scandal [...] We should think of all the murder there is in death: every death is a murder, is premature, and there is the responsibility of the survivor." (Levinas 2000, 72)

194

Thus, in contrast to Heidegger, Levinas underlines the eternal responsibility that I have for the "Other" before any response or calling. God does not force me to be responsible for the death of the other; He just shows me the way through the face and the fate of the other, and it is me who is responsible for fulfilling this ethical responsibility.

Levinas also provides a criticism of Kierkegaard's religious ethics, which for Levinas cannot ethically justify the death of the other. Insisting on faith in a God who is reduced to immanence, according to Levinas, isolates the individual from society through a mystical (or, better, sacred) obedience: "The suffering [religious] truth does not open us out to others, but to God in isolation" (Levinas 1998c, 30). Laura Llevadot provides us with a valuable statement concerning one of the most crucial discrepancies between Kierkegaard and Levinas on the issue of death: "Levinas articulates ethics from the viewpoint of dying for the Other, while in Kierkegaard's interpretation of the biblical passage about Abraham, what is in question [...] is 'killing' the Other in response to a 'superior' request" (Llevadot 2011, 208). This request makes Levinas skeptical about the notion of God in Kierkegaard's thought.[245] For Levinas, in no way can God be understood by humans as a punisher or "butcher" who reduces His essence and infinite attributes in order to perform in a scenario which fits into the human's finite mind. This is why Levinas stresses that "the priority of the Other over the self, even in the

---

[245] Especially concerning the paradigm of Abraham, Levinas interprets it through the order of ethics and not as a matter of blind faith. Mjaaland states that for Levinas "it is precisely in such an understanding of ethics, where one does not spare oneself, but discovers the meaning of existence and finds one's own identity in the encounter with the face of the other, that the religious dimension too becomes visible" (Mjaaland 2008, 109).

extreme case of death, expresses the self's humanity when he responds to the call of the Other: 'here I am' (*me voici*)" (ibid., 207). But the phrase "here I am" expresses no egoistic conditions of the self and indicates no priority of the self over the "Other", but on the contrary, in accusative form, opens the way for the other. It is exactly the same process in the death for the other, where I am responsible for the death of the other and suffer her casualty.

3.9 Kierkegaard on Death[246]

Kierkegaard proved in his works, especially *Works of Love*, *Sickness unto Death*, and *Concluding Unscientific Postscript*, that death is inseparable from existence and thus death must be studied in terms of existence. Kierkegaard adds that self-knowledge is integrated with death, and the more I am concerned about death, the more I am aware of selfhood.[247] As Simon Podmore underlines, "death is the secret 'unknown' that simultaneously holds the key to self-knowledge, and also to the self's own destruction" (Podmore 2011b, 45). Several contemporary Kierkegaardian thinkers have taken two major separate lines of thought about death. On the one hand, immanentists claim that Kierkegaard emphasizes only

---

[246] From my point of view, the most comprehensive study concerning Kierkegaard's notion of death was edited by P. Stokes and A. J. Buben: *Kierkegaard and Death* (2011). It explores several valuable themes from the most renowned Kierkegaardian scholars of the 20th and 21st centuries.

[247] However, as J. Watkin mentions, Kierkegaard understands death through a postmodern existence where he prefers to go back to an ancient/subjective consideration of death. Borrowing a Socratic dialectic of death, Kierkegaard claims that our deeds and actions in this world impact our character in the afterlife. He characterizes the afterlife as eternal life, immortality, resurrection, eternal happiness, etc. For further discussion, see J. Watkin, "Dying and Eternal Life as Paradox", 189–190. However, Socrates, in contrast to Christian faith, rejected resurrection and eternal salvation (Marks 2011, 275).

ontological presuppositions of death, that is, that we live just once as a being-in-the-world, and they reject the claim that there is life after death. A classic example of this line of thought is, of course, Heidegger, who explores a positive response to death that is the end of life and ontology. On the other hand, transcendentalists claim that there is definitely "a higher order of existence" (Watkin 1990, 65) above and beyond the life we live in the cosmos.

Kierkegaard's notion of death is discussed in terms of objective and subjective truth. Death plays a decisive role in the existential line of thought as a truth of reality. On the one hand, several atheist existential thinkers claim that we are merely, as finite beings, "bones and flesh". Death, teleologically speaking, is just the end of organic life, something that must be considered an objective truth[248] without any cause and effect in our subjectivity. On the other hand, Kierkegaard, as a Christian thinker, provides a different dialectic in order to present a subjective truth of death. Before examining the notion of death as it was explored by Kierkegaard, it is worth discussing the significant difference between objective and subjective truth.[249]

Objective truth for Kierkegaard is a necessary but insufficient condition for selfhood as well as for understanding and overcoming the notion of death. Since objective truth is

---

[248] By saying objective truth, as Kierkegaard defines it, we mean a theory "which requires statements to be verified or proven by the facts—judgements, statements or propositions are correct or true only if they factually match the object or situation they are referring to" (Watts 2014, loc. 1423).

[249] A very consistent work concerning modern/objective and ancient/subjective ethics and Kierkegaard's defense of the latter is D. D. Possen's "Death and Ethics in Kierkegaard's Postscript", 122-132. Kierkegaard, through his pseudonym Johannes Climacus, attacks modern/objective ethics in order to defend ancient/subjective ethics exploring several case studies (ibid., 124-127).

based only on a theoretical or factual framework; that is, we can justify something as it is only by explaining it either with epistemic experiment or through physical norms, "the objective approach cancels out or ignores the essential significance of the individual existence" (Watts 2014, loc. 1448) and does not assist us in understanding the real meaning of death. As a Protestant, Kierkegaard alleges that the only person able to know the truth of my existence is myself, and this existential self-knowledge[250] necessarily passes through the direct divine communication between me and God: faith.[251] For

---

[250] Though Kierkegaard rejects epistemological criteria of selfhood and its relation to God, he insists that mind is of immense importance only if it is related to pure heart. In contrast to Orthodox tradition, which gives priority to the self-emptying heart as the starting point of contemplation and communication with God (Sakharov 2002, 166-169), Kierkegaard contends that a collected mind which "has collected itself from every distraction, from every relation, in order to center itself upon this relation to itself as an individual who is responsible to God (Kierkegaard 1956, 215)", must be integrated in self-emptying contemplation. At this point, Levinas would reject both views. For Levinas, human beings are firstly and most importantly responsible to the face of the other, and, in this way, they are indirectly responsible to God as well. As Kierkegaard notes, "purity of heart is to will one thing. Every call from God is always addressed to one person, the single individual" (Kierkegaard 1967-78, I. 100).

[251] This is a quite crucial point for distinguishing Kierkegaard's and Levinas's views as regards the relation between humans and God. For Levinas, God commands me through the face of the other, but it is my responsibility to understand and answer. However, Kierkegaard explores a different approach concerning the man-God relation: I am responsible directly to Him and my responsibility is a matter of faith (Abraham's paradigm); the religious life does not coincide with ethics, which is sometimes absurdity if it is measured by ethical norms. For Levinas "the Self is infinitely responsible when it stands before the Others [...] Subjectivity exists within this responsibility, and only an irreducible subjectivity can take on a responsibility. That is the meaning of the ethical" (Levinas 1998c, 32-33). At this point I would like to express my acknowledgement to M. Dimitrova, who helped me to understand this important difference between Levinas and Kierkegaard's notion of responsibility. M. Mjaaland strongly agrees with Dimitrova's claim by underlining that after Kierkegaard transcends the ethical for the sake of absolute religion—through the violent paradigm of Abraham, which infringes any form of ethics—he (Kierkegaard) exceeds "every human authority". Mjaaland, like Dimitrova, stresses that "according to Levinas, there cannot be any absolute instance outside the human community that can legitimize a break with the ethical. It is rather the other

Kierkegaard, comprehension of oneself is a necessary and sufficient condition to understand our existence and thus to reflect the notion of death. This comprehension, however, is based not on objectively measurable exterior properties, but exists inside me and can be revealed through religious presuppositions that are, for Kierkegaard, Christian ethics and faith.

But how can we escape objective truth since we live in the real world in which all facts are imbued with reality and facticity? As Kierkegaard admits, objective truth is quite useful for speaking about math, science, history, and sociology but is not enough to deal with subjectivity and the way of being. Considering objective arguments, epistemologically or physiologically speaking, we can speak about theories of life, reality, and how things are in the world as it is. As Michael Watts correctly states, the "human being cannot find truth separate from the subjective experience of his own individual existing" (ibid., loc. 1473-1477). Objective truth can answer questions dealing with the facts of our being (subject-object relation) whereas subjective truth answers questions regarding our way of being in terms of our values (subject-subject relation).[252]

---

way around, so that the absolute other – God – only becomes visible in the face of the other, not as immediately present, but hiding himself while leaving a trace in the face of the other" (Mjaaland 2008, 108). In contrast, Kierkegaard insists on a direct absolute relation between the self and God, something that for Levinas is impossible due to human finitude and the human inability to understand God merely through knowledge.

[252] Levinas would partly agree as regards the above argument. On the one hand, he would not raise any objection to the assertion that "objective truth is concerned with the facts of our being" (Watts 2003, 82), that is, ontology. Nor would he have any severe problems with adopting metaphysical ethics, such as values to the search of subjectivity. He would positively view the position that it is impossible to experience our way of being objectively. On the other hand,

Kierkegaard combines subjectivity with inwardness. This point needs to be thoroughly examined since there is a danger of considering Kierkegaard's notions of subjectivity and death as ontological.[253] This inwardness has nothing to do with ontological introspective reflection which emerges from mental and emotional properties. It is not even psychological cognitive states that can be processed with epistemological analytic criteria. Kierkegaard refers to active involvement with one's innermost moral or spiritual commitments (ibid., loc. 1501). However, Kierkegaard's insistence on subjective truth is not as clear as it seems. Active involvement or religious truth cannot be confused with ethical truth. There is a paradox which can only be understood in the inner state of deep silence. Kierkegaard underlines that it is via silence that religious active involvement justifies subjectivity and therefore death as well.

Kierkegaard considers, especially in his later writings, that silence is better understood as religious silence, while

---

he would strongly reject that "the existing individual cannot separate from himself and observe his existing from an outside vantage point" (ibid., loc. 1484-1488) Levinas surely would give immense credit to Kierkegaard's notion of subjectivity, but what really matters in Levinasian ethics is exactly the opposite: "subjective experience is — eternally and without conditions — in the process of becoming through the face of the other. It is the outsider who calls me to subjective truth and not my inner egotic representation.

[253] Levinas, as well as Kierkegaard, takes a similar line as regards the matter of death and the involvement of ontotheology; however, they explore their arguments, as we shall see, within different frameworks. Levinas prefers ethics and Kierkegaard religious faith. Nevertheless, they both raise objections to that Hegelian standpoint which, erroneously, they allege, defends the integration of immanence and transcendence. As J. Watkin correctly puts it, "if the nature order, immanence, is identified with the religious, the actual transcendent, nationality and religion can be equated and God made into the image of man as a 'man-god' so that all theology becomes anthropology [...] Personal immortality is not included in the speculative metaphysical system, while what is called immortality is not what Christians have traditionally understood it" (Watkin 1990, 67-68).

during his early and middle works, silence deals with aesthetics and ethics.[254] The fundamental tone of Kierkegaard's authorship is the communication of silence (Nelson 2006, 83), where it serves as a divine ground of self. Religious silence therefore does not coincide with ethical or aesthetic silence; "a direct encounter with God is possible, which would do without all the vagaries of words" (Shakespeare 2001, 64). For Kierkegaard, silence is the basis of personhood where an individual has the authority to act freely as long as he remains silent and "only the person who can remain essentially silent can speak essentially, can act essentially" (Kierkegaard 1978, 97). Divinity can be achieved by being silent and not through speaking, as God's words are hidden in secrecy. As Johnson states, "this divine silence provides the basis for the religious life for Kierkegaard, which should be characterized by silence rather than talkativeness" (Johnson 2019, 202). Kierkegaard adds that silence is a divine paradox from which the self can escape from social talkativeness in order to open the way for personal communication with God. Therefore, for Kierkegaard, religious silence is a paradox (Taylor 1981, 182).[255]

According to Kierkegaard, true prayer presupposes passionate silence, which is a subjective mood imbued with an "irrational mind". True prayer is before God; it is only if "a human realizes that he stands naked before God that he becomes a fully fledged human being" (Watts 2014, loc. 1741).

---

[254] As C. Johnson argues, "in his early and middle works, Kierkegaard considers silence mostly as an aesthetic and ethical problem, while his later writing deals extensively with the possibility and necessity of religious silence" (Johnson 2019, 200).

[255] Kierkegaard, in contrast to Heidegger's insistence on the fact that death is a compulsory interior to the order of being, "sees death as a paradoxical expression for the fact that human self-understanding is impossible to conform to a question of ontology" (Mjaaland 2008, 100).

Prayer in silence "requires an intensity of inwardness sufficient to sustain belief that is against reason [...] [and] utterly absurd" (ibid., loc. 1652). For Kierkegaard, prayer does not need any icons, depictions, or church commandments. There is not even the need for speaking or communal gathering but for silence: "Prayer is neither speaking nor not speaking but is receptivity, passivity, and waiting on God, which is also true silence or to make thyself nothing, become nothing before God [...] To pray is not merely to be silent but to hear. And so it is; to pray is not to hear oneself speak, but it is to be silent, and to remain silent, to wait, until the man who prays hears God" (Kierkegaard 1940, 322-323).

A characteristic paradigm of Kierkegaard's preference and prophetic "voice of silence" is mentioned in his *Writings* where he opposes people's tragic drama of illusory objective truth in the new technology of postmodern 20th-century societies. It is urgently necessary for us in the present age, Kierkegaard underlines, to "create silence" in order to approach subjective truth which is a necessary and sufficient condition to understand our existence as human beings.

> "Ah, everything is noisy. . . and man, this clever fellow, seems to have become sleepless in order to invent even new instruments to increase noise, to spread noise and insignificance with the greatest possible haste and on the greatest possible scale. Yes, everything is soon turned upside down: communication is indeed soon brought to its lowest point with regard to meaning and simultaneously the means of communication are indeed brought to their highest with regard to speedy and overall circulation for what is publicized with such hot haste and, on the other hand, what has greater circulation than—rubbish! Oh, create silence." (Kierkegaard 1990, 48).

Silence, Kierkegaard states, is the beginning of understanding subjectivity. Language also begins with silence. The more silence there is, the more subjectivity unveils its meaning. As Michael Strawser observes, "silence begins when speech has ended [...] It [silence] is the absolute beginning of the communication of that meaning which is essentially related to existence — ethical-religious meaning; it is the beginning of the word. In other words, silence is the condition of subjectivity and inwardness. It makes possible the internal secret of an individual existence" (Strawser 2006, 56). Kierkegaard advocates a deep silence because God's voice can be heard in it.

> "In observing the present state of the world and life in general, from a Christian point of view one had to say (and from a Christian point of view with complete justification): it is a disease. And if I were a physician and someone asked me 'What do you think should be done?' I would answer, 'The first thing, the unconditional condition for anything to be done, consequently the very first thing that must be done is: create silence, bring about silence [...]'" (Kierkegaard 1976, 46).

Abraham, commanded by God to sacrifice Isaac, remained silent, ready to obey God's commandment until the end. Kierkegaard's principle is not far from this paradigm. Silence is the door opening our relation to God. We can hear the Lord's voice through silence and modesty, but modesty does not mean servitude or passivity. Paradoxically, silence and modesty lead us to eternal communication with God through faith. For Kierkegaard, silence is a main characteristic of divine language. Abraham made a movement of faith through silence because God's commandment presupposed Abraham's acting this way. As Strawser correctly underlines, "silence is clearly a source of enormous powers, the condition for the reception of the word" (ibid., 62).

> "Silence is the condition for cultured conversation between human and human. The more a person has ideality and ideas in silence, the more she will be able even in her daily associations to reproduce her daily life and that of

others in such a way that she seems to be speaking only at a distance even about specific matters [...] The inward orientation of silence is the condition for cultured conversation; chattering is the caricatured externalization of inwardness, and is uncultured" (Kierkegaard 1987, 87)

In contrast to Levinas's otherness, exteriority, and passivity,[256] Kierkegaard, through silence (as a prerequisite of inwardness), intends to develop a model of active interiority which is activated in a secrecy (Mazouji and Jahromi 2019, 12-13) in which "'God calls me,' for it is on that condition that I can call myself or that I am called in secret. God is in me, he is the absolute 'me' or 'self,' he is that structure of invisible interiority that is called, in Kierkegaard's sense, subjectivity" (Derrida 1995, 109).[257] However, Levinas, like Kierkegaard, sometimes makes a special mention of silence in relation to habitation, familiarity, and language.

"The simple living from ... the spontaneous agreeableness of the elements is not yet habitation. But habitation is not yet the transcendence of language. The Other who welcomes in intimacy is not the you [*vous*] of the face that reveals itself in a dimension of height, but precisely the thou [*tu*] of familiarity: a language without teaching, a silent language, an understanding

---

[256] Levinas contends that "responsibility for the other, [that is subjectivity] in its antecedence to my freedom, is a passivity more passive than all passivity" (Levinas 1991, 15), and not actual transcendence, as Kierkegaard alleged.

[257] This is one of the most controversial differences between Levinas and Kierkegaard regarding God. On the one hand, Kierkegaard believes that God has a direct relation to mankind, and He "resides" inside us. We can meet Him through religious faith, particularly through our "isolation" in prayer. God for Kierkegaard is the "absolute me or self". God, Strawser asserts, is "the transcendent source of the self or subjectivity" (Strawser 2006, 64). On the other hand, for Levinas, God is the absolute Other, whose essence and properties cannot be revealed to humans, but we as finite beings are able to see His trace through the face of the other person. "The direct comprehension of God is impossible for a look directed upon him [...] because the relation with infinity respects the total Transcendence of the other without being bewitched by it, and because our possibility of welcoming him in man goes further than the comprehension that thematizes and encompasses its object [...] The Other is the very locus of metaphysical truth, and is indispensable for my relation with God" (Levinas 1969, 78).

without words, an expression in secret [....] In human welcome the language that keeps silence remains an essential possibility" (Levinas 1969, 155-156).

What we need to surpass death, according to Kierkegaard, is the highest subjective truth — (repetition of) faith, necessarily far from the church's stereotype and Hegelian positivism, integrated with (subjective) passion and absurdity.[258]

> "There is no meditation between the individual self and God by priest or by logical system (contra Catholicism and Hegelianism respectively). There is only the individual's own repetition of faith. This repetition of faith is the way the self relates itself to itself and to the power which constituted it, i.e. the repetition of faith is the self [...] We must [therefore] believe by virtue of the absurd [...] Absurdity requires faith that we believe that for God even the impossible is possible, including the forgiveness of the unforgivable" (McDonald 2017, ch. 5).

Of course, if we view death objectively, we are merely flesh and bones. However, it is worth noting that the early Kierkegaard, who started his philosophical accounts giving priority to aesthetics, paid particular attention to the enjoyment of life, as did the Greek philosopher Epicurus. Kierkegaard's aesthetic norm was that "man is meant to be as happy as possible in this life" (Watkin 1990, 68), spending his life in joy, pleasure, and even hedonism. When Kierkegaard "converted" to ethics, he realized that "even life's highest and richest moment of enjoyment is accompanied by death" (ibid., 66) and that "real pleasure consists not in what one takes pleasure in but in the mind. If I had in my service a humble spirit who, when I asked for a glass of water, brought me all the world's most expensive wines nicely blended in a

---

[258] Watts defines absurdity by saying that "the absurd is that the eternal truth has come into existence in time, that God has come into existence, has been born, has grown up etc., has come into existence exactly as an individual human being, indispensable from any other human being" (Watts 2014, loc. 1619-1623).

goblet, I would dismiss him until he learned that the pleasure consists not in what I enjoy but in having my way" (Kierkegaard 2004, ch. 1). It is crucial to understand that Kierkegaard's initial ethics supports the immanentist line of thought, which gives priority to the mind and inwardness.

The crucial moment in Kierkegaard's philosophy was his decision to make a sharp distinction between the immanentist and the transcendentalist lines of thought. He was first dedicated to ethics and then (from Christian ethics) to Christian religion in order to transpose his philosophical aspects in favor of transcendentalism. This confident transition was made when he realized the paramount importance of silence as a transcendental language of faith. Silence is the transcendental tool that gives Kierkegaard the opportunity to apply a non-abstract way of thinking, a leap to faith from which "humans promote their reality as individuals only by constructing a private relationship with the infinite" (Mazouji and Jahromi 2019, 1). In addition, for Kierkegaard, this leap to faith "requires divine assistance — a prior transformation of the individual's nature through God's grace" (Watts 2014, loc. 1627). This is of course rejected by Levinas, who admits that for God as the Absolute it is nonsense to enter the temporal sphere of existence directly. God's essence is unknowable to human beings, and thus it is "banned" for us to meet Him directly face-to-face. However, God gives us the opportunity to find his trace through the face of our neighbor, the meek, the stranger, and the last. It is hence our duty to reflect God's presence in His absence.

Death, thus, for Kierkegaard, is a temporary silence, a paradoxical silence (Mazouji and Tahromi 2019, 11-12) overcoming the objective, rational analysis of knowledge. This, for Kierkegaard, is linked to God's ability to enter the mortality of human existence through silence. Kierkegaard insists that "silence must be maintained in order to constantly be open to God's word" (ibid., 2). Kierkegaard's most noted example of silence was his description of Abraham's decision to sacrifice Isaac in silence. Both Isaac and his mother Sara have no idea about this tragic event since Abraham takes full responsibility, ignoring all universal norms of morality. Abraham chooses to act in silence once he realizes that God's command is a paradox which, however, completely depends on faith. Faith dominates ethical norms in Abraham's mind. The triptych silence-paradox-faith is always integrated in Kierkegaard's Christian dialectics. Understanding how to surpass death, Kierkegaard uses the same Christian dialectic; that is, the "leap of faith" is a necessary and sufficient condition to understand, justify, and surpass death. Kierkegaard, however, did not at first glance take this path in his philosophical writing since, as we discussed above, he initiated his thought through aesthetics, where death is a tragic universal event without metaphysical repercussions.

Kierkegaard also provides us information on how he considers the notion of the self-denying condition in order to see death in a Christian perspective: "Christian love is self-denying love" (Kierkegaard 1949, 43), and "if one concentrates upon but one thought, one must in relation to it consider discovering self-denial, and it is the self-denial which discovers that God exists [...] Still only in self-denial can a man completely recommend love" (Kierkegaard 1995, 292, 293). He also separates the aesthetic notion of love (the poet) that is erotic love and friendship from the Christian kenotic self-denial which is a characteristic of Christian ethics. Kierkegaard gives priority to love as the Gospels explore it in order to understand the meaning of death in relation to our "duty" toward the other. He highlights that what really matters is Christian, not aesthetic, love: "Erotic love and friendship are preferential love [*Forkjerlighed*] and the passion of preferential love; Christian love [*Kjerlighed*] is self-denial's love, for which this *shall* vouches. To deprive these passions of their strength is the confusion. But preferential love's most passionate boundlessness in excluding means to love only one single person; self-denial's boundlessness in giving itself means not to exclude a single one" (Quinn 1998, 357). In contrast to Levinas, Kierkegaard declares that self-denial is related also to death but within a process where "the individual should have an absolute relationship to the absolute [that is God] and a relative one to what is relative [human beings and oneself]" (Watkin 1990, 72-73).

From my point of view, the above discussion of silence as a necessary and sufficient condition of our relation to God, as Kierkegaard expresses it, provides us a clearer picture of how Kierkegaard presents death and its relation to subjectivity through pure faith, something that is not a priority in Levinasian thought. It is worth noting that Derrida (Derrida 1995; idem. 1978, 79-153; Rée and Chamberlain [eds.] 1998, 151-174) endeavors to present a reconciliation between Kierkegaard and Levinas on the issue of death and how Kierkegaard's second ethics must be reexamined in order to justify that he did not try to abandon ethics in favor of Christian religion but to implement it.

Derrida, thoroughly reexamining Kierkegaard's *Fear and Trembling* (Hong [ed.] 1983), claims that Abraham's paradigm of absolute duty to God does not infringe ethics, as Levinas falsely alleges. Derrida believes that Kierkegaard provides us a "second ethics"[259] through his religious ethics in order to explain that he does not intend to abandon ethics but rather to reconcile ethics with religion: "To say that it is a duty to love God means something different from the above, for if this duty is absolute, then the ethical is reduced to the relative. From this it does not follow that the ethical should be invalidated; rather, the ethical receives a completely different expression, a paradoxical expression, such as, for example, that love to God may bring the knight of faith to give his love to the neighbor" (ibid., 70). Of course, Levinas's objection to that statement remains: Levinas on the one hand has no problem with Kierkegaard believing in God, and Abraham faithfully obeying God's "cruel" command: "sacrifice your son to your Lord". On the other hand, Levinas insists that Kierkegaard gives priority to the universal and not to the singular. Levinas would not accept Kierkegaard's "wholly other", which is not even present here and now. The other in Kierkegaard is a universal symbolic "Other", something that is not acceptable for Levinas. What really matters, according to Levinas, is not universal ethics but specifically the face, and

---

[259] L. Llevadot provides a comprehensive answer concerning the difference between first and second ethics, according to Kierkegaard: "Love for the present, the priority of the living over the dead, responsibility toward the real, expresses the submission of the first ethics (which Derrida criticizes) to the logic of interchange. On the other hand, love for one's neighbor, the duty to love the dead, and the duty to love the living as if they were dead (before consideration of any preferences), points to the possibility of a second ethics" (Llevadot 2011, 215).

here, the death of the singular "Other", and not generally the presence in the domain of the masses.

On the one hand, Levinas would agree with Kierkegaard's absence; that is, absolute ethics rejects phenomenality and presence in-the-world, as Heidegger claims with certainty. On the other hand, Levinas would reject silence and the impossibility of speech, since he gives priority to the dialogical process between me and the other, through the saying and not the said. Highlighting the significance of language as a dialogical process of communication and not of silence, Llevadot contends that "the communicative language, which occupies this space in relation to ethics, is not the totalitarian language of ontology, but it is nevertheless the communicative *saying*[260] that condemns the silence of Abraham" (Llevadot 2011, 208).

By developing the theory of second ethics which "has the actuality of sin within its scope" (Kierkegaard 1980, 23), Kierkegaard intends to show, in contrast to Levinas, that what really matters regarding death is not "thou shalt not kill" or "dying for the other", but, as Llevadot states, "the [Kierkegaardian] second ethics revolves around our relationship with the dead, the way we live with the death of the Other" (Llevadot 2011, 212). For Kierkegaard, in loving the dead, we develop a true subjectivity beyond despair where "the extreme opposite of this despair is constituted by faith"

---

[260] Concerning the importance of *saying*, Levinas underlines that "the relationship of responsibility with another signifies as Saying. The Saying, prior to any language that conveys information or content, prior to language as a Said, is exposure to that obligation for which no one can replace me, and which strips the subject right down to his passivity as a hostage. In the Saying, the way in which I appear is an appearing-before or a co-appearing: I am placed in the accusative case [me]" (Levinas 2000, 161).

(ibid., 213). Losing a beloved person or a friend, our subjectivity penetrates the domain of despair where selfhood suffers this casualty. Kierkegaard's second ethics is beyond any objective criteria of "fake" preferential love. This is the reason that Kierkegaard insists on the notion of love-toward-death and not being-toward-death, as Heidegger claims. Kierkegaard says: "Write! For whom? For the dead, for those whom you have loved, in the past, and in loving them I shall also meet together with the dearest my contemporaries" (Kierkegaard 1995, 292). This "shall" plays a decisive role in Kierkegaard's thought about death (Llevadot 2011, 213).

CONCLUSION

In this study I have tried to explore a vital element which is found in Levinas and Kierkegaard: a philosophical response beyond fundamental ontology and reason. Our consideration of ourselves, subjectivity, and God goes beyond the analytical subject. Metaphysical arguments which have been explored by empiricists, idealists, and experimental thinkers in analytic philosophy are — from my point of view — incapable of justifying the so-called "total being" of Hegelian and post-Hegelian philosophy. For instance, according to Levinas and Kierkegaard, Locke's empirical understanding of being, Copernicus's and Laplace's quantum mechanics, Descartes's insistence on an ideal *cogito* which is seen and reflected only through oneself, Hegel's totality and recollection, and Heidegger's *Dasein*, as well as Husserl's *noetic* and *noematic* phenomenology, lack an essential ethical presupposition: infinity.

The subject is in doubt once it returns to itself. On the one hand, Levinas proposes, as is discussed in the main body of this study, biblical[261] and not experimental evidence to discuss subjectivity, which can be justified only by prioritizing the "Other" and not the self. Levinas vehemently opposes the total enforcement of the I. It is the other who always comes first. There is an intersubjective dissymmetry that is mistakenly avoided in analytical philosophy. Whereas the analytic

---

[261] Levinas's biblical notion of God, subjectivity, and selfhood must be interpreted on the basis of ethics and not through positive or apophatic theology. It is ethics that shows us the way to understand ourselves and God's trace in the world and not theology.

line of thought provides autonomy, Levinas speaks about heteronomy, and where the former insists on totality of the self, Levinas asserts vulnerability: "Only a vulnerable *I* can love his neighbor" (Levinas 1998b, 91).[262] For Levinas, what matters is not the priority of the I in relation to the other, but the priority of the other in relation to me without any absorption. For Levinas, we need to dramatically reverse the traditional hierarchy "where the self takes precedence over the other" (Casey 2003, 384) by introducing the idea of the infinite beyond the subject and the world.

On the other hand, Kierkegaard, even if he started his philosophical thought by passing from aesthetics το ethics, finally argued that it is only through personal religious faith that one can meet God. Kierkegaard's philosophical thought about subjectivity ends up not far from Levinas's selfhood. He rejects any epistemological and experimental accounts of personhood and insists that psychological and ontological criteria are not enough to speak about ourselves. However, his main difference regarding selfhood and subjectivity is that we need ourselves more than the other. Like Levinas, Kierkegaard asserts that we ought to be moral persons, but this morality does not depend on others but on us. Subjectivity is something that starts from the inner part of my relation between me and God, and God is the main mediator between me and the other. Moreover, according to Kierkegaard, God's instrument to approach the other is love, but love also is an

---

[262] Specifically, Levinas states that "the Bible [and not any experimental cognitive evidence] is the priority of the Other in relation to me. It is in another that I always see the widow and the orphan. The other always comes first. This is what I have called [...] the dissymmetry of interpersonal relationship [...] and this is vulnerability. Only a vulnerable I can love his neighbor" (Levinas 1998b, 91).

instrument of myself which increases through a personal direct relation between me and God through honest prayer.

Both thinkers pay particular attention to the idea and the ideal of infinity, which plays a decisive role in understanding their philosophical accounts of God and selfhood. As is mentioned in the bulk of this research, Levinas, even if he derives several ideas from his mentor, Husserl, then admits that infinity is not understood as a denial of the finite. The phenomenological process of *noesis* and *noema*, as Husserl claimed, is not enough to explain infinity. Levinas points out that even though Husserl was the principal founder of phenomenology and the first thinker of understanding being *qua* being by integrating psychology and cognitive studies with philosophy, he was incapable of expressing the major importance of the alterity of the "Other" because he focused only on knowledge and experience while ignoring the significant role of ethics. Levinas attempted to go further by proposing, in contrast to Husserl, that infinity is "an idea signifying with a significance prior to presence, to all presence, prior to every origin in consciousness, and so an-archic, accessible only in its trace" (Levinas 1998b, 64). Thus, Levinas infers that infinity is an idea above and beyond consciousness, something that cannot be integrated into a totality. The structure of the idea of infinity appears in its exteriority, which is quite crucial in Levinasian thought because it confines the intentional apprehension of consciousness to return to itself, which is ontology. Infinity extends subjectivity and consciousness as well as surpassing recollection and memory. A nonspatial immemorial dimension breaks up the dogmatic presuppositions of consciousness.[263] It is thus for Levinas something other than intentionality that matters, the alterity of the "Other". It is not enough to speak about the transcendence of the ego's consciousness. Levinas is not interested in applying intentional criteria to describe infinity since "the experience of infinity is not the consciousness of something" (Casey 2003, 390).

Levinas insists that infinity echoes as a humility[264] in which any ontological reduction is unacceptable, especially in God. Infinity is not a concept that belongs to knowledge but to ethics. Thus, we cannot speak about the idea of infinity without ethics. It is worth mentioning that Levinas draws from Kierkegaard's notion of the other to explore infinity; apart from their different starting points, that is, the former is Jewish and other-centered and the latter is Protestant and God-centered, we can note several similarities. For instance, they both raise objections to the functional utility of *conatus essendi*, which mistakenly puts the self first. Thus, both Kierkegaard's idea of God and Levinas's idea of infinity do not

---

[263] Levinas underlines that "in thinking infinity the *I* from the first *thinks more than it thinks*. Infinity does not enter into the idea of infinity, is not grasped; this idea is not a concept. The infinite is the radically, absolutely, other. The transcendence of infinity with respect to the ego that is separated from it and thinks it constitutes the first mark of its infinitude [...] The thinker who has the idea of infinity *is more than himself*, and this inflating, this surplus, does not come from within, as in the celebrated project of modern philosophers, in which the subject surpasses himself by creating" (Levinas 1987a, 54).

[264] By humility Levinas means the opposition of absolute knowledge which lies in reason. Reason, according to Levinas, intends to absorb mystery and intuition. Presumably influenced by Herbert Marcuse's works *One-Dimensional Man* (2006) and *Eros and Civilization* (1974), Levinas denies reason's hostility to humility and vulnerability. He argues, like Marcuse, that reason must cooperate with humility by accepting its inability to understand everything. Decentering thus the subject from its own substance, we open a new ethical horizon for the self to move beyond rationality. The industrial new world order and its manifestation in mass production inevitably absorbed human's multidimensional capabilities in an isolated enclosed unit, creating a one-dimensional self focused only on the totality of her own self.

depend on rational exegesis. They both challenge consciousness by providing the role of the "Other". Unreasonableness hence transcends consciousness and reason to a different way of thinking that is metaphysical ethics.

For both thinkers, desire is the starting point to reflect the notion of infinity: "Desire is the means to access the infinite" (Casey 2003, 395). We can reflect metaphysics by only adopting desire as a way of abandoning the realm of theory and epistemology. We also need to get rid of the presuppositions of ontology that begins with the self, seeks the self, and returns to the self. On the other hand, metaphysical ethics seeks the "Other" beyond history and never returns to the same. Levinas and Kierkegaard, both anti-Hegelians, assert that the totality of consciousness and negation[265] cannot explain infinity. Levinas's conception of infinity beyond reason and consciousness is revealed by Derrida, who points out that "for Levinas, on the contrary, desire is the respect and knowledge of the *other as other*, the ethico-metaphysical moment whose transgression consciousness must forbid itself"

---

[265]   Negativity, as Levinas alleges, is an ontological term which surfaces only egoitic repercussions. For instance, Derrida refers that for Levinas "the work of identification and the concrete production of egoity, it entails a certain negativity. A finite negativity, an internal and relative modification through which the ego affects itself by itself, within its own movement of identification. Thus, it alters itself toward itself within itself The resistance to work, by provoking it, remains a moment of the same, a finite moment that forms a system and a totality with the agent" (Derrida 1978, 116). Hegelian negation is at present. Levinas intends to surpass this procedure by introducing otherness and closeness of ethics beyond history. Levinas proposes that negativity must be overcome; the status of totality and ontology encounter not only the *cogito* of the ego as an isolated self-enclosed unit, but the other as well. Derrida adds that for Levinas "if negativity (work, history, etc.) never has a relation to the other, if the other is not the simple negation of the same, then neither separation nor metaphysical transcendence can be conceived under the category of negativity. Just as [...] other, so the ego cannot engender alterity within itself without encountering the Other" (ibid., 117).

(Derrida 1978, 115). Levinas draws from Kierkegaard's work *Fear and Trembling*, claiming that "the movement of desire can be what it is only paradoxically, as the renunciation of desire" (ibid., 115). For Kierkegaard desire is a religious term while for Levinas it is an ethical term. This is one of the most important differences between them regarding metaphysics. However, we can assert that Levinas would have no objection to desire as a religious term meaning "the surplus possible in a society of equals, that of glorious humility, responsibility and sacrifice, which are the condition for equality itself" (Levinas 1969, 64).

Furthermore, Kierkegaard and Levinas also agree that the way of being cannot be harmonized with Odyssey's aim of returning to Ithaca. The self must recognize its humility in order to accept that its subjectivity depends on the other first and then itself. It is through the eschatology of the other that I am called as a subject. By decentering the subject, the I can find herself through the face of the other. At this point, Kierkegaard distinguishes the priority of religion over ethics by claiming that there is need first to "sign a religious contract between me and God" in which the self must start with faith and a direct relation to God and then seek the other. In contrast, Levinas contends that it is our duty to understand what God wants for us through his traces: the other human who waits for me to make the first step towards him. For Levinas there is no land occupied by me. There is no desire without the desire of the other. Every metaphysical notion of the beyond depends on the face of the other and her demand for relation with her, even the most wretched and the meekest.

Levinas explains that infinity (no matter how it is construed, Levinasian ethics or metaphysical ethics) is not a field of knowledge which can define the epistemological implications assimilated by the subject, but rather "it is absolute alterity, complete heterogeneity with respect to the order of the same; it elevates consciousness so that a new awareness gives birth which leads to a new way of being, a humility before immeasurable immensity. If the infinity of the infinite could be measured, it would be measurable through desire [and not reason] [...] According to Levinas the inordinateness measured by desire is the face" (Casey 2003, 397).

Kierkegaard, though he supports the idea of infinity against reason, prefers to develop his arguments in favor of religion rather than ethics. For instance, he insists that infinity is inseparable from divinity and that Christianity is integrated with infinity. He infers that infinity comes to the mind through prayer and the direct relation to God first and not through the face of the other. Thus, God is the mediator between me and the other. Personal contemplation through faith is a necessary condition of getting to know myself, but this procedure does not depend on established criteria like those of the Western church and the historicity of religion. It mostly depends on subjective realism, that is, the experience of divinity.

Both thinkers try to define subjectivity beyond any causal effects such as apprehension and individualism. Subjectivity echoes to infinity beyond reason. Outside being, subjectivity abandons egoism, and it becomes goodness. Goodness is relevant to desire as a non-desire, which means that I must not seek desire for the sake of materialism, that is, due to utilitarian repercussions, but rather focus on ethical and (not ontological) transcendence. We need to transcend thinking as well as Hegelian self-consciousness of the subject, detaching the ego from its own self-interest for the sake of the face of the other. Finally, as Levinas infers, "the face of the Other at each moment destroys and overflows the plastic image it leaves me, the idea existing to my own measure and to the measure of its *ideatum* [...] It does not manifest itself by these qualities [...] It *expresses itself*. The face brings a notion of truth which, in contradistinction to contemporary ontology, is not the disclosure of an impersonal *Neuter*, but *expression*" (Levinas 1969, 50-51).

BIBLIOGRAPHY OF WORKS CITED

Ables, T. A. 2011. "On the Very Idea of an Ontology of Communion: Being, Relation and Freedom in Zizioulas and Levinas", *The Heythrop Journal* 52: 672-683.

Adams, R. M. 1977. "Kierkegaard's Arguments Against Objective Reasoning in Religion", *The Monist* 60(2): 228-243.

Adorno, T. 1989. *Kierkegaard: Construction of the Aesthetic*, translated by R. Hullot-Kentor, Minneapolis: University of Minnesota Press.

Ahbel-Rappe S. and Kamtekar R. (eds.). 2006. *A Companion to Socrates*, Oxford: Blackwell.

Alford, H. (ed.) 1839. *John Donne: The Works of John Donne*, volume 3, London: John W. Parker,

Allen, P. and Neil, B. 2002. *Maximus the Confessor and His Companions: Documents from Exile*, Oxford: Oxford University Press.

Anton, J. and Preus, A. (eds.). 1992. *Essays in Ancient Greek Philosophy*, 4 volumes, New York: State of University of New York Press.

Aristotle 2008. *Φυσικά*, Books III-IV, translated by V. Betsakos, Thessaloniki: Zitros.

Aristotle 2006. *Nicomachean Ethics*, (in Greek), volumes 1-4, Thessaloniki: Zitros.

Aristotle. 2006. *Physics*, Books 1-VIII, translated by R.P. Hardie and R.K. Gaye, London: Neeland Media.

Aristotle. 1995. *Politics*, Books I-II, translated by T.J. Saunders, Oxford: Clarendon Press.

Aronoff, G. L. 2010. *Guilt, Persecution and Atonement: Moral Responsibility in Loewald and Lévinas*, unpublished Ph. D. thesis, Concordia University.

Atterton, P. 2004. "Face-to-Face with the Other Animal?" in P. Atterton, M. Calarco and M. Friedman (eds.) *Levinas and Buber: Dialogue and Difference*, Pittsburgh: Duquesne University Press, 262-81.

Augustine. 1987. *Confessions*, translated by R.S. Pine-Coffin, New York: Penguin.

Augustine. 1984. *City of God*, translated by H. Bettenson, New York: Penguin.

Baird, M. L. 2007. "Whose Kenosis? An Analysis of Levinas, Derrida, and Vattimo on God's self-emptying and the Secularization of the West", *The Heythrop Journal* 48: 423-437.

Bajzek, B. 2016. "Intersubjectivity, Illeity and Being-in-love: Lonergan and Levinas on Self-Transcendence", *The Heythrop Journal* 57: 1-11.

Baracat Jr, J.C. 2017. "Ennead IV.7: On the Immortality of Soul", *The International Journal of the Platonic Tradition* 11: 205-245.

Barber, M. D. 2008. Autonomy, "Reciprocity and Responsibility: Darwall and Levinas on the Second Person", *International Journal of Philosophical Studies* 16(5), 629-644.

Bataille, G. 1962. *Eroticism*, translated by M. Dalwood, London and New York: Marion Boyars.

Baumann, Z. 1993. *Postmodern Ethics*, Cambridge: Blackwell.

Bayer, T. I. 2014. "Socrates' Profession", *Sophia Philosophical Review* 8(2): 83-95.

Bergo, B. 2005. "What Is Levinas Doing? Phenomenology and the Rhetoric of an Ethical Un-Conscious", *Philosophy and Rhetoric* 38(2): 122-144.

Bergo, B. 1999. *Levinas between Ethics and Politics: For the Beauty that Adorns the Earth*, Springer- Kluwer Academic Publishers, Dordrecht.

Bernasconi, R. 2000. "The Alterity of the Stranger and the Experience of the Alien", in J. Bloechl (ed.) *The Face of the Other and the Trace of God*, New York: Fordham University Press, 62-89.

Bernasconi, R. 1998. "Different Styles of Eschatology: Derrida's Take on Levinas' Political Messianism", *Research in Phenomenology* 28(1), 3-19.

Bernasconi, R. 1995. "'Only the Persecuted': Language of the Oppressor, Language of the Oppressed," in A. Peperzak (ed.) *Ethics as First Philosophy: The Significance of Emmanuel Levinas for Philosophy, Literature and Religion*, London: Routledge, 77-86.

Bernasconi, R. 1988. "Levinas: Philosophy and Beyond" in H. J. Silveiman (ed.) *Philosophy and Non-Philosophy since Merleau-Ponty*, London and New York: Routledge, 232-58.

Bernasconi, R. 1986. "Levinas and Derrida: The Question of the Closure of Metaphysics" in R.A. Cohen (ed.) *Face to Face with Levinas*, New York: State University of New York Press, 181-202.

Bernasconi, R. 1985. "The Trace of Levinas in Derrida" in D. Wood and R. Bernasconi (eds.) *Derrida and Difference*, Warwick: Parousia Press, 17-44.

Bernasconi, R. and Wood, D. (eds.). 1988. *The Provocation of Levinas: Rethinking the Other*, London-New York: Routledge.

Bernet, R. 2004. "Levinas Critique on Husserl", in S. Critchley and R. Bernasconi (eds.) *The Cambridge Companion to Levinas*, Cambridge: Cambridge University Press, 82-99.

Bernet, R. 2000. "The Encounter with the Stranger: Two Interpretations of the Vulnerability of the Skin", in J. Bloechl (ed.) *The Face of the Other and the Trace of God*, New York: Fordham University Press, 43-61.

Berry, W. W. 1981. "Kierkegaard's Existential Dialectic: The Temporal Becoming of the Self", *Journal of Religious Thought* 38: 20–41.

Bettina, B. 2005. "Ontology, Transcendence, and Immanence in Emmanuel Levinas' Philosophy", *Research in Phenomenology* 35: 141-180.

Bloechl, J. 2000. "Ethics as First Philosophy and Religion", in J. Bloechl (ed.) *The Face of the Other and the Trace of God: Essays on the Philosophy of Emmanuel Levinas*, New York: Fordham University Press, 130-164.

Boothroyd, D. 2011. "Off the Record: Levinas, Derrida and the Secret of Responsibility", *Theory Culture and Society* 28, 41-59.

Braine, D. 2019. "Negative theology", in *Routledge Encyclopedia of Philosophy*, London: Taylor and Francis.

Brothers, R. 1999. "Ethics of Ethics, Law of Laws: Kierkegaard, Levinas and the Aporia of Substantive Identity", *Sophia 38(2)*: 54-68.

Bruns, G. L. 2004. "On the Coherence of Hermeneutics and Ethics: An Essay on Gadamer and Levinas", in Krajewski, B. (ed.) *Gadamer's Repercussions: Reconsidering Philosophical Hermeneutics*, California: California University Press, 30-54.

Bryson, K. A. 2017. "The Ways of Spirituality", *Sophia Philosophical Review* 10(2): 5-37.

Buben, A. 2011. "Christian Hate: Death, Dying, and Reason in Pascal and Kierkegaard", in P. Stokes, and A.J. Buben (eds.), *Kierkegaard and Death*, Bloomington and Indianapolis: Indiana University Press, 65-80.

Buber, M. 1968. "Dialogue", in *Between Man and Man*, translated by R.G. Smith, New York: Macmillan, 1-45.

Bukdahl, J. 2001. *Søren Kierkegaard and the Common Man*, Grand Rapids: Eerdmans Publishing.

Busch, T. W. 1992. "Ethics and Ontology: Levinas and Merleau-Ponty", *Man and World* 25: 195-202.

Bussanich, J. 1996. "Plotinus's Metaphysics of the One", in L.P. Gerson (ed.) *The Cambridge Companion to Plotinus*, Cambridge: Cambridge University Press, 38-65.

Caputo, J. 2007. *How to read Kierkegaard*, New York and London: W.W. Norton.

Caputo, J. 2000. "Adieu-sans Dieu: Derrida and Levinas", in J. Bloechl (ed.) *The Face of the Other and the Trace of God*, New York: Fordham University Press, 276-312.

Caruana, J. 2007. "The Drama of Being: Levinas and the History of Philosophy", *Continental Philosophical Review* 40: 251-273.

Caruana, J. 2006. "'Not Ethics, Not Ethics Alone, but the Holy': Levinas on Ethics and Holiness", *The Journal of Religious Ethics* 34(4): 561-583.

Caruana, J. 2002 "Levinas's Critique of the Sacred", *International Philosophical Quarterly* 42(4): 519–34.

Casey, T. G. 2003. "Levinas' Idea of the Infinite and the Priority of the Other", *Gregoriarum* 84(2): 383-417.

Chalier, C. 2004. "Levinas and the Talmud", in S. Critchley and R. Bernasconi (eds.) *The Cambridge Companion to Levinas*, Cambridge: Cambridge University Press, 100-118.

Chappell, T. S-G. 2013. "Knowledge of Persons", *European Journal for Philosophy of Religion* 5(4): 31-56.

Chappell T. S-G. 2012. "The Goods and the Persons They Are Goods For", *Philosophical News* 5: 1-70

Chappell, T. S-G. 2011. "On the Very Idea of Criteria of Personhood", *The Southern Journal of Philosophy* 49(1): 1-27.

Christensen, C.B. 2008. *Self and World: From Analytic Philosophy to Phenomenology*, Berlin-New York: Walter de Gruyter.

Churchland, P. M. 1999. *Matter and Consciousness: A Contemporary Introduction to the Philosophy of Mind*, Massachusetts: MIT Press.

Cicero, M. T. 2005. *Tusculan Disputations: On the Nature of Gods and on Commonwealth*, translated by C.D. Yonge, New York: Cosimo Classics.

Clair, A. 1976. *Pseudonymie Et Paradoxe: La Pensee Dialectique De Kierkegaard*, Paris: J. Vrin.

Coe, C. D. 2018. *Levinas and the Trauma of Responsibility: The Ethical Significance of Time*, Indianapolis: Indiana University Press.

Cohen, J. 2012. "Levinas and the Problem of Phenomenology", *International Journal of Philosophical Studies* 20(3): 363-374.

Cohen, R. A. 2006. "Levinas: thinking least about death—contra Heidegger", *International Journal of Philosophy of Religion* 60: 21-39.

Corrigan, K. 1996. "Essence and Existence in the Enneads", in L.P. Gerson (ed.), *The Cambridge Companion to Plotinus*, Cambridge: Cambridge University Press, 105-129.

Costello, P. 2014. "Towards a Phenomenology of Religion Across the Limits of Reason Alone", *Sophia Philosophical Review* 8.2: 106-126.

Courtney, D. F. 2014. "The Teleology of Freedom: The Structure of Moral Self-Consciousness in the Analytic", in *The Teleology of Reason: A Study of the Structure of Kant's Critical Philosophy*, Berlin: De Gruyter, 248-291.

Critchley S. 2004. "Introduction", in S. Critchley and R. Bernasconi (eds.) *The Cambridge Companion to Levinas*, Cambridge: Cambridge University Press, 2004, 1-32.

Crowell, S. 2012. "Why is Ethics First Philosophy? Levinas in Phenomenological Context", *European Journal of Philosophy* 23(3): 1-25.

Dalton, S., 2001. "Kierkegaard's Repetition as a Comedy in Two Acts", *James Head* 4(2): 1-18.

Davenport, J. 2012. *Narrative Identity and Autonomy: from Frankfurt and MacIntyre to Kierkegaard*, New York and Abingdon: Taylor and Francis.

Davenport, J. 2001. Alastair MacIntyre, Philip Quinn, Anthony Rudd, (eds.), *Kierkegaard After MacIntyre: Essays on Freedom, Narrative and Virtue*, Peru, Ill. Open Court Publishing.

De Witt, N. W. 1954. *Epicurus and his Philosophy,* Minneapolis: University of Minnesota.

Demirel, E., "The Subject-Matter: The Subject", *Sophia Philosophical Review XII.1* (2019), pp. 75-98.

Derrida, J. 1999. *Adieu: To Emmanuel Levinas*, translated by P-A., Brault and M. Naas. Stanford: Stanford University Press.

Derrida, J. 1998. "Whom to Give to (Knowing Not to Know)," in J. Rée and J. Chamberlain (eds.) *Kierkegaard: A Critical Reader*, translated by D. Wills, Oxford: Blackwell, 151-174.

Derrida, J. 1995. *The Gift of Death*, translated by D. Wills, Chicago: Chicago University Press.

Derrida, J. 1978. *Writing and Difference*, translated by A. Bass, Chicago: The University of Chicago Press.

Derrida, J. and Ferraris, M. 2001. *A Taste for the Secret*, translated by G. Donis, Cambridge: Polity Press.

Derrida, J. and Vattimo, G. (eds.). 1998. *Religion*, Cambridge: Polity Press.

Descartes R. 1644. *Principia Philosophiae*, Amsterdam: Louis Elzevir.

Dimitrova, M. & Pietrzak P. 2018. "Interview with Maria Dimitrova on Emmanuel Levinas's Philosophy", *In Statu Nascendi* 1(1): 181-189.

Dimitrova, M. 2016. *Sociality and Justice*, Stuttgart: Ibidem-Verlag.

Dimitrova, M. 2013a. "Responsibility and Justice: Beyond Moral Egalitarianism and Rational Consensus", *Sophia Philosophical Review* 7(1): 5-11.

Dimitrova, M. 2013b. "The Language of Dialectics", *Sophia Philosophical Review* 7.2: 89-94.

Dimitrova, M. 2011. *In Levinas' Trace*, Cambridge: Cambridge Scholars Publishing.

Dimitrova M. 2009. "Levinas' Outrageousness as a Grotesque: in Response to Jacob Rogozinski", *Sofia Philosophical Review* 3.2: 50-57.

Dimitrova M. 2006. "Levinas: How to Think *Humanitas* of *Homo Humanus?*", *Sofia Philosophical Review*, 1(1): 15-29.

Dooley, M. 2001. *The Politics of Exodus: Kierkegaard's ethics of responsibility*, New York: Fordham University Press.

Dostoevsky, F. 1970. *The Brothers Karamazov*, translated by A.R. MacAndrew, New York: Bantam.

Dowden, B. 2009. *The Metaphysics of Time: A Dialogue*, Rowman & Littlefield Publishers, Inc.

Dowden, B. "Time", in B. Dowden, and J. Feiser (eds.) *Internet Encyclopedia of Philosophy*, ISSN 2161-0002, https://www.iep.utm.edu/17/06/2020.

Dreyfus, H. L. 2012. "'What a monster then is man": Pascal and Kierkegaard on being a contradictory self and what to do about it", in S. Crowell (ed.) *Cambridge Companion to Existentialism*, Cambridge: Cambridge University Press, 96-110.

Dreyfus, H. L., "Kierkegaard on the Self", in E.F. Mooney (ed.) *Ethics, Love and Faith in Kierkegaard: Philosophical Engagements*, Bloomington and Indianapolis: Indiana University Press, 2008, pp. 11-23.

Drossev, D. 2012. "The Grotesque "I" before the Face of the Other: The Eschatology of the Grotesque", *Sophia Philosophical Review 6(I)*: 56-65.

Dunne, J. 1993. *Back to the Rough Ground: 'Phronesis' and 'Techne' in Modern Philosophy and Aristotle*, Notre Dame: University of Notre Dame Press.

Dunning, S. 1985. *Kierkegaard's Dialectic of Inwardness*, Princeton: Princeton University Press.

Edelglass, W. 2006. "Levinas on Suffering and Compassion", *Sophia* 45.2: 43-59.

Epicurus. 1957 "Letter to Menoekeus", tr. C. Bailey, in W.J. Oates (eds.) *The Stoic and Epicurean Philosophers*, New York: Modern Library, 1957.

Eskin, M. 2000. "A language before words: Levinas's ethics as a semiotic problem", *Semiotica* 129(1): 29-49.

Evans, C. S. 2006. *Kierkegaard: on Faith and the Self*, Texas: Baylor University Press.

Evans, C. S. 2004. *Kierkegaard's Ethic of Love: Divine Commands and Moral Requirements*, Oxford: Oxford University Press.

Fagenblat, M. 2002. "*Il y a* du quotidien: Levinas and Heidegger on the self", *Philosophy and Social Criticism* 28.5: 578-604.

Ferreira, M. J. 2001. *Love's Grateful Striving: A Commentary on Kierkegaard's Works of Love*, Oxford: Oxford University Press.

Ferreira, M. J. 1998. "Faith and the Kierkegaardian Leap", in A. Hannay and G. Marino (eds.), *The Cambridge Companion to Kierkegaard*, New York: Cambridge University Press, 207-234.

Ferro, F. 2012. "Beyond subjectivity: Levinas, Kierkegaard and the absolute other", *Nordicum-Mediterraneum* 7(1): 26-51.

Fink, H. 2000. "From the Aesthetic to the Ethical: A Kierkegaardian Reading of Blok's "Neznakomka", *The Slavic and East European Journal* 44.1: 79-91.

Flyvbjerg B. 1993. "Aristotle, Foucault and Progressive Phronesis: Outline of an Applied Ethics for Sustainable Development" in E. R. Winkler and J. R. Coombs (eds.), *Applied Ethics: A Reader*, Massachusetts: Blackwell, 11-27.

Fowler, H. W. 1965. *A Dictionary of Modern English Usage*, Oxford: Oxford University Press.

Fox-Muraton, M. 2012. "Election or the Individual? Levinas on Kierkegaard's Challenges to Judaism", *Kierkegaard Studies* 1: 367-386.

Franck, D. 2000. "The Body of Difference", in J. Bloechl (ed.) *The Face of the Other and the Trace of God*, New York: Fordham University Press, 3-29.

Frank, J. 2002. *Dostoevsky: The Mantle of the Prophet, 1871-1881*, Princeton: Princeton University Press.

Frankfurt H. 1971. "Freedom of the Will and the Concept of a Person", *Journal of Philosophy* 1: 5-20.

Gadamer, H-G. 1998. "Culture and the World," in H-G. Gadamer, *Praise of Theory: Speeches and Essays*, translated by C. Dawson, Yale University: New Haven.

Gallagher, M. 1968. "Wittgenstein's Admiration for Kierkegaard", *The Month* 39: 43-49.

Gardiner, M. 1996. "Alterity and Ethics: A Dialogical Perspective", *Theory, Culture and Society* 13(2): 121-43.

Goodman, L. E. 1996. *God of Abraham*, New York and Oxford: Oxford University Press, 1996.

Grimsley, R. 1966. *Søren Kierkegaard and French Literature: Eight Comparative Studies*, Cardiff: University of Wales Press.

Grøn, A. 2008. *The Concept of Anxiety in Søren Kierkegaard*, translated by J.B.L. Knox, Macon: Mercer University Press.

Grondin, J. 2012. *Introduction to Metaphysics: from Parmenides to Levinas*, translated by L. Soderstrom, New York: Columbia University Press.

Gschwandtner, C. M. 2007. "The neighbor and the infinite: Marion and Levinas on the encounter between self, human other, and God", *Continental Philosophical Review* 40: 231-249.

Guenther, L. 2009. "'Nameless Singularity': Levinas on Individuation and Ethical Singularity", *Epoché* 14(1): 167-187.

Guignon, C. 2011. "Heidegger and Kierkegaard on Death: The Existentiell and the Existential", in P. Stokes, and A.J. Buben (eds.), *Kierkegaard and Death*, Bloomington and Indianapolis: Indiana University Press, 184-203.

Hall, R. L., *Word and Spirit: A Kierkegaardian Critique of the Modern Age*, Bloomington: Indiana University Press, 1993.

Halteman, M. 2019. "Ontotheology", in *Routledge Encyclopedia of Philosophy*, London: Taylor and Francis.

Hamilton, C. 1998. "Kierkegaard on Truth as Subjectivity: Christianity, Ethics and Asceticism," *Religious Studies* 34: 61–79.

Hand, S. (ed.). 1989. *The Levinas Reader*, Oxford: Basil Blackwell.

Hanlon, S. 2009. *Levinas Singularity and the Restless Subject*, unpublished PhD Dissertation, Ontario: McMaster University.

Hannay A. 1982. *Kierkegaard: The Arguments of the Philosophers*, London: Routledge and Kegan Paul.

Hansel, J. 1999. "Utopia and Reality: The Concept of Sanctity in Kant and Levinas", *Philosophy Today* 43(2): 168–75.

Harris, J. 1985. *The value of life*, London: Routledge, 1985.

Hegel, G. W. F. 1979. *Phenomenology of Spirit*, translated by A. Miller, Oxford: Oxford University Press.

Heidegger, M. 1962. *Being and Time*, translated by J. Macquarrie and E. Robinson. Oxford: Basil Blackwell.

Heidegger, M. 1978. "Letter on Humanism", in *Basic Writings: Nine Key Essays, plus the Introduction to Being and Time*, translated by D. Farrell Krell, London: Routledge.

Heng, W. 2008. "Levinas' Phenomenology of Sensibility and Time in His Early Period", *Journal of Chinese Philosophy* 35: 105-121.

Hirst, B. A. 2014. "After Levinas: Assessing Zygmunt Bauman's 'ethical turn'", *European Journal of Social Theory* 17(2): 184-198.

Hodge, J. 1995. *Heidegger and Ethics*, London: Routledge.

Höffding, H. 1923. "Pascal and Kierkegaard", *Revue de Métaphysique et de Morale* 30.2: 221-246.

Hofmeyr, B. 2005. *Ethics and Aesthetics in Foucault and Levinas*, Nijmegen: Print Partners Ipskamp.

Holquist, M. 1977. *Dostoevsky and the Novel*, Princeton: Princeton University Press.

Hollander, L. M. (ed.). 1960. *Selections from the Writings of Kierkegaard*, New York: Doubleday.

Hong, H. V. and Hong, E. H. (eds.). 2000. *The Essential Kierkegaard*, Princeton: Princeton University Press.

Husserl, E. 1931. *Ideas: General Introduction to Pure Phenomenology*, translated by W.R.B. Dixon, London: George Allen and Unwin.

Hurst, A. 2000. "Kierkegaard, Levinas and the Question of Escaping Metaphysics", *South African Journal of Philosophy* 19(3): 168-187.

Jackson, T. 1998. "Arminian edification: Kierkegaard on grace and free will," in A. Hannay and G. Marino (eds.), *The Cambridge Companion to Kierkegaard*, New York: Cambridge University Press, 235-256.

Joakim, G. 2005. *Kierkegaard: A Biography*, translated by B. H. Kirmmse. Princeton, Princeton University Press.

Jodalen, H. and Vetlesen J. (eds.). 1997. *Closeness: An Ethics*, Oslo: Scandinavian University Press.

Johnson, C. 2019. "The Silent Tone of the Eternal: Søren Kierkegaard and John Climacus on Silence", *Spiritus* 19(2): 199-216.

Jothen, P. 2014. *Kierkegaard, Aesthetics and Selfhood: The Art of Subjectivity*, London: Ashgate.

Kant, I. 1996. *Religion within the Boundaries of Mere Reason*, translated by A. Wood and G. di Giovanni, Cambridge: Cambridge University Press.

Kanton, A. 1996. "Time of ethics: Levinas and the éclectement of time", *Philosophy and Social Criticism* 22(6): 19-53.

Kearney R. and Rainwater M. (eds.). 1996. *The Continental Philosophy Reader*, London and New York: Routledge.

Kearney, R. (ed.). 2003. *Continental Philosophy in the 20th century*, Routledge History of Philosophy, volume 8, London-New York: Routledge, (paperback edition).

Kemp, P. 1997. "Another Language for the Other: From Kierkegaard to Levinas", *Philosophy and Social Criticism* 23(6): 5-28.

Khrapovitski, A. 1963. *"The Moral Idea of the Trinitarian Dogma"*, in N. Rkhrski (ed.), The Moral Idea of the Most Important Christian Orthodox Dogma, Montreal, 1963, 3-24.

Kierkegaard, S. 2009a. *Concluding Unscientific Postscript*. Translated by A. Hannay, Cambridge: Cambridge University Press.

Kierkegaard, S. 2009b. *Kierkegaard's Writings, XIV: Two Ages: "The Age of Revolution" and the "Present Age": A Literary Review,* translated and edited by. H. V. Hong and E. H. Hong, Princeton: Princeton University Press.

Kierkegaard, S. 2004. *Either/or: A fragment of life,* edited by A. Hannay, London: Penguin classics, 2004. [kindle version]

Kierkegaard, S. 1995. *Works of Love,* translated by H. V. Hong and E. H. Hong, Princeton: Princeton University Press.

Kierkegaard, S. 1991a. *Attack Upon Christendom,* translated by W. Lowrie, Princeton: Princeton University Press.

Kierkegaard, S. 1991b. *Practice in Christianity: The Categories of Offense,* translated by H. V. Hong and E. H. Hong, Princeton: Princeton University Press.

Kierkegaard, S. 1990. *Kierkegaard's Writings, XXI: "For Self-Examination",* translated by H. V. Hong and E. H. Hong, Princeton, N.J.: Princeton University Press.

Kierkegaard, S. 1980 and 1989. *The Sickness unto Death: A Christian Psychological Exposition for Edification and Awakening by Anti-Climacus,* translated by H. V. Hong and E. H. Hong, Princeton: Princeton University Press; translated by A. Hannay, Harmondsworth and New York: Penguin Books.

Kierkegaard, S. 1987. *Two Ages,* translated and tr. H. V. Hong and E. H. Hong, Princeton: Princeton University Press.

Kierkegaard, S. 1985. *Philosophical Fragments and Johannes Climacus,* translated by H. V. Hong and E. H. Hong. Princeton: Princeton University, Press.

Kierkegaard, S. 1983. *Repetition: A Venture in Experimenting Psychology,* translated by H. V. Hong and E. H. Hong. Princeton: Princeton University Press.

Kierkegaard, S. 1980. *The Concept of Anxiety,* translated by R. Thomte in collaboration with A. B. Anderson, Princeton: Princeton University Press.

Kierkegaard, S. 1978. *Two Ages: The Age of Revolution and The Present Age–A Literary Review,* translated and edited by H. V. Hong and E. H. Hong, Princeton: Princeton University Press.

Kierkegaard, S. 1976. *For a Self-Examination,* edited and translated by H. V. Hong and E. H. Hong, Princeton: Princeton University Press.

Kierkegaard, S. 1970. *Journals and Papers,* edited and translated by H. V Hong and E. H Hong, Bloomington: Indiana University Press.

Kierkegaard, S. 1956. *Purity of Heart Is To Will One Thing,* translated by D. V. Steere, New York: Harper & Row Publishing.

Kierkegaard, S. 1951. *Journals*, translated by A. Dru, London: Oxford University Press.

Kierkegaard, S. 1949. *Works of Love*, tr. D. F. Swenson and L.M. Swenson, Princeton: Princeton University Press.

Kierkegaard, S. 1944. *For Self-Examination and Judge Yourselves*, translated by W. Lowrie, Princeton: Princeton University Press.

Kierkegaard, S. 1940. *Christian Discourses*, translated by. W. Lowrie, Princeton: Princeton University Press.

Kirmmse, B. H. 2008. "Affectation, or the Invention of the Self: A Modern Disorder" in E. F. Mooney (ed.) *Ethics, Love and Faith in Kierkegaard: Philosophical Engagements*, Bloomington and Indianapolis: Indiana University Press, 24-38.

Kleinberg-Levin, D. M. 2008. *Before the Voice of Reason: Echoes of Responsibility in Merleau-Ponty's Ecology and Levinas's Ethics*, New York: State University of New York Press.

Knoll, M. 2014. "To Philosophize or not to Philosophize", *Sophia Philosophical Review* 8.2: 96-105.

Kojeve, A. 1980. *Introduction to the Reading of Hegel: Lectures on the Phenomenology of Spirit*, translated by J. Nichols, London-Ithaca: Cornel University Press.

Kosch, M. 2006. *Freedom and Reason in Kant, Schelling and Kierkegaard*, New York: Oxford University Press.

Kosky, J. L. 1996. "After the Death of God: Emmanuel Levinas and the Ethical Possibility of God", *The Journal of Religious Ethics* 24(2): 235-259.

Kosky, J. L. 2001. *Levinas and the Philosophy of Religion*, Indianapolis: Indiana University Press.

Larchet, J-C. 2007. "Suffering in Spiritual Life and Teaching of Elder Sophrony (in Greek)", Πρακτικά Διορθόδοξου Επιστημονικού Συνεδρίου: Γέροντας Σωφρόνιος. Ο Θεολόγος του Ακτίστου Φωτός, 435-456.

Large, W. 2015. *Levinas' Totality and Infinity*, London-New York: Bloomsbury.

Large, W. 2013. "The Name of God: Kripke, Levinas and Rozenweig on Proper Names", *Journal of the British Society of Phenomenology* 44.3: 321-334.

Large, W. 2011. "On the Two Meanings of the Other in Levinas' Totality and Infinity", *Journal of the British Society of Phenomenology* 42.3: 243-254.

Large, W. 2000. "God and the Philosophy of Emmanuel Levinas: A Nietzschean Response", *Literature & Theology* 14.3: 335-349.

Law, D. R. 2013. *Kierkegaard's Kenotic Christology*, Oxford: Oxford University Press.

Leatherbarrow, W.J. 1992. *Fyodor Dostoevsky: "The Brothers Karamazov"*, Cambridge: Cambridge University Press.

Levinas, E. 2004. "Secularism and the Thought of Israel.", translated by N. Poller, in *Unforeseen History*, Urbana, Ill.: University of Illinois Press, 113-124.

Levinas, E. 2003. *Humanism of the Other*, translated by N. Poller, Chicago: University of Illinois Press.

Levinas, E. 2001. "Interview with Francois Poirie (1986)", in J. Robbins (ed.) *Is It Righteous to Be: Interviews with Emmanuel Levinas*, Stanford: California University Press, 23-83.

Levinas, E. 2000. *God, Death and Time*, California: Stanford University Press.

Levinas, E. 1999. *Alterity and Transcendence*, translated by M. B. Smith, New York: Columbia University Press.

Levinas, E. 1998a. *Entre Nous: On Thinking-of-the-Other*, translated by M. B. Smith and B. Harshav, New York: Columbia University Press.

Levinas, E. 1998b. *Of God Who Comes to Mind*, translated by B. Bergo, Stanford: Stanford University Press.

Levinas, E. 1998c. "Existence and Ethics.", in J. Rée and J. Chamberlain (eds.) *Kierkegaard: A Critical Reader*, Oxford: Blackwell, 26-38.

Levinas, E. 1996a. *Basic Philosophical Writings*, A. Peperzak, S. Critchley, and R. Bernasconi (eds.), Indianapolis: Indiana University Press.

Levinas, E. 1996b. *Proper Names*, London: The Athlone Press, 1996b.

Levinas, E. 1995. *The Theory of Intuition in Husserl's Phenomenology*, translated by A. Orianne, Illinois: Northwestern University Press.

Levinas, E. 1994a "The Temptation of Temptation", in *Nine Talmudic Readings*, translated by A. Aronowicz, Bloomington: Indiana University Press, 30-50.

Levinas, E. 1994b. *In the Time of the Nations*, translated by M.B. Smith, Indianapolis: Indiana University Press.

Levinas, E. 1994c. *Outside the Subject*, translated by M.B. Smith, Stanford: Stanford University Press.

Levinas, E. 1994d. "Spinoza's Background", in *Beyond the Verse: Talmudic Readings and Lectures*, translated by G. D. Mole, Bloomington: The Athlone Press, 168-173.

Levinas, E. 1994c. "The Name of God According to a few Talmudic Texts", in *Beyond the Verse: Talmudic Readings and Lectures*, translated by G. D. Mole, Bloomington: The Athlone Press, 116–128.

Levinas, E. 1994d. "In the Image of God, According to Rabbi Hayyim Voloshiner", in *Beyond the Verse: Talmudic Readings and Lectures*, tr. G. D. Mole, Bloomington: The Athlone Press, 151-167.

Levinas, E. 1991. *Otherwise Than Being, or, Beyond Essence*, translated by A. Lingis, The Netherlands: Springer.

Levinas, E. 1990. *Difficult Freedom: Essays on Judaism*, translated by S. Hand, Baltimore: The Athlone Press and John Hopkins University Press.

Levinas, E. 1987a. *Collected Philosophical Papers*, translated by A. Lingis, Dordrecht: Martinus Nijhoff.

Levinas, E. 1987b. *Time and the Other (and additional essays)*, translated by R. A. Cohen, Pittsburg: Duquesne University Press.

Levinas, E. 1986. "The Trace of the Other," translated by A. Lingis, in Mark C. Taylor (ed.) *Deconstruction in Context: Philosophy and Literature*, Chicago: University of Chicago Press, 345-359.

Levinas, E. 1985. *Ethics and Infinity*, translated by R. A. Cohen, Pittsburg, PA: Duquesne University Press.

Levinas, E. 1978. *Existence and Existents*, translated by A. Lingis, The Hague: Martinus Nijhoff.

Levinas, E. 1974. *Autrement qu'être ou au-delà de l'essence*, translated by B. Bettina, The Hague: Martinus Nijhoff.

Levinas, E. 1972. *Humanisme de l'autre homme*, Montpellier: Fata Morgana.

Levinas, E. 1969. *Totality and Infinity*, tr. A. Lingis, Pittsburg, PA: Duquesne University Press.

Lewis D. 1989. "Dispositional Theories of Value", *Proceedings of the Aristotelian Society*, Supplementary Volume: 113-38.

Li, J. 2002. *Can Death be a Harm to the Person who Dies?*, Dordrecht: Springer-Science+Business Media, B.Y.

Lippitt, J. 2013. *Kierkegaard and the Problem of Self Love*, Cambridge: Cambridge University Press.

Lippitt, J. 2000. *Humour and Irony in Kierkegaard's Thought*, London: Macmillan & New York: St. Martin's Press.

Llevadot, L. 2011. "Kierkegaard, Levinas, Derrida: The Death of the Other", in P. Stokes, and A. J. Buben (eds.), *Kierkegaard and Death*, Bloomington and Indianapolis: Indiana University Press, 204-218.

Llewelyn, J. 1995. *Emmanuel Levinas: The Genealogy of Ethics*, London and New-York.

Loudovikos, N. 2010. *A Eucharistic Ontology: Maximus the Confessor's Eschatological Ontology of Being as Dialogical Reciprocity*, Cambridge: Holy Cross Orthodox Press.

Mackinlay, S. 2017. "Hermeneutic Perspectives on Ontology, After Metaphysics has Been Overcome: From Levinas to Merleau-Ponty", *Sophia* 56: 115-124.

Mackinnon, A. 1993. "Kierkegaard and the Leap of Faith", *Kierkegaardiana* 16: 107-125.

Malantschuk, G. 1971. *Kierkegaard's Thought*, edited and translated H. V. Hong and E. H. Hong, Princeton: Princeton University Press.

Manderson, D. 2005. "Proximity: The law of ethics and the ethics of law". *Law Journal* 28.3: 696–719.

Mantzarides G. (ed.). 2008. *Elder Sophrony: A Theologian of The Uncreated Light* (in Greek), Thessaloniki: Saint Mountain.

Marcus, P. 2008. *Being for the other: Emmanuel Levinas, ethical living and psychoanalysis*, Milwaukee: Marquette University Press.

Marcus, P. 2007. "'You are Therefore I am', Emmanuel Levinas and Psychoanalysis", *Psychoanalytic Review* 94(4): 515-527.

Marcuse, H. 2006. *One-dimensional Man*, London: Routledge.

Marcuse, H. 1974. *Eros and Civilization: A Philosophical inquiry into Freud*, Boston: Beacon Press.

Marion, J.-L. 2001. *The idol and distance: Five studies*, tr. T.A. Carlson, New York: Fordham University Press.

Marion, J.-L. 1991. *God without being: Hors-Texte*, tr. T.A. Carlson, Chicago: University of Chicago Press.

Marks, T. M. 2011. "Kierkegaard's Understanding of the Afterlife", in P. Stokes, and A.J. Buben (eds.), *Kierkegaard and Death*, Bloomington and Indianapolis: Indiana University Press, 274-297.

Martinich, A. P. 2005. *Philosophical Writing: An Introduction*, London: Blackwell Publishing.

Matravers, D. (ed.). 2008. *A850 Postgraduate foundation module in Philosophy: Study Guide*, London: Open University Press.

Mayson, R. 2007. *The God of Spinoza: a Philosophical Study*, Cambridge: Cambridge University Press.

Mazouji, R. and Jahromi M. R. 2019. "Silence as a Language of Faith and Being: A Comparative Study of Kierkegaard's and Heidegger's uses of Silence", *The Heythrop Journal* 60: 1-14.

McDonald, W. 2017. "Søren Kierkegaard", *The Stanford Encyclopedia of Philosophy*, E. N. Zalta, (ed.), (online source).

McLachlan, J. 2010. "Beyond the Self, Beyond Ontology: Levinas' Reading of Shestov's Reading of Kierkegaard", *Comparative and Continental Philosophy* 2(2): 179-196.

Mensch, J. 2018. "Life and Horizon", *Sophia Philosophical Review* 11(2): 7-18.

Milbank, J. 1996. "The Sublime in Kierkegaard," *The Heythrop Journal* 37: 298-321.

Min, A. K. 2006. "Naming the Unnamable God: Levinas, Derrida and Marion", *International Journal for Philosophy of Religion* 60(3): 99-116.

Minister, S. and Murtha J. 2010. "Levinas and the Philosophy of Religion", *Philosophy Compass* 5.11: 1023-1033.

Mjaaland, M. T. 2011. "Suicide and Despair", in P. Stokes, and A.J. Buben (eds.), *Kierkegaard and Death*, Bloomington and Indianapolis: Indiana University Press, 81-100.

Mjaaland, M. T. 2008. *Autopsia: Self, Death and God after Kierkegaard and Derrida*, translated by B. McNeil, Berlin-New York: Walter de Gruyter.

Mooney, E. F. 2008a. "A Socratic and Christian Care for the Self", in E.F. Mooney (ed.) *Ethics, Love and Faith in Kierkegaard: Philosophical Engagements*, Indianapolis: Indiana University Press, 1-8.

Mooney E. F. 2008b. "Postscript Ethics: Putting Personality on Stage", in E.F. Mooney (ed.) *Ethics, Love and Faith in Kierkegaard: Philosophical Engagements*, Indianapolis: Indiana University Press, 39-47.

Moore, C. E. (ed). 2002. *Provocations: Spiritual Writings of Kierkegaard*, Farmington: The Bruderhof Foundation.

Morgan, M. L. 2007. *Discovering Levinas*, New York: Cambridge University Press.

Moyaert, P. 2000. "The Phenomenology of Eros: A Reading of Totality and Infinity", in J. Bloechl (ed.) *The Face of the Other and the Trace of God*, New York: Fordham University Press, 30-42.

Moyn, S. 2004. "Transcendence, Morality, and History: Emmanuel Levinas and the Discovery of Soren Kierkegaard in France", *Yale French Studies* 104: 22-54.

Muench, P. 2011. "Thinking Death into Every Moment: The Existence-Problem of Dying in Kierkegaard's *Postscript*", in P. Stokes, and A. J. Buben (eds.), *Kierkegaard and Death*, Bloomington and Indianapolis: Indiana University Press, 101-121.

Murphy, D. 2007. "Levinas and Kierkegaard on Divine Transcendence and Ethical Life: Response to Donald L. Turner and Ford Turrell's 'The Non-Existent God'", *Philosophia* 35: 383-385.

Nealon, J. T. 1997. "The Ethics of Dialogue: Bakhtin and Levinas", *College English* 59(2): 129-148.

Nelson, C. 2006. "Soundings of Silence: The Lily, the Bird, and the Dark Knight of the Soul in the Writings of Søren Kierkegaard," in R. L. Perkins (ed.) *International Kierkegaard Commentary Vol. 18: Without Authority*, Macon, GA: Mercer University Press.

Neto, J. R. M. 1995. *The Christianization of Pyrrhonism: Scepticism and Faith in Pascal, Kierkegaard and Shestov*, Dordrecht-Boston-London: Kluwer Academic Publishers.

Newman, M. 2000. "Sensibility, Trauma, and the Trace: Levinas from Phenomenology to the Immemorial", in J. Bloechl (ed.) *The Face of the Other and the Trace of God*, New York: Fordham University Press, 90-129.

O' Meara, D. 2015. "Consciousness of Self, of Time and of Death in Greek Philosophy", *ΣΧΟΛΗ* 9(2): 283-291.

Olson, E. 1997. *The Human Animal: Personal Identity without Psychology*, Oxford: Oxford University Press.

Oppy, G. and Tsakakis, N. N. (eds..). 2013. *The History of Western Philosophy of Religion*, 5 volumes, London and New York: Routledge.

Papastephanou, M. 2005. "Onto-theology and the incrimination of ontology in Levinas and Derrida", *Philosophy and Social Criticism* 31(4): 461-485.

Pareyson, L. 1998. *Kierkegaard e Pascal*, Mursia: Gruppo Ugo Mursia Editore.

Patrick, D. 1947. *Pascal and Kierkegaard: a Study in the Strategy of Evangelism*, 2 volumes, London: Lutterworth.

Pattison, G. 1998. "Kierkegaard and the Sublime" in N. J. Cappelorn and H. Deuser (eds.), *Kierkegaard Studies Yearbook*, Boston: Walter De Gruyter, 245-275.

Pattison, G. 1992. *Kierkegaard: The Aesthetic and the Religious*, London: Macmillan.

Pattison, G. and Shakespeare, S. (eds.). 1998. *Kierkegaard: the self in society*, New York: St. Martin's Press.

Peperzak, A. 2007. "From Politics to Ethics (Hegel) or From Ethics to Politics?", *Levinas Studies* 2: 197-214.

Peperzak, A. 1997. *Beyond: The Philosophy of Emmanuel Levinas*, Evanston, IL: Northwestern University Press.

Peperzak, A. (ed.). 1995. *Ethics as First Philosophy: The Significance of Emmanuel Levinas for Philosophy, Literature and Religion*, London: Routledge.

Peperzak, A. (ed.). *To the Other: An Introduction to Philosophy of Levinas*, Indiana: Purdue University Press, 1993.

Peperzak, A. 1983. "Phenomenology — Ontology — Metaphysics: Levinas' Perspective on Husserl and Heidegger", Man and World 16: 113-127.

Pirhayati, A. and Rezaei, Z. 2019. "On the Proper Scope of Philosophy of Religion", *Sophia Philosophical Review* 12(1): 68-74.

Plant, B. 2005. *Wittgenstein and Levinas: Ethical and Religious thought*, London-New York: Routledge.

Plato. 1990. *Λάχης, Μένων, Παρμενίδης*, in Greek, translated by B. Tatakis, Athens: Daidalos.

Plato 2005. *Euthyphro, Apology, Crito, Phaedo, Phaedrus*, [Loeb Classical Library], translated by H. N. Fowler, Harvard University Press: Massachusetts.

Plotinus. 2018. *The Enneads*, edited by L.P. Gerson and translated by G. Boys-Stones et al., Cambridge: Cambridge University Press.

Podmore, S. D. 2011a. *Kierkegaard and the Self Before God: Anatomy of the Abyss*, Bloomington & Indianapolis: Indiana University Press.

Podmore, S. D. 2011b. "To Die and Yet Not Die: Kierkegaard's Theophany of Death", in P. Stokes, and A.J. Buben (eds.), *Kierkegaard and Death*, Bloomington and Indianapolis: Indiana University Press, 44-64.

Possen, D. D. 2011. "Death and Ethics in Kierkegaard's Postscript", in P. Stokes, and A.J. Buben (eds.), *Kierkegaard and Death*, Bloomington and Indianapolis: Indiana University Press, 122-132.

Prosser, B. T. 2002. "Conscientious Subjectivity in Kierkegaard and Levinas", *Continental Philosophy Review* 35: 397-422.

Purcell, M. 2006. *Levinas and Theology*, Cambridge: Cambridge University Press.

Purcell, M. 1998. *Mystery and Method: The Other in Rahner and Levinas*, Milwaukee: Marquette University Press.

Purcell, M. 1996. "The ethical significance of Illeity", *Heythrop Journal* 37: 125-138.

Putnam, H. 2004a. "Levinas and Judaism", in *S. Critchley and R. Bernasconi (eds.) The Cambridge Companion to Levinas*, Cambridge: Cambridge University Press, 33-62.

Putnam, H. 2004b. *Ethics without Ontology*, Massachusetts: Harvard University Press.

Putnam H. 1999. *The Threefold Cord: Mind, Body and World*, New York: Columbia University Press.

Quinn, P. L. 1998. "Kierkegaard's Christian Ethics", in A. Hannay and G. Marino (eds.), *The Cambridge Companion to Kierkegaard*, New York: Cambridge University Press, 349-375.

Rasmussen, J. 2005. *Between Irony and Witness: Kierkegaard's Poetics of Faith, Hope, and Love*, New York: Bloomsbury T&T Clark.

Rawls, J. 1971. *A Theory of Justice*, Massachusetts: Harvard University Press.

Raz, J. 1986. *The Morality of Freedom*, Oxford: Clarendon Press.

Reed, R. C. 2017. "The Binding of Abraham: Levinas's Moment in Kierkegaard's Fear and Trembling", *Sophia* 56(1): 81-98.

Richard, B. 2006. "Socrates and Skepticism", in S. Ahbel-Rappe and R. Kamtekar (eds.) *A Companion to Socrates*, Oxford: Blackwell, 298-311.

Robbins, J. W., *Between Faith and Thought: An Essay on the Ontotheological Condition*, Charlottesville: University of Virginia Press, 2003.

Robbins, J. W. 2002. "The Problem of Ontotheology: Complicating the Divine between Theology and Philosophy", The *Heythrop Journal* 48: 139-151.

Ruti, M. 2015. *Between Levinas and Lacan: Self, Other, Ethics*, London and New York: Bloomsbury.

Sakharov, N. V. 2002. *I Love Therefore I am: the Theological Legacy of Archimandrite Sophrony*, New York: St Vladimir's Seminary Press.

Sandford, S. 2000. *The Metaphysics of Love: Gender and Transcendence in Levinas*, London: The Athlone Press.

Saracino, M. 2003. *On Being Human: A Conversation with Lonergan and Levinas*, Milwaukee: Marquette University Press.

Sartre, J-P. 1956. *Being and Nothingness*, translated by H.E. Barnes, New York: Philosophical Library.

Schiller, F. 1954. *On the Aesthetic Education of Man*, tr. R. Snell, London: Routledge and Kegan Paul Ltd.

Schrijvers, J. 2011. *Ontotheological Turnings: the decentering of the modern subject in recent French phenomenology*, New York: Suny Press.

Schrijvers, J. 2010. "Marion, Levinas and Heidegger on the question concerning ontotheology", *Continental Philosophical Review* 43: 207-239.

Schrijvers, J. 2006. "On Doing Theology 'After' Ontotheology: Notes on a French Debate", *New Blackfriars* 87: 302-314.

Scruton, R. 2012. *The Face of God: The Gifford Lectures*, London: Continuum, 2012.

Shakespeare, S. 2001. *Kierkegaard, Language and the Reality of God*, Burlington, VT: Ashgate.

Sheil, P. 2010. *Kierkegaard and Levinas: The subjunctive mood.* Burlington: Ashgate.

Simmons, A. and Wood, D. (ed.). 2008. *Kierkegaard and Levinas: Ethics, Politics and Religion*, Indianapolis: Indiana University Press.

Singer, P. 1993. *Practical ethics*, Cambridge: Cambridge University Press.

Skorupski, J. (ed.). 2010. *The Routledge Companion to Ethics*, London and New York.

Smith, F. 2016. "Gadamer and Levinas on the topic of Sociality", *Sophia Philosophical Review* 9(2): 95-109.

Sorell, T. and Rogers, G. A. J. (eds.). 2003. *Analytic Philosophy and the History of Philosophy*, Oxford: Clarendon Press.

Spinoza, B. 2000. *Ethics: Concerning God*, tr. R.H.M. Elwes, Pennsylvania: the Pennsylvania State University.

Spinoza, B. 1992. *The Ethics*, tr. S. Shirley, Indianapolis: Hackett, 1992.

Stamatellos, G. 2007. *Plotinus and Pre-Socratics*, New York: State University of New York Press.

Stauffer, J. and Bergo, B. G. 2009. *Nietzsche and Levinas: "After the Death of a Certain God"*, New York: Columbia University Press.

Stern, R. 2020. "How Is Love of the Neighbour Possible? A Løgstrupian Response to a Lutheran Critique of Levinas – and Vice Versa", *The Monist* 103: 83-101.

Stewart, J. 2003. *Kierkegaard's Relation to Hegel Reconsidered*, New York: Cambridge University Press.

Stokes, P. 2015. *The Naked Self: Kierkegaard and Personal Identity*, Oxford: Oxford University Press.

Stokes, P. and Buben, A. J. (eds.). 2011. *Kierkegaard and Death*, Bloomington and Indianapolis: Indiana University Press.

Strawser, M. 2006. "Gifts of Silence from Kierkegaard and Derrida", *Soundings: An Interdisciplinary Journal* 89(1): 55-72.

Strawson, P. 2008. *Freedom and Resentment and Other Essays*, London: Taylor and Francis.

Strawson P. 1962. "Freedom and Resentment", *Proceedings of the British Academy xlviii*, 1-25.

Strhan, A. 2012. *Levinas, Subjectivity, Education: Towards an Ethics of Radical Responsibility*, London: Wiley-Blackwell.

Sugarman, R. I. 2013. "Through the Lens of Levinas: Preliminary Reflections on Holiness (Leviticus 19)", *Levinas Studies* 8(1), 129-143.

Tajalli, P. and Segal, S. 2018. "Levinas, Weber, and a Hybrid Framework for Business Ethics", *Philosophy of Management* 18: 71–88.

Taminiaux, J. 1997. "The early Levinas's reply to Heidegger's fundamental ontology", *Philosophy and Social Criticism* 23(6): 29-49.

Taylor, M. C. 1981. "Sounds of Silence" in R.L. Perkins (ed.) *Kierkegaard's Fear and Trembling: Critical Appraisals*, Tuscaloosa, AL: University of Alabama Press.

Taylor, M. C. 1980. *Journeys to Selfhood: Hegel & Kierkegaard*, Berkeley, Los Angeles, London: University of California Press.

Theisohn, P. 2008. "Reading the Beyond. Lévinas – Literature, Holiness, and Politics", *Naharaim* 2(1): 61-80.

Theunissen, M., 2005, *Kierkegaard's Concept of Despair*, tr. B. Harshav and H. Illbruck, Princeton: Princeton University Press.

Thomas, E. 2005. *Emmanuel Levinas: Ethics, Justice and the Human Beyond Being*, New-York and London: Routledge.

Thompson, I. 2005. *Heidegger on Ontotheology: Technology and the Politics of Education*, Cambridge: Cambridge University Press.

Thulstrup, N. 1980. *Kierkegaard's Relation to Hegel*, tr. G. Stengren, Princeton: Princeton University Press, 1980.

Tollefsen, T. T. 2008. *The Christocentric Cosmology of St Maximus the Confessor*, Oxford: Oxford University Press.

Tooley, M. 1986. "Abortion and infanticide", in P. Singer (ed.) *Applied ethics*, Oxford: Oxford University Press, 57-86.

Tumayan, A. 2004. "'I more the Others': Dostoevsky and Levinas", *Encounters with Levinas* 104, 55-66.

Van Riessen, R. D. N. 2007. *Man as a Place of God: Levinas' Hermeneutics of Kenosis*, The Netherlands: Springer.

Vinokurov, V. 2003. "Levinas's Dostoevsky: A Response to 'Dostoevskis Derrida", *Common Knowledge* 9(2): 318-340.

Verene, D. P. 2007. *Hegel's Absolute: An Introduction to Reading of Phenomenology of Spirit*, New York: State University Press.

Verene, D. P. 1985. *Hegel's Recollection: A Study of Image in the Phenomenology of Spirit*, New York: State University Press.

Urbano, R. 2012. "Approaching the divine: Levinas on God, Religion, Idolatry and Atheism", *Logos* 15(1): 50-81.

Uttley, S. R. 2016. '*Exorcising the Curse of Sisyphus': English Catholic education and the possibility of authenticity. A philosophical study after Heidegger, Derrida, Lonergan and Boeve*, unpublished PhD thesis, Nottingham: Nottingham Trent University.

Walsh, S. 2005. *Living Christianly: Kierkegaard's Dialectic of Christian Existence*, Pennsylvania State University Press.

Walsh, S. 1994. *Living Poetically: Kierkegaard's Existential Aesthetics*, University Park, Pennsylvania: Pennsylvania State University Press.

Walter, B. A. 2014. *Communication and Response-ability: Levinas and Kierkegaard in Conversation*, unpublished PhD Dissertation, Duquesne University: Duquesne Scholarship Collection.

Wandelfels B. 2004. "The Face of the Other", in S. Critchley and R. Bernasconi (eds.) *The Cambridge Companion to Levinas*, Cambridge: Cambridge University Press, 63-81.

Ward, G. 1995. *Barth, Derrida and the Language of Theology*, Cambridge: Cambridge University Press.

Warren, J. 2004. *Facing Death: Epicurus and his Critics*, Oxford: Clarendon Press.

Warren, M. A. 1997. "On the moral and legal status of abortion", in H. Lafollette (ed.) *Ethics in practice: An anthology*, Oxford: Blackwell, 91-102.

Watkin, J. 1990. "Kierkegaard's View of Death", *History of European Ideas* 12(1): 65-78.

Watkin, J. 1979. *Dying and Eternal Life as Paradox*, unpublished PhD dissertation, University of Bristol.

Watson G. 1975. "Free Agency", *Journal of Philosophy* 72(8): 205-20.

Watts, M. 2014. *Kierkegaard: An Essential Introduction*, Oxford: Oneworld Publications (Kindle version).

Watts, M. 2003. *Kierkegaard*, Oxford: Oneworld.

Weimin, M. 2008. "Phenomenology or Anti-Phenomenology? – The Ethical Subject in Lévinas", *Journal of Chinese Philosophy* 35(1): 61-78.

Wells, A. 2012. "On Ethics and Christianity: Kierkegaard and Levinas", *The Heythrop Journal* 53: 71-80.

Welz, C. 2007. "The presence of the transcendent – transcending the present. Kierkegaard and Levinas on subjectivity and the ambiguity of God's transcendence", in A. Grøn, I. Damgaard, & S. Overgaard (eds.), *Subjectivity and transcendence*, Mohr Siebeck: Tubingen, 149-176.

Welz, C. 1997. "Present within or without Appearances? Kierkegaard's Phenomenology of the Invisible: Between Hegel and Levinas", in S. Heiko, J. Stewart, K. Verstrynge (eds.). *Kierkegaard Studies Yearbook*, Boston: Walter De Gruyter, 470-513.

Welz, C. and Verstrynge, K. (eds.). 2008. *Despite oneself: Subjectivity and its secret in Kierkegaard and Levinas*, London: Turnshare, 2008.

Wertheimer R. 1993. "Socratic Skepticism" in E. R. Winkler and J. R. Coombs (eds.) *Applied Ethics: A Reader*, Massachusetts: Blackwell, 143-163.

West, D. 1996. *An Introduction to Continental Philosophy*, Cambridge: Polity Press.

Weston, M. 1994. *Kierkegaard and Modern Continental Philosophy*, London: Routledge.

Westphal, M. 2008a. *Levinas and Kierkegaard in Dialogue*, Indianapolis: Indiana University Press.

Westphal, M. 2008b. "The Many Faces of Levinas as a Reader of Kierkegaard", *Revista Portuguesa de Filosofia* 64.2: 1141-1162.

Westphal, M. 2000. "Commanded Love and Divine Transcendence in Levinas and Kierkegaard", in J. Bloechl (ed.) *The Face of the Other and the Trace of God*, New York: Fordham University Press, 200-223.

Westphal, M. 1996. *Becoming a Self: A Reading of Kierkegaard's Concluding Unscientific Postscript*, Indiana: Purdue University Press.

Westphal, M. 1992. "Levinas, Kierkegaard and the Theological Task". *Modern Theology* 8.3: 241-261.

Westphal, M. and Matustik, M. J. 1995. *Kierkegaard in Post/Modernity*, Bloomington & Indianapolis: Indiana University Press.

Wheeler, M. 2011. "Martin Heidegger", *The Stanford Encyclopedia of Philosophy*, E.N. Zalta (ed.), (online source).

White, R. 2012. "Levinas, the Philosophy of Suffering and the Ethics of Compassion", *The Heythrop Journal* 53: 111-123.

Wittgenstein, L. 1958. *Philosophical Investigations*, translated by G.E.M. Anscombe, Oxford: Basil Blackwell.

Wyschogrod, E. 1999. "Ethics as First Philosophy: Levinas reads Spinoza", *The Eighteenth Century* 40(3): 195-205.

Xiushan, Y. 2008. "Levinas faces Kant, Hegel and Heidegger: Debates of contemporary philosophy on ontology", *Frontiers of Philosophy in China* 3.3: 438-454.

Yampolskaya, A. 2019. "Prophetic Subjectivity in Later Levinas: Sobering up from One's Own Identity" *Religions* 10(1): 1-12.

Yandell, K. E. (ed.), *Philosophy of Religion: A Contemporary Introduction*, New-York and London: Routledge, 1999.

Yannaras, C. 2013. *Against Religion: The Alienation of the Ecclesial Event*, translated by N. Russell, Brookline-Massachusetts: Holy Cross Orthodox Press.

Yannaras, C. 2005. *On the Absence and Unknowability of God*, translated by H. Ventis, London-New York: T&T Clark International.

Yannaras, C. 2004. *Postmodern Metaphysics*, tr. N. Russell, Brookline-Massachusetts: Holy Cross Orthodox Press.

Zaborowski, H. 2000. "On Freedom and Responsibility: Remarks on Sartre, Levinas and Derrida", *The Heythrop Journal* 41: 147-165.

Online Sources

https://www.youtube.com/watch?v=qbGaXEqxSvU

https://www.youtube.com/watch?v=wBk4nlPd_24